Controlling In-Plant
Airborne Contaminants

MECHANICAL ENGINEERING

A Series of Textbooks and Reference Books

EDITORS

L. L. FAULKNER
Department of Mechanical Engineering
The Ohio State University
Columbus, Ohio

S. B. MENKES
Department of Mechanical Engineering
The City College of the
City University of New York
New York, New York

OTHER VOLUMES IN PREPARATION

Controlling In-Plant Airborne Contaminants

SYSTEMS DESIGN AND CALCULATIONS

John D. Constance

Consulting Engineer

CRC Press
Taylor & Francis Group
Boca Raton London New York

CRC Press is an imprint of the
Taylor & Francis Group, an **Informa** business

First published 1983 by Marcel Dekker, Inc.

Published 2019 by CRC Press
Taylor & Francis Group
6000 Broken Sound Parkway NW, Suite 300
Boca Raton, FL 33487-2742

© 1983 by Taylor & Francis Group, LLC
CRC Press is an imprint of Taylor & Francis Group, an Informa business

First issued in paperback 2019

No claim to original U.S. Government works

ISBN 13: 978-0-367-45191-2 (pbk)
ISBN 13: 978-0-8247-1900-5 (hbk)

**Visit the Taylor & Francis Web site at
http://www.taylorandfrancis.com**

**and the CRC Press Web site at
http://www.crcpress.com**

Library of Congress Cataloging in Publication Data

Constance, John Dennis, [date]
Controlling in-plant airborne contaminants.

(Mechanical engineering ; 21)
Bibliography: p.
Includes index.
1. Air–Pollution, Indoor. 2. Factories–Design
and construction. 3. System design. I. Title.
II. Series.
TD883.1.C656 1983   628.53   83-6589
ISBN 0-8247-1900-X

To our daughter
Anita Marie

PREFACE

This book was written with a special purpose in mind: to provide a useful reference work for the practicing engineer in his evaluation and design of systems for the control of the industrial in-plant environment. Designers, contractors, operators, and maintenance personnel will find the book replete with work-a-day information that will give them that "at home" feeling on the job. Technicians and technologists, as well as students, will find the material most helpful to their introduction to the field of making the industrial plant more liveable. With this thought in mind, time-saving approaches are emphasized through the use of charts, graphs, tables, and tested samples of actual workable designs. This book picks up from where the run-of-the-mill data handbook and guide leave off and fills in the voids.

It is not within the scope of this book to include detailed discussions of the special fields of fume, gas, and dust sampling and analysis, duct system design, system balancing, and air-moving equipment. Nor can space be devoted to air scrubbing and methods of air cleaning; valuable sources are listed for these specialties in the reference and bibliography sections of the book. Rather, we will devote our pages to systems design criteria and useful calculations and proven techniques to control the in-plant environment in the oil refinery and chemical plant industries. Much of the material will also have applications in other industries which have similar problems.

This book is necessary in view of the increasing importance of in-plant air pollution—before it gets beyond the confines of the processing plant.

Much has been written on the subject of this book, but it is scattered throughout a large variety of publications. The book's contents are based primarily on the experiences of the author in the oil refinery and chemical plant design field. The methods used have been field tested and have stood up under actual operation. During the course of design the one major consideration was to intertwine actuality with basic theory to arrive at the most economical solution to design for economy and safety. For many years the volume of outside air used to pressurize a space was a guess based in most cases on the design engineer's experience. This author developed an approach to solving the problem of pressurizing air quantities by calculating the outflow rate of air while still maintaining pressure. The method was tested in a number of installations, and it proved workable.

When one considers that for every 1000 ft^3/min of air used for pressurization, 5 tons of refrigeration are required at approximately $1500 per ton,
the savings from efficient ventilation can be considerable. It is for this
reason that this book has been written—to make available to design and
plant engineers, to construction and consulting engineering firms, and to
experienced industrial hygiene engineers, in condensed, practical, and
useful fashion, a summary of the information and data needed to determine
what control measures should be employed and how control systems should
be designed so that when installed they have a fair chance of performing
satisfactorily.

Pertinent references are listed, and the pagination is cross refer-
enced. Appendixes have been included to focus attention on design criteria
and problem solving.

John D. Constance

INTRODUCTION

Health and safety hazards associated with certain occupations were probably recognized even before the dawn of history. Throughout antiquity,
however, little interest was shown in protecting worker health and safety,
perhaps because the dangerous trades were usually restricted to slave
labor. Hippocrates, in the fourth century B.C., recognized the toxic
properties of lead and recorded a series of attacks of lead colic in a miner.
Pliny the Elder, a Roman scholar of the first century A.D., referred to
the hazard of handling sulfur and zinc and also described a protective mask,
made from a bladder, which was used by workers in dusty trades. About
100 years later Galen accurately described the pathology of lead poisoning.

In 1473, Ulrich Ellenborg produced the first publication on the subject,
a pamphlet on occupational diseases and injuries among gold miners. He
also wrote about the toxic actions of carbon monoxide, mercury, lead, and
nitric acid. In addition, he offered instruction in hygiene and other preventive measures. In 1556, the German scholar Agricola described the
diseases of miners and prescribed preventive measures.

The first comprehensive book on occupational medicine was published
in Italy by the "father of industrial medicine" Bernardino Ramazzini. His
De Morbis Artificum Diatriba, interpreted as The Diseases of Workmen,
contained accurate descriptions of the occupational diseases of most of the
workers of his time. Ramazzini was perhaps the first person to describe
accurately the pathology of silicosis. Unfortunately, his suggested "cau-
tions" were to be largely ignored for several centuries.

In England, Charles Thackrah (1795-1833) devoted his life to the study
and prevention of occupational hazards associated with industrialization,
and his influence was felt in both medical and political spheres. In 1837 the
first article on occupational disease appeared in America and relied heavily
on Thackrah as an authority.

Early in twentieth-century America, Dr. Alice Hamilton observed industrial conditions first hand and startled mine owners, factory managers,
and state officials with evidence of illness correlated with toxic exposures.
She presented concrete proposals for the elimination of unhealthful conditions and exercised tremendous influence on both industrial leaders and
lawmakers.

The mechanization which accompanied the Industrial Revolution brought
new and more varied hazards and intensified old ones. More importantly,

the number of industrial workers increased markedly in this period. The resultant increase in injuries eventually brought about legislation, such as the Factory Acts of Great Britain. The Health and Morals of Apprentices Act was passed in 1802, and the Child Labor Laws in 1833. In 1901, a law protecting the health of adult workers was successfully passed.

This is history; now the Occupational Safety and Health Act (OSHA) in the United States has established both safety standards for industry and their means of enforcement.

What makes a good in-plant environment to protect worker health and safety? The answer is that in a controlled environment dust, gases, smoke, and fumes must be kept under control, and noise sources must be reduced to acceptable levels through the use of absorbing systems of baffles and curtains.

Fumes and Gases Irrespective of all that has been claimed to have been done, there is still a large percentage of industrial plants in the United States where such pollutants are not controlled.

Smoke The cause is often the lack of makeup air; but in many cases there is also a lack of understanding and consideration of all the factors causing the problem.

Heat Radiant heat from the processes and heat from the sun have been found to create uncomfortable conditions that lead to worker fatigue and discomfort.

Dusts These are left to disperse into the workroom without consideration to the health of the worker.

Improper Ventilation A new plant may start off by providing ventilation to accomplish a certain level of comfort, but as changes take place within the workplace and in the process itself, ventilation needs are overlooked or not appreciated. Then the original design conditions drop off.

Noise This can be the industrial plant's most difficult problem, but with the right approach to the problem, it need not be.

Why does the in-plant environment fall short of the design? Perhaps, the following reasons will provide an insight:

Economics will not justify a new design. How often have you asked someone why in-plant conditions are not made better and received the answer that "if I spend our money there, I won't be owning the business anymore." There are situations where this may be true.

"Our manufacturing process does not require anything better than the present system" may be another answer.

The type of labor required will put up with the present conditions. This has been a common reason in heavy industry and elsewhere.

Even though the intent is to improve the inplant environment, only a partial job is done. Often this is because a complete study was not made, and all bases were not touched.

Sometimes, obviously selfish interests control the plant and the person in charge of the project focused on a particular aspect of the environment; for example, the well-ventilated plant with a noise problem.

Finally, the entire plan for a plant simply may not work. The industrial engineer planned a well-organized layout, the chemical engineer eliminated the fumes and smoke, the architect used real imagination in the colors selected for the equipment and the building, and the mechanical engineer did an excellent job of controlling the in-plant atmosphere. The people involved seem to have done their jobs; however, they did not work together.

Contaminated air may be injurious to workers, deleterious to the manufactured product, and costly to plant operations. Contaminated air may also be unsafe to worker well being. Contaminated air can cause corrosion of operating equipment with resulting injury to the worker. It is essential that contaminant control systems be effective and economical. Although some dusts, vapors, and gases may be nontoxic, they may be explosive or flammable, and it is advisable to control them to provide an acceptable and safe in-plant environment.

Then there are the interests of good housekeeping, which are important for several reasons. First, the quality of the products being processed or manufactured in a contaminated area may be affected through the lack of control. Second, corrosive vapors and gases, if uncontrolled, can materially shorten the life of structures and manufacturing equipment.

We should not overlook the importance of controlling dust, vapors, and gases to minimize fire and explosion hazards. Insurance underwriters are well aware of the possible losses due to the lack of control, and, consequently, specify minimum standards of ventilation. If a plant owner does not meet these standards, he may not qualify as an insurable risk. And then he must also contend with OSHA.

The last, but not the least, factor to be considered is the control of air pollution outdoors. This means the presence in the outdoor atmosphere of one or more contaminants such as dust, fumes, gases, mist, odor, smoke, or vapor in quantities, of characteristics, and of duration such as to be injurious to human, plant, or animal life, or to property, or that reasonably interferes with the comfortable enjoyment of life and property by plant neighbors. Thus, it behooves plant owners and operators to control these contaminants at the source.

The first question the design engineer should raise before undertaking a contaminant-control system is, therefore, can the contaminant be eliminated, or can less toxic or less obnoxious or less hazardous chemicals be used in the process? The industrial health engineer, drawing from past experiences, should be able to estimate the approximate cost of the contaminant-control system. This estimated cost should be given to the development and research people within the company so that they may review the costs of research and development to find substitute chemicals or even a new process.

If their findings do not prove fruitful, or if it is not practical to spend research time to develop a new process, then the next approach is to see what can be done to contain the contaminants to minimize ventilation requirements. If the sources of contamination are scattered throughout the plant manufacturing area, and it is not practical to collect these contaminants at their source, the dilution method of control may be applicable. However, generally speaking, the preferred method of control is to collect them at their source. Then, perhaps, the dilution method may be used as an auxiliary requirement of the insurance company to dilute flammable vapors and gases should an accidental spill occur.

Thus, we see that there is a great deal that has to be done in the field of controlling in-plant airborne contaminants, and that much work is needed to clarify the legal, control, operating, engineering, and test aspects. Systems design demands that operating plant management be made aware of the conditions of all air vapors, gases, liquids, and airborne particulates that could leave plant buildings. This responsibility is solely theirs. Plant management must also be cognizant of the condition of the air as it enters the buildings or is recirculated, so that design steps will provide for a safe and healthful internal environment for the worker.

ACKNOWLEDGMENTS

In preparing this book for controlling the in-plant environment for safety and health, the author drew copiously from his experience in industry and from his published works which reflected that experience.

The author gratefully acknowledges the help and cooperation he received from the publishers and editors of the published material presented below.

Chapter 5

"Mixing factor is guide to ventilation," reprinted with permission of Power (February, 1970), Copyright © 1970, McGraw-Hill, Inc., New York.

"When to use dilution ventilation," reprinted with permission of Power (February, 1976), Copyright © 1976, McGraw-Hill, Inc., New York.

"How to apply dilution ventilation," reprinted with permission of Power (January, 1975), Copyright © 1975, McGraw-Hill, Inc., New York.

Chapter 6

"Estimating exhaust-air requirements for processes," reprinted by special permission from Chemical Engineering (August 10, 1970), Copyright © 1970, McGraw-Hill, Inc., New York.

Chapter 9

"Pressure ventilate for explosion protection," reprinted by special permission from Chemical Engineering (September 20, 1971), Copyright © 1971, McGraw-Hill, Inc., New York.

"How to pressure-ventilate large motors for corrosion, explosion and moisture protection," reprinted by special permission from Chemical Engineering (February 27, 1978), Copyright © 1978, McGraw-Hill, Inc., New York.

Chapter 10

"Clearing the air in laboratories," reprinted by special permission from
Research/Development (September, 1972), Copyright © 1972, Technical
Publishing Company, A Company of Dun & Bradstreet Corporation, Barring-
ton, Illinois, all rights reserved.

Chapter 11

"Plant-area design to prevent air-moisture condensation," reprinted by
special permission from Chemical Engineering (October 5, 1970), Copyright © 1970, McGraw-Hill, Inc., New York.

"Stop condensation underground," reprinted with permission of Power
(February, 1975), Copyright © 1975, McGraw-Hill, Inc., New York.

"Removing moisture from buildings by exhaust ventilation," reprinted by
special permission from Chemical Engineering (May 19, 1980), Copyright
© 1980, McGraw-Hill, Inc., New York.

Chapter 12

"Noise criteria: Their evaluation and use," reprinted from Consulting
Engineer (December, 1973), Vol. XLI, No. V.I, pp. 58-63, Copyright ©
1973, Technical Publishing Company, A Company of Dun & Bradstreet
Corporation, Barrington, Illinois, all rights reserved.

Appendix A

"Solve gas purging problems graphically," reprinted by special permission
from Chemical Engineering (December 29, 1980), Copyright © 1980,
McGraw-Hill, Inc., New York.

"Control of explosive or toxic air-gas mixtures," reprinted by special permission from Chemical Engineering (April 19, 1971), Copyright © 1971,
McGraw-Hill, Inc., New York.

"Calculating sound levels from octave-band analyses," reprinted by special
permission from Chemical Engineering (February 18, 1974), Copyright ©
1974, McGraw-Hill, Inc., New York.

"Cost estimates by use of six-tenths factor," reprinted from Consulting Engineer (September, 1973), Vol. XLI, No. III, pp. 84-86, Copyright © 1973, Technical Publishing Company, A Company of Dun & Bradstreet Corporation, Barrington, Illinois, all rights reserved.

Lastly, the author is indebted to the editors and publishers in all phases of engineering and environmental control, especially the editors of Chemical Engineering, Power, Consulting Engineer, and Research/ Development.

John D. Constance

CONTENTS

Controlling In-Plant
Airborne Contaminants

1

THEORY IN PRACTICE

1.1.   INTRODUCTION

The object of this chapter is to refresh the reader in matters of theory and practice pertaining to the field of contaminant control.   Furthermore, engineering problems encountered involve a knowledge of certain fundamental scientific principles. Therefore, this chapter can be considered as a foundation upon which our structure of in-plant environmental control expertise is to be built. During the course of a design problem these matters crop up, and an understanding of basic principles will be helpful.

When dealing with gases and vapors of a chemical and organic nature, we must understand their behavior to help in arriving at design decisions. The composition of matter and the behavior of gases and vapors, gas laws, and states of aggregation can do much to guide the designer to in-plant environmental control systems.

This chapter will review these important matters in a quick review of basic theory, and most subjects will be reinforced with examples and their solutions. In all cases the practical aspects of each example are reviewed, and the necessary practical formulas are given with explanations. See Baumeister, T. et al. (1978) and Perry, R. and Chilton, C. (1978).

1.2. SHORT OUTLINE OF BASIC CHEMISTRY AND PHYSICS

Chemical Principles

Chemistry is the science which deals with changes in the composition and constitution of substances and with the alteration in properties which accompanies and gives evidence of these changes. There are about 92 kinds of matter, known as elements, existing as minute atoms which form relatively stable molecules. Molecules are pure substances composed of the same kind. Molecules containing atoms of different elements are called compounds.

Most Common Elements

Some of the most common elements together with their atomic weights are as follows:

Aluminum	Al	27.0	Nickel	Ni	58.7
Calcium	Ca	40.1	Nitrogen	N	14.0
Carbon	C	12.0	Oxygen	O	16.0
Chlorine	Cl	35.5	Phosphorus	P	31.0
Copper	Cu	63.6	Potassium	K	39.1
Gold	Au	197.2	Silicon	Si	28.1
Hydrogen	H	1.0	Silver	Ag	107.9
Iron	Fe	55.9	Sodium	Na	23.0
Lead	Pb	207.2	Sulfur	S	32.1
Magnesium	Mg	24.3	Tin	Sn	118.7
Mercury	Hg	200.6	Zinc	Zn	65.4

The above values are rounded off to the nearest tenth. More accurate tables are available in standard textbooks of chemistry.

Properties of Matter

Atoms The smallest particle of any element is known as an atom. It cannot be broken down or further subdivided by chemical means. No apparatus can measure the weight of an atom directly. It is possible, however, to compare large multiples of atoms with the same multiple of other atoms and thus establish the rate of weights.

<u>Molecular weight</u>   The weight of a molecule must be the sum of all the atomic weights contained in it. Thus, the weight of sulfuric acid, H_2SO_4, is calculated as

Two atoms of hydrogen   (2)(1) =   2.0

One atom of sulfur   32.1

Four atoms of oxygen   (4)(16) = 64.0

Total   98.1

The same applies to the molecule of a pure substance. Oxygen (O_2) has a molecular weight of (2)(16) = 32.

<u>Pound mol</u>   It is often found convenient to use as many pounds of a given substance as there are units in its molecular weight. This amount is called a pound mol (pound molecule). Thus, 1 pound mol of oxygen is 32 pounds; 1 pound mol of sulfuric acid is 98.1 pounds.

<u>Valence</u>   Elements differ in their methods of combining with other elements. One atom of hydrogen can never combine with more than one other atom of any kind; oxygen can combine with two hydrogen atoms. Thus, hydrogen has only one point of attachment which is called its valence. Some elements have two or more valences. Carbon may form carbon monoxide (CO) and carbon dioxide (CO_2).

Chemical Equations

When atoms and molecules react to form new molecules, a chemical equation may be written. This is a statement in chemical symbols of the number and kind of molecules or atoms reacting with each other during a chemical change and of the products resulting from this reaction. Thus, the formation of carbon monoxide by burning carbon in oxygen is expressed as $2C + O_2 = 2CO$. In terms of atomic weights, it means that 24 parts by weight of carbon react with 32 parts by weight of oxygen to produce 56 parts by weight of carbon monoxide. Note that both sides of the equation must balance. On each side of the equation there must be the same number of atoms of a particular kind. The weight relationships expressed by such equations hold true for any uniform system of weights. Accordingly, the above equation is true whether the parts by weight are pounds, ounces, or tons. In other words, 24 lb carbon react with 32 lb oxygen to yield 56 lb carbon monoxide.

EXAMPLE 1.1.   If 100 pounds carbon are burned to form CO, how many pounds of oxygen are used up and how many pounds CO are produced?

SOLUTION   The reaction is expressed as above discussed. Then

$$\frac{24 \text{ parts carbon}}{32 \text{ parts oxygen}} = \frac{100 \text{ parts C}}{x \text{ parts O}_2}$$

$$x = \frac{(32)(100)}{24} = 133 \text{ lb oxygen}$$

Also

$$y = \frac{(56)(100)}{24} = 233 \text{ lb CO generated}$$

Weight

Weight is the attraction of gravity for a given mass and is expressed in pounds, tons, ounces, etc.

Specific Gravity

Specific gravity is the weight of a material in pounds, that would occupy a certain space under a definite set of conditions. The numerical value of the specific gravity is obtained by dividing by the weight of water that would occupy the same space under identical conditions.

Volume

Volume is the space occupied by a given quantity of matter, and is measured in cubic feet, cubic inches, gallons, etc. The specific volume of a material is the number of cubic feet occupied by one pound of the material under a certain set of conditions of temperature and pressure.

Density

Density is the inverse of specific volume and is expressed in pounds per cubic foot.

Temperature

Temperature is a measure of the average heat content of matter. Heat flows from a material of a higher temperature to a material of a lower temperature; this difference is required for heat to flow. Heat cannot flow uphill, that is, to a material of a higher temperature. Temperature is expressed in degrees Fahrenheit (°F) in the English system.

Pressure

Pressure is a property of matter which represents the force per unit area
exerted against other matter. The units of measurement in common use
include atmospheres, pounds per square inch, pounds per square foot, and
equivalent heights of material which exert definite pressures, such as
inches of mercury or feet of water.

Enthalpy

Enthalpy, also known as heat content, a property of matter that often concerns engineers. Its addition or removal causes changes in other properties of that matter. For instance, a change in the heat content of a solid
may change the temperature, the magnetic properties, the color, or even
the state of the material.

Specific Heat

The quantity of heat required to change the temperature of various substances differs according to the properties of those substances. Accordingly, the specific heat is used to represent, for any given material, the
ratio of the quantity of heat required to change its temperature by 1°F to the
heat required to change the temperature of the same weight of water through
1°F. For example, if it requires 100 Btu to heat a certain weight of oil
from 75 to 76°F, and it requires 200 Btu to heat the same weight of water
through the same range of temperature, the ratio is 1:2, and we may say
that the specific heat of the oil is 0.5.

Vaporization

Vaporization is the change in state from the liquid to the vapor that takes
place at constant temperature.

Vapor Pressure

The pressure at which vaporization takes place and at which the vapor completely fills the space over the vaporizing liquid is the vapor pressure at the
existing temperature. Vapor pressure varies with the temperature and is
different for each different liquid. The presence of any other gas in the
space above the liquid does not change the effect at all, so long as the other
gas remains insoluble in the liquid. Water at a temperature of 80°F exerts
a pressure of 0.51 psia against the surrounding surfaces of the container,
whether it is the only vapor present or whether the space also contains air
at a pressure of 100 psia. See the steam tables for water (Keenan, J. H.
et al., 1978).

Boiling Point of a Liquid

Whenever the vapor pressure of a liquid equals the total pressure of its environment, any further vaporization will cause a slight excess pressure
and will push back the atmosphere. This condition is known as boiling, and
the temperature at which this takes place is known as the boiling point.

Condensation

Condensation, the change of state from a vapor to a liquid, is the reverse
of vaporization and, likewise, occurs at constant temperature. The heat
required to cause condensation is exactly the same as that which must be
removed for condensation. Thus, the latent heat of vaporization is equal to
the heat of condensation.

Dew Point

The temperature at which condensation first occurs is the dew point. Boiling point and dew point are the same. The dew point of a mixture of gases
and vapors is that temperature at which the first droplets of liquid are
formed. The system must be chemically nonreactive. See a temperature-
entropy diagram (T-S) for a pure fluid (Baumeister, T. et al., 1978).

Saturated and Superheated Vapor

When the vapor pressure equals the total pressure (sum of all pressures),
the vapor is said to be saturated. When the vapor pressure is less than the
total pressure, the vapor is said to be superheated.

Fusion and Solidification

Direct conversion of a solid into a liquid is known as fusion. The heat required to cause this change is called the heat of fusion. The temperature at
which this takes place is called the melting point. The reverse of fusion is
called solidification, the change from a liquid to a solid. The corresponding temperature is known as the freezing point.

Gas Laws

So many engineering operations involve the handling of gases that special
attention must be given to the properties of matter in the gaseous state.
These behaviors are so consistent for certain gases at moderate pressures
and have been found so useful that they are known as the gas laws. For all
work involving gases, these laws hold for perfect gases and also for all

gases under moderate pressure and temperature and not close to condensation. They can apply to vapors near the dew point if no other data are
available, but could involve an error.

Boyle's Law

Boyle's law is a gas law stating that at any given temperature the volume
(v) of any given weight of a gas, multipled by the pressure (p), is a constant.
Thus, pv = constant.

Avogadro's Law

Avogadro's law states that at any specified temperature and pressure, a
given volume of one gas will contain the same number of molecules of that
gas as are contained in the same volume of any other gas at the same temperature and pressure. This holds true whether we have a single gas or a
mixture of gases, or a mixture of vapors in a superheated state. Thus, 100
ft^3 oxygen at 50°F and 1 atm pressure contains the same number of molecules as 100 ft^3 nitrogen or as 100 ft^3 air at the same temperature and
pressure. The same law holds for pound molecules (pound mols) of any gas
vapors, or a mixture of these.

Pound Molecular Volume

It has been found, using Avogadro's law as a basis, that one pound mol of a
perfect gas occupies a volume of 379 cubic feet at 60°F and one atmosphere
pressure (14. 7 psia). This relation may be used for actual gases or vapors
when there is no change in state or chemical reaction. Thus 1 lb mol carbon dioxide (CO_2) (molecular weight of 44) occupies 379 ft^3 at the above
conditions. The weight of gas in that volume is 44 lb. The weight of oxygen
is 379 ft^3 at these conditions of temperature and pressure is its molecular
weight of 32 lb.

Charles' Law

Charles law states that for any specified weight of a given gas, the product
of its volume and existing pressure is proportional to the absolute temperature (T, which is °F + 460), and is given in degrees Rankine. Thus, pv =
KT. The constant K does not change as long as we deal with the same number of pounds of the same gas and that the dimensions of p and v do not
change.

Dalton's Law of Partial Pressures

Dalton's law of partial pressures states that, in a mixture of gases, each
gas exerts the same pressure as it would exert if it were present alone in

the occupied volume of the mixture. Each component gas exerts its own "partial pressure." The sum of their pressures equals the total pressure (P). Thus

$$P = P_1 + P_2 + P_3 + \cdots + P_n \tag{1.1}$$

Mol Fraction of a Gas in a Mixture of Gases

The mol fraction of a gas in a mixture of gases is equal to the moles of the gas divided by the total number of moles of all gases in the mixture. We may also say that the partial pressure exerted by a gas in a mixture is equal to its mol fraction multiplied by the total pressure. Accordingly, the mol fraction of any gas in a mixture is numerically equal to the fraction of the total pressure that is exerted by the gas.

The Law of Perfect Gases

Practically all of the laws discussed so far may be combined in the useful expression known as the perfect gas law. This law states that the product of the pressure times the volume equals the product of the number of mols present (N), the absolute temperature, and a gas constant (R). Thus

$$pv = NRT \tag{1.2}$$

where p = psia, v = ft^3, N = lb mol, R = 10.71, and T = °F + 460.

Deviation from the Perfect Gas Law

It was soon found that the expression for the perfect gas law was only an approximation to the actual behavior of real gases. At high densities, the variations may be very great depending on the character of the particular gas under consideration. The equation pv = NRT represents a limiting case that all real gases approach as their pressures are lowered or their temperatures increased. Depending upon the character of the gas, pressure, and temperature, this deviation is known as the compressibility factor (Z), and now the adjusted equation becomes

$$pv = ZNRT \tag{1.3}$$

EXAMPLE 1.2. At what pressure will 88 lb carbon dioxide gas occupy a volume of 100 ft^3 when the temperature of the system is 10°F? Assume that the compressibility factor (Z) is unity. Molecular weight of CO_2 is 44.

SOLUTION

$$p = \frac{ZNRT}{v} = \frac{(1)(88/44)(10.71)(10 + 460)}{100} = 100.7 \text{ psia}$$

EXAMPLE 1.3.   A cylinder with a net volume of 1.54 ft^3 is filled
with nitrogen at a pressure of 2000 psig and 80°F. How many
cubic feet of "free" nitrogen will the cylinder discharge if the
compressibility factor of the gas at the filling condition is 1.125?
Molecular weight of N_2 is 28.

SOLUTION   The number of pound mols at filling must first be
calculated

$$N = \frac{pv}{ZRT} = \frac{(2000 + 14.7)(1.54)}{(1.125)(10.71)(540)} = 0.477 \text{ lb mol}$$

The volume available for discharge to the "free" condition is v =
(1)(0.477)(10.71)(530)/(14.7) = 184 ft^3. However, since 1.54 ft^3
still remains within the cylinder after the pressure drops to atmospheric (14.7 psia) due to lack of pressure differential from
cylinder to atmosphere, we must deduct the volume of the cylinder to get the net amount of gas released. Thus, 184 - 1.54 =
182.46 or 182.5 ft^3.

1.3. BEHAVIOR OF GASES AND VAPORS

We have already covered the gas laws and problems related to them. Here
we will discuss the matter of the behavior of gases and vapors more
completely.

Critical Temperature of a Gas

If the temperature of a gas is below a certain temperature, known as the
"critical" temperature, an increase in pressure will lead eventually to condensation. When a gas has dropped below the critical point, it is known as
a vapor. When a gas is increased in both temperature and pressure above
the critical it is known as a gas. Above the critical a gas may be compressed indefinitely without liquefaction. In this way gases have been
caused to increase in density above the normal liquid density. For example, hydrogen at 149°F and 1500 atm pressure has a density of 0.1301 g/
cm^3. The normal density of liquid hydrogen is 0.071 g/cm^3.

Gas Mixtures

In a homogeneous mixture of different gases the molecules of each component gas are uniformly distributed throughout the entire volume of the containing vessel and the molecules of each component gas contribute, by their
impacts, to the total pressure exerted by the entire mixture. Dalton's law
states that the total pressure is the sum of the pressures exerted by
the molecules of each component gas. These statements apply to all
gases, whether or not their behavior is ideal. The partial pressure of a

component gas which is present in a mixture of gases is the pressure that
would be exerted by that component gas if it alone were present in the
same volume as the mixture. The partial volume of a component gas
which is present in a mixture of gases is the volume that would be occupied
by that component gas if it alone were present at the same pressure and
temperature as the mixture.

Volumetric Analysis

A volumetric analysis gives a description of the mixture. It is commonly
used in practice and expresses the amount of a particular gas in the mixture
by the percentage of the total volume which the gas would occupy if the various gases were placed in separate compartments at the same temperature
and pressure as the mixture. If an analysis is given simply as percent it
is assumed in practice to be by volume, unless stated otherwise.

Gravimetric Analysis

A gravimetric analysis describes the gas mixture by giving the percentage
by weight of each component gas.

Converting Volumetric to Gravimetric Analysis

Given the composition of a gas mixture by volume, the percentage by
weight is determined by using as a basis 1 lb mol of the mixture.

> EXAMPLE 1.4. A mixture of gases has the following composition
> by volume: oxygen 6.3%, sulfur dioxide 14.6%, nitrogen 79.1%.
> Calculate the composition by weight of this mixture. Note gases
> will not react chemically.
>
> SOLUTION   Basis: 1 lb mol of the mixture. Since volume per-
> cent equals mol percent, mol fraction equals mol percent/100,
> and mol fraction multiplied by molecular weight gives weight in
> pounds. Then

Gas	Mol fraction		Mol wt.		Pounds
Oxygen	0.063	X	32	=	2.02
Sulfur dioxide	0.146	X	64.1	=	9.36
Nitrogen	0.791	X	28	=	22.15

Total weight is 33.53 lb, or the weight of 1 lb mol of the mixture.
Composition by weight may be found in the usual manner.

$$\text{Oxygen} = 2.02/33.53, \text{ or } 6\% \text{ by weight}$$
$$\text{Sulfur dioxide} = 9.36/33.53, \text{ or } 27.9\% \text{ by weight}$$
$$\text{Nitrogen} = 22.15/33.53, \text{ or } 66.1\% \text{ by weight}$$

Converting Gravimetric to Volumetric Analysis

Given the composition by weight of a gas mixture, the percent by volume may be determined by using as a basis 1 lb of the mixture.

EXAMPLE 1.5.   A mixture of nonreactive gases has a composition by weight as follows: oxygen 10.7%, carbon monoxide 0.9%, nitrogen 88.4%.   Calculate the composition by volume of the mixture.

SOLUTION   Basis: 1 lb of the mixture.

Gas	Weight fraction		Mol wt.		Lb/mol
Oxygen	0.107	÷	32	=	0.00335
Carbon monoxide	0.009	÷	28	=	0.000321
Nitrogen	0.884	÷	28	=	0.0316
Total lb mol					0.035171

Since mol percent equals volume percent, determine mol percent.

$$\text{Oxygen} = 0.00335/0.035171, \text{ or } 9.5\%$$
$$\text{Carbon monoxide} = 0.000321/0.035171, \text{ or } 0.9\%$$
$$\text{Nitrogen} = 0.0315/0.035171, \text{ or } 89.6\%$$

Average Molecular Weight of a Gas Mixture

A certain group of components of a mixture of gases may pass through a process without being changed in composition or weight. For example, in a drying process, dry air merely serves as a carrier for the vapor being removed and undergoes no change in composition or weight. It is frequently convenient to treat such a mixture as though it were a single gas and assign to it an average molecular weight which may be used for calculation of its weight and volume relations. Such an average molecular weight has no physical significance from the standpoint of the molecular theory and is of no value if any component of the mixture takes part in a reaction or is altered in relative quantity. The average molecular weight is calculated by adopting a unit molal quantity of the mixture as a basis of calculation. The weight of this molal quantity is then calculated and will represent the average molecular weight. By this method the average molecular weight of air is found to be 29 for all practical purposes.

EXAMPLE 1.6.   Calculate the average molecular weight of a flue gas mixture having the following composition by volume: carbon monoxide 0.1%, carbon dioxide 13.0%, oxygen 7.7%, nitrogen 79.2%.

SOLUTION   Basis: 1 lb mol of the mixture.

Carbon monoxide	(0.001) (28)	=	0.028
Carbon dioxide	(0.13) (44)	=	5.72
Oxygen	(0.077) (32)	=	2.46
Nitrogen	(0.792) (28)	=	22.18
Total			30.39 (the average molecular weight)

Specific Heat of a Gaseous Mixture

The heat transferred to a mixture is the sum of the heats transferred to each constituent of the mixture. Where G is the weight fraction of the gas in the mixture and c is its specific heat, the specific heat of the mixture is given by

$$c_m = G_x c_x + G_y c_y + G_z c_z \qquad \text{Btu/lb/°F} \qquad (1.4)$$

for gases x, y, and z.

EXAMPLE 1.7.   A boiler flue gas analysis shows, after converting to gravimetric analysis, carbon dioxide 19.5%, carbon monoxide 0.1%, oxygen, 6.2%, nitrogen 74.2%. Find the instantaneous specific heat of the mixture at constant pressure and 500°F if specific heats for the various gases at constant pressure are 0.235 for carbon dioxide, 0.251 for carbon monoxide, 0.22 for oxygen, and 0.256 for nitrogen, all at 500°F.

SOLUTION   Basis: 100 lb flue gas.

Carbon dioxide	(0.195) (0.235)	=	0.0458
Carbon monoxide	(0.001) (0.251)	=	0.000251
Oxygen	(0.062) (0.22)	=	0.01346
Nitrogen	(0.742) (0.256)	=	0.19
Total			0.25 Btu/lb/°F

Gas Constant and Specific Heat Relationships

When making thermodynamic calculations for a given gas, it is quite convenient to have available the established relations that exist for a gas between its specific heat and its individual gas constant (R).

$$c_p = c_v + \frac{R}{778} = c_v + AR \qquad (1.5)$$

$$c_v = \frac{R}{778} \times \frac{1}{k-1} = \frac{AR}{k-1} \qquad (1.6)$$

$$c_p = \frac{R}{778} \times \frac{k}{k-1} = AR \times \frac{k}{k-1} \qquad (1.7)$$

Densities of Gas Mixtures

If the composition of a gas mixture is expressed in molal or weight units, the density is readily determined by selecting a unit molal quantity or weight as the basis and calculating the volume at the specified conditions of temperature and pressure. This method may be applied to gas mixtures which do not follow the perfect gas law.

> EXAMPLE 1.8. A tank 36 in. in diameter by 108 in. long contains air at 80 psig and 65°F. Find the weight and density of air in the tank. How many cubic feet of "free" air is stored in the tank?
>
> SOLUTION Tank volume is $(0.785)(3)^2(9) = 63.6$ ft^3. Air density at tank conditions using 29 for the molecular weight of air, a molal volume of 379 ft^3, and an atmospheric air pressure of 15 psia is
>
> $$\frac{29}{379} \times \frac{80+15}{15} \times \frac{60+460}{65+460} = 0.48 \text{ lb/ft}^3$$
>
> Weight of the air in the tank is $(0.48)(63.6) = 30.5$ lb. "Free" air stored in the tank is $30.5/29\ (379) = 399$ ft^3 at 60°F and 14.7 (approximately) at 15 psia. Note that the actual volume of air that will leave the tank is $399 - 63.6 = 335.4$ ft^3.

1.4. MIXTURES OF GASES AND VAPORS

General

Many problems in the chemical process industries (CPI) involve mixtures of gases and vapors. Even the air we breathe is a mixture of a gas (air) and vapor (water), the air containing oxygen and nitrogen. In an automobile engine a mixture of gasoline vapor and air are exploded. Flue gases leaving furnaces contain moisture as vapor from the combustion of air and hydrocarbons. Air leaving a compressor may be considered as saturated with water vapor. Our discussion here will focus on atmospheric air only. However, many of the principles and equations will also apply generally to a mixture of any vapors and gases. Dalton's law of partial pressures is assumed to hold for these mixtures, although only as an approximation.

Dew Point

If an unsaturated mixture of vapor and gas is cooled, the relative amounts of the components and the percentage by volume composition will at first remain unchanged. Assuming that the various components follow the behavior of a perfect gas, it follows that, if the total pressure is constant, the partial pressure of the vapor will remain unchanged by the cooling. This will be the case until the temperature is lowered to such a value that the vapor pressure of the liquid at this temperature is equal to the existing partial pressure of the vapor pressure in the mixture. The mixture will then become saturated, and any further cooling will result in condensation. The temperature at which the equilibrium vapor pressure of the liquid is equal to the existing partial pressure of the vapor is the dew point. At saturation the dew point is equal to the existing temperature of the gas. As the mixture becomes less saturated, the dew point is lowered. The vapor content of a vapor-gas mixture may be calculated from dew point data, or conversely, the dew point may be predicted from the composition of the mixture.

EXAMPLE 1.9. Water vapor is mixed with nitrogen at a temperature of 80°F and a pressure of 14.7 psia. The dew point of the mixture is 70°F. (1) Calculate the partial pressure of the water vapor, and (2) calculate the volumetric composition of the mixture.

SOLUTION   From steam tables the saturation pressure of water at 70°F is 0.3628 psia, and at 80°F it is 0.5067 psia.

1. Partial pressure water vapor is 0.3628 psia.
2. Composition by volume: water vapor 0.3628/14.7 = 2.47%; nitrogen = 97.53%.

Relative humidity   If a gas contains a vapor in such proportions that its partial pressure is less than the saturation pressure of the liquid at the existing temperature, the mixture is but partially saturated. The relative saturation (relative humidity; RH) of such a mixture may be defined as the percentage ratio of the partial pressure of the vapor to the vapor pressure of the liquid at the existing temperature. Thus relative humidity is a function of both composition of the mixture and its temperature as well as the nature of the vapor, since the nature of the liquid is the most important factor determining the magnitude of the equilibrium vapor pressure.

EXAMPLE 1.10. A mixture of acetone vapor and nitrogen contains 14.8% acetone by volume. Calculate the relative saturation at a temperature of 68°F and 745 mmHg (millimeters of mercury).

SOLUTION   Vapor pressure of acetone at 68°F is 184.8 mmHg. Partial pressure of acetone = (0.148)(745) = 110 mmHg. Relative saturation = 110/184.8 = 0.595, or 59.5%.

Note: relative humidity is relative saturation term applied to water vapor.

Humidity ratio   It is convenient to base calculations on a unit weight of dry gas because the weight of the vapor and, therefore, of the mixture so often varies, while the weight of the dry gas remains constant. Thus,

$$w_v = \frac{\text{vapor density}}{\text{dry gas density}}$$

$$= 0.622 \left(\frac{\text{partial pressure of vapor}}{\text{total pressure - partial pressure of vapor}} \right) \qquad (1.8)$$

where 0.622 = molecular weight of vapor/molecular weight of air. If any other vapor were involved with another gas, their respective molecular weights would be substituted in the ratio.

EXAMPLE 1.11.   How many pounds of moisture must be added each hour to the air entering a building (air is initially 32°F and 60% relative humidity) to produce an inside relative humidity of 30% and 70°F? Building volume is 500,000 ft^3 and there are three air changes taking place each hour. Specific volume of air may be taken as 13.8 ft^3/lb.

SOLUTION   Pressures are so low that the vapor-gas mixture may be considered to be following the perfect gas law. Referring to the steam tables, at 32°F the vapor pressure of water is 0.180 in.Hg. The partial pressure of water in the air at 60% relative humidity is (0.60)(0.180) = 0.108 in.Hg. The humidity ratio becomes applicable to

$$w_v = \frac{(0.622)(0.108)}{29.92 - 0.108} = 0.00226 \text{ lb water per pound of dry air}$$

This is the entering condition for the air-vapor mixture at 32°F. At 70°F vapor pressure of water is found to be 0.739 in.Hg. At 30% RH, the partial pressure of water in the atmosphere is

$$(0.30)(0.739) = 0.221 \text{ in.Hg.}$$

Humidity ratio under the new conditions is

$$\frac{(0.622)(0.222)}{29.92 - 0.222} = 0.00465 \text{ lb water per pound dry air}$$

Water to be added is

$$\frac{500,000 \times 3}{13.8} (0.00465 - 0.00226) = 260 \text{ lb/hr}$$

Vapor content of a saturated gas   When a gas or a gaseous mixture remains in contact with a liquid surface, it will acquire vapor from the liquid until the partial pressure of vapor in the gas mixture equals the vapor pressure of liquid at its existing temperature. When the vapor concentration reaches this equilibrium value, the gas is said to be saturated with vapor. It is not possible for the gas to contain a greater concentration of vapor because, as soon as the vapor pressure of the liquid is exceeded by the partial pressure of the vapor, condensation will take place. The vapor content of a saturated gas is determined by the vapor pressure of the liquid and may be predicted directly from vapor pressure data which, for water, can be found in the steam tables. For ammonia we can use the ammonia tables, and so on. In most cases, at low pressures the partial volume of vapor in a saturated gas may be calculated from

$$V_v = \frac{V\, p_v}{P} \tag{1.9}$$

where V_v is partial volume in cubic feet, P_v is partial pressure in pounds per square inch absolute, V is total volume in cubic feet, and p is total pressure in pounds per square inch absolute. From this equation the percent composition by volume of a vapor-saturated gas may be calculated. The composition on a weight basis may be obtained as heretofore discussed.

EXAMPLE 1.12.   An air compressor is required to deliver 11,200 standard cubic feet per minute (scfm) of dry air measured at 70°F and 14.7 psia. What would be the rating for air entering that is saturated with water vapor at 60°F and 14.25 psia?

SOLUTION   The weight of dry air does not change at constant conditions. The density of air at 70°F and 14.7 psia is given in the tables as 0.07495.

(11,200)(0.07495) = 840 lb per minute of dry air

Obtain the pounds of moisture per pound of dry air by using humidity ratio.

$$\frac{\text{saturation vapor pressure at 60°F}}{14.25 - \text{saturation vapor pressure at 60°F}} \times 0.622$$

$$= \frac{0.2563}{14.25 - 0.2563} \times 0.622$$

$$= 0.01139 \text{ lb water per pound dry air}$$

The weight of the moisture attached to 840 lb dry air under these conditions is

(840)(0.01139) = 9.6 lb water

The total weight of dry air and water = 840 + 9.6 = 849.6 lb. Using the tables, we find that the specific volume of a saturated mixture is 0.07353 lb/ft^3. Therefore

$$\frac{849.6}{0.07353} = 11,554 \text{ scfm rating}$$

1.5. FUELS AND COMBUSTION PRODUCTS

Fuels

The source of heat which is used to produce steam in a boiler is the fuel.
The cost of fuel is by far the greatest single expenditure in the production
of power. Fuels may be solid, liquid, or gaseous. The principal solid
fuels are coal, wood, and lignite. The principal liquid fuels are Bunker
"C" oil, light and heavy oils, and other unrefined petroleum products.
Gaseous fuels are principally natural gas, refinery gas, coke oven gas,
and blast furnace gas. Sawdust, bagasse (sugar cane), garbage, and
sewage disposal wastes may be included, among others. The principal
ingredients of these fuels are hydrogen and carbon.

Combustion Reaction

Compared with the slow oxidation of the rusting of iron, combustion is a
rapid oxidation accompanied by the evolution of heat. The three elements
in fuels which have heating value are carbon, hydrogen, and sulfur. Carbon may combine chemically with air to form either carbon monoxide,
carbon dioxide, or both. Hydrogen forms water. Sulfur forms sulfur
dioxide or the trioxide and, if moisture is present as it usually is in the
stack, sulfurous and sulfuric acids are formed, with resultant corrosion
of the exposed metal surfaces. The average heating value of coal may be
taken as 12,000 Btu/lb. Oxygen for combustion is derived from the air.

Combustion Data in Convenient Form

Much can be written concerning combustion of the common fuels listed
above. Most combustion problems involving mols may be solved simply
by remembering that gas volumes are directly proportional to moles.
Thus, 100% by volume of any gas mixture may be taken as 100 mol. Then
5% becomes 5 mol, and so on. After figuring the amount of atmospheric
oxygen used in combustion, it is often desirable to determine the amount
of nitrogen or air this involves. Here are the conversion factors based on
the fact that air is 21% oxygen by volume and 23% oxygen by weight: air
volume equals volume of oxygen divided by 0.21; weight of air equals
weight of oxygen divided by 0.23. Table 1.1 provides consolidated combustion data.

Oxygen for Combustion

Oxygen for combustion is derived from the atmosphere which is composed
of 21% oxygen and 79% nitrogen by volume. Accordingly, there are $0.79/0.21 = 3.76$ ft^3 (or mol) nitrogen per cubic foot (or mole) of oxygen. To
show how nitrogen goes through the combustion process unchanged, let's

TABLE 1.1 Consolidated Combustion Data: Air Required and Combustion Products [table gives required combustion air and products for common combustibles burned with theoretical air requirements—air and products are given in mols, cu ft and lb (see right-hand column) for 1 mol, 1 cu ft, and 1 lb of fuel]

Fuel	For 1 mol of fuel — Air O_2	N_2	Other products CO_2	H_2O	SO_2	For 1 cu ft of fuel — Air O_2	N_2	Other products CO_2	H_2O	SO_2	For 1 pound of fuel — Air O_2	N_2	Other products CO_2	H_2O	SO_2	
C	1.0	3.76	1.0								.0833	.313	.0833			Mols
	379	1425	379								31.6	118.8	31.6			Cu ft
	32.0	105	44.0								2.67	8.78	3.67			Pounds
H_2[a]	0.5	1.88		1.0		.00132	.00496		.00264		.250	.940		0.5		Mols
	189.5	712		379b		0.5	1.88		1.0b		94.8	356		189.5b		Cu ft
	16.0	52.6		18.0		.0422	.139		.0475		8.0	26.3		9.0		Pounds
S	1.0	3.76			1.0						.0312	.1176			.0312	Mols
	379	1425			379						11.84	44.6			11.84	Cu ft
	32.0	105			64						1.0	3.29			2.0	Pounds
CO	0.5	1.88	1.0			.00132	.00496	.00264			.0179	.0672	.0357			Mols
	189.5	712	379			0.5	1.88	1.0			6.77	25.4	13.53			Cu ft
	16.0	52.6	44.0			.0422	.139	.116			.571	1.88	1.57			Pounds
CH_4	2.0	7.52	1.0	2.0		.00528	.0198	.00264	.00528		.125	.470	.0625	.125		Mols
	758	2850	379	758*		2.0	7.52	1.0	2.0b		47.4	178	23.7	47.4b		Cu ft
	64.0	210	44.0	36.0		.169	.556	.116	.0950		4.0	13.17	2.75	2.25		Pounds
C_2H_2	2.5	9.40	2.0	1.0		.0066	.0248	.00528	.00264		.0962	.362	.0769	.0385		Mols
	947	3560	758b	379b		2.5	9.40	2.0	1.0b		36.4	137	29.15	14.58b		Cu ft
	80.0	263	88.0	18.0		.211	.694	.232	.0475		3.08	10.13	3.38	.692		Pounds
C_2H_4	3.0	11.29	2.0	2.0		.00792	.0298	.00528	.00528		.1071	.403	.0714	.0714		Mols
	1137	4280	758	758*		3.0	11.29	2.0	2.0*		40.6	153	27.1	27.1b		Cu ft
	96.0	316	88.0	36.0		.253	.834	.232	.0950		3.43	11.29	3.14	1.286		Pounds
C_2H_6	3.5	13.17	2.0	3.0		.00923	.0347	.00528	.0079		.1167	.439	.0667	.10		Mols
	1326	4990	758	1137b		3.5	13.17	2.0	3.0*		44.2	166.3	25.3	37.9b		Cu ft
	112.0	369	88.0	54.0		.296	.972	.232	.1425		3.73	12.29	2.93	1.8		Pounds

*The volumes shown for H_2O apply only where the combustion products are at such high temperatures that all the H_2O is a gas.

**Varying assumptions for molecular weight introduce a slight inconsistency in the values of air and combustion products from the burning of hydrogen. True molecular weight of hydrogen is 2.02 but the approximate value of 2 is used in figuring the air and combustion products.

Source: Consolidated combustion data: air required and combustion products, Power, Sept. 1945, p. 106.

examine the combustion of hydrogen with air using the ratios just determined.

$$2H_2 + O_2 + 3.76N_2 \rightarrow 2H_2O + 3.76N_2 \qquad (1.10)$$

The composition of air by weight is used here as 23.13% oxygen and 76.87% nitrogen. From this we can calculate that there are 3.32 lb H_2 per pound of O_2. In practice a fuel will not burn completely when mixed with no more than the theoretical amount of air. The desirable amount of air will depend on the combustion conditions.

Gross Heating Value of Fuels

The gross heating value of fuels is used in all combustion calculations and is the amount of heat evolved by one pound of fuel when the products of combustion are returned to their original temperature before combustion. These values are usually given at 60°F.

Water vapor appears in the products of combustion whenever the fuel contains hydrogen in combined (C_2H_2) or free form (H_2). This vapor condenses when the stack gases are cooled below the dew point, giving up heat, the amount of which depends upon the weight condensed. If all the vapor is condensed, the maximum amount of heat is given up by the products of combustion, and the corresponding heating value is called the gross or higher heating value. However, in the actual operation of a boiler or gas engine, the exhaust temperature is above the boiling point of water at atmospheric pressure and, therefore, the actual heat available is the net or lower heating value.

Information on the higher heating values of selected fuels can be found in Table 1.2.

Air Required for Combustion

In the selection of combustion equipment, theoretical air requirements are used. Table 1.1 gives complete data for this purpose.

In practice an amount of air in excess of that required theoretically is introduced with the fuel to influence complete combustion. While this theoretical value is easily calculated when the fuel analysis is given, the amount of air actually required for a given installation will be known by experience and influenced by economical limitations. Table 1.3 gives practical percentage values of excess air by weight for different fuels.

The amount of air needed to burn a fuel completely is very small, but in order to obtain maximum steam output, insure complete combustion, avoid smoking, avoid overheating, minimize slagging when burning coal, and insure adequate mixing of the combustion gases with air, it is necessary to use from 10 to 75% excess air by weight. If this is not done, some of the oxygen will escape without combining with its allotted share of the

TABLE 1.2 Higher Heating Values of Selected Fuels

Combustible	Gross heating value (Btu/lb)	Combustible	Gross heating value (Btu/lb)
Carbon to CO	4,350	Acetylene	21,465
Carbon to CO_2	14,544	Ethane	22,226
Hydrogen	61,523	Hydrogen sulfide	7,459
Methane	23,838	Octane	20,550
Propane	21,651	Coal	12,000
Bunker "C" oil	18,000		

combustible matter, some of the hydrogen will escape unburned, or the partial combustion of the carbon in the fuel to carbon monoxide or even carbon alone will result.

Preventable Fuel Loss

The potential reduction in the loss of fuel is indicated by the percentage CO_2 in the flue or stack gases. Table 1.4 shows this when ashpit or solid carbon loss are not included.

Best Combustion Conditions

When CO_2 percentage is as high as possible, one would think that boiler economy is as high as possible. This is not true, especially when the

TABLE 1.3 Excess Air by Weight for Different Fuels

Fuel	Percent excess	Fuel	Percent excess
Bunker "C" oil	20	Bagasse (sugar cane)	50
Natural gas	15	Blast furnace gas	20
Refinery gas	15	Coke oven gas	20
Tar	30	Coal, pulverized	25
Wood	50	Coal, stoker	40

TABLE 1.4   Preventable Fuel Loss

Percent CO_2	Percent loss	Percent CO_2	Percent loss
14	0	7	13.30
13	1.03	6	17.72
12	2.22	5	23.94
11	3.63	4	33.23
10	5.33	3	48.80
9	7.39	2	79.90
8	9.97	1.8	90.30

Orsat analysis shows no CO and only a reasonable amount of free O_2, not over 6%. The presence of any CO represents a heat loss up the stack. In some boiler plants, especially those with large combustion chambers, the percentage CO_2 will run high, say up to 13%, and yet no CO will be present in the stack gas. In installations with small furnace volumes, as soon as the CO_2 runs above 6-8%, CO begins to show in the stack gases with attendant heat loss up the stack. Therefore, keep CO_2 as high as possible, with CO and O_2 never over 6%. Smoke is the result of incomplete combustion and, for the most part, is made up of combustibles which are distilled from the fuel but were not mixed with air and ignited in the furnace. Perfect or near perfect combustion of any fuel will give off a very slight haze which usually indicates proper firing. For good combustion, time, temperature, turbulence, and uniformity must be attained.

Minimum Temperature

A minimum temperature is required to bring about the important chemical reactions in a furnace. We install refractory brack and refractory arches to reflect heat and keep temperatures up until combustible gases have been burned. Turbulence is important in bringing about intimate mixing of gases and air. This is effected by the use of steam or air jets, wing walls, and arches. Uniformity of fire bed in stoker firing and a uniform supply of fuel and air are important but are most frequently violated.

   EXAMPLE 1.13.   Calculate the pounds of air and the products of combustion required and formed, respectively, when 1 lb of a gasoline composed of 85% carbon and 15% hydrogen is burned with the theoretical amount of air. What percentage of CO_2 exists in the products of combustion by volume?

SOLUTION   Basis: 1 lb fuel and standard gas conditions. Make up the table below and refer to Table 1.1.

Fuel	Wt. %	Wt. fract. lb	Theoretical air lb/lb	lb	CO_2 lb/lb	lb	H_2O lb/lb	lb	N_2 lb/lb	lb
C	85	0.85	11.54	9.8	3.7	3.12	–		8.87	7.52
H_2	15	0.15	34.6	5.4	–	–	9.0	1.35	26.56	4.0
Total				15.2		3.12		1.35		11.52

Orsat analyzer shows no water vapor due to condensation at room temperature. Since water vapor condenses out, only CO_2 and H_2 remain. We now calculate volumes that the weight of each gas will occupy at standard conditions and divide each volume so obtained by the total volume to obtain the volume fraction or percent.

$$\text{Volume } CO_2 = \frac{3.12}{44} \times 379 \text{ (molal volume)} = 27 \text{ ft}^3$$

$$\text{Volume } H_2 = \frac{11.52}{28} \times 379 \text{ (molal volume)} = 156 \text{ ft}^3$$

Then $(27)/(27 + 156) = 0.148$ or 14.8% CO_2

EXAMPLE 1.14.   A steam boiler flue gas analysis shows 14% CO_2, 2% CO, 5% O_2, and 79% N_2. Calculate the percent heat lost in the unburned CO as stack loss.

SOLUTION   Solution scheme:

$$\frac{\text{Heat given if all C burned to } CO_2 - \text{ actual heat generated}}{\text{Heat given if all C burned to } CO_2}$$

Set down theoretical combustion reactions for complete or partial combustion.

$$C + O_2 = CO_2 + 14{,}544 \text{ Btu per pound of carbon}$$

$$2C + O_2 = 2CO + 4{,}350 \text{ Btu per pound of carbon}$$

On a basis of 100 mol flue gas as analyzed, there are 14 mol

CO_2 and 2 mol CO. Since there are 16 lb atoms in 14 mol CO_2 and 2 mol CO, we can substitute in the heat generation ratio above as follows:

$$\frac{(14 + 2)(12)(14,544) - [(2)(12)(4,350) + (14)(12)(14,544)]}{(14 + 2)(12)(14,544)} \times 100$$

$$= 8.8\% \text{ lost}$$

EXAMPLE 1.15.   Three pounds of carbon are burned in air to carbon dioxide. What will be the weight of the products of combustion if twice the theoretical quantity (100% excess) of air is used?

SOLUTION   Set up the theoretical combustion equation.

$$C + O_2 = CO_2$$

Nitrogen from the air will also be included. Now refer to Table 1.1.

$$CO_2 = 3.67 \times 3 = 11 \text{ lb}$$

$$O_2 = 2.67 \times 3 = 8 \text{ lb}$$

$$N_2 = 8.78 \times 3 \times 2 = 52.68 \text{ lb}$$

The above O_2 weight is the excess or 100% overage. The total weight of products = 11 + 8 + 52.68 = 71.68 lb.

EXAMPLE 1.16.   What volume of oxygen will be required to burn 5 lb carbon to carbon dioxide? What weight of air is required? How much nitrogen does this represent?

SOLUTION   Refer to Table 1.1.

1. $(5)(31.6) = 158 \text{ ft}^3$ oxygen.
2. $(5)(2.67 + 8.87) = 57.70$ lb air.
3. $(5)(8.87) = 44.35$ lb nitrogen is represented.

2
IDENTIFYING SOURCES OF AIR CONTAMINANTS

2.1. INTRODUCTION

Operations of the petroleum industry can be divided into production, refining, and marketing. In this book we will concern ourselves with controlling the in-plant environment for the refining phase, which extends to the conversion of crude oil to a finished saleable product and also includes oil refining and petrochemical processing or the manufacture of various chemicals derived from petroleum. This is also represented by the chemical process industries (CPI) and their contributions to the in-plant contaminant problem. Control of contaminants outside the plant and affecting the neighborhood will not be treated, but the reader is referred to the bibliography hereinafter documented.

2.2. REFINING

Surely the petroleum industry has installed equipment in its plants or modified existing equipment not only to prevent economic losses but also to try

TABLE 2.1. Potential Sources of Emissions from Oil Refineries

Emission	Potential source
Hydrocarbons	Air blowing, barometric condensers, blind changing, blowdown systems, boilers, catalyst regenerators, compressors, cooling towers, decoking operations, flares, heaters, incinerators, loading facilities, processing vessels, pumps, sampling operations, tanks, turnaround operations, vacuum jets, waste-effluent handling
Sulfur oxides	Boilers, catalyst regenerators, decoking operations, flares, heaters, incinerators, treaters, acid-sludge disposal
Carbon monoxide	Catalyst regenerators, compressor engines, coking operations, incinerators
Nitrogen oxides	Boilers, catalyst regenerators, compressor engines, flares
Particulate matter	Boilers, catalyst regenerators, coking operations, heaters, incinerators
Odors	Air blowing, barometric condensers, drains, process vessels, steam blowing, tanks, teaters, waste effluent-handling equipment
Aldehydes	Catalyst regenerators, compressor engines
Ammonia	Catalyst regenerators

to improve community relations, prevent fire hazards, and comply with air pollution laws. The air contaminants emitted from piping and processing equipment associated with the CPI and oil refining include hydrocarbons, carbon monoxide, sulfur and nitrogen compounds, malodorous materials, particulate matter, aldehydes, organic acids, and ammonia. The potential sources of these pollutants are shown in Table 2.1. See Marchello, J. M. (1976).

Flares and Blowdown Systems

In order to prevent unsafe operating conditions of excessive pressure build-up in processing units during start-up and shutdown and to safely handle extraneous hydrocarbon leaks, a refinery must provide a means of venting hydrocarbon vapors safely. This can be accomplished by using either a properly sized elevated flare stack using steam injection or a series of venturi burners actuated by pressure variations. Good instrumentation and properly balanced steam-to-hydrocarbon ratios are prime factors in the design of a safe, smokeless flare. See Brumbaugh, A. K., Jr. (1947).

Pressure Relief Valves

In refining operations, pressure vessels are protected from overpressure by relief-valve systems. The relief valves themselves are normally spring loaded. Corrosion and improper reseating of the valve seat results in leakage. Proper maintenance through routine inspection, the use of rupture discs, or manifolding the discharge or downstream side to a vapor recovery system or to a flare, will minimize air contamination from this source.

Storage Vessels

Tankage and other storage vessels used to store crude oil and volatile petroleum distillates are a large potential source of hydrocarbon emissions. Hydrocarbons can be discharged to the atmosphere from such sources as a result of diurnal temperature changes, filling operations, and general volatilization. High control efficiencies can be realized by incorporating properly designed vapor recovery or disposal systems, floating-roof tanks, or pressure tanks.

Bulk-loading Facilities

The filling of vessels or tank trucks used for transporting petroleum products is a potential large source of hydrocarbon emissions. As the product is being loaded, it displaces gases containing hydrocarbons which then can escape to the atmosphere. A tested method of preventing these emissions is by collecting the vapors by enclosing the filling hatch and piping the captured vapors to recovery or disposal equipment. The use of submerged filling and bottom loading can also reduce the amount of displaced hydrocarbons.

Catalyst Regenerators

Modern refining processes include many operations using solid-type catalysts. These catalysts become contaminated with coke buildup during operation and must be regenerated or discarded. For certain processes to be economically feasible, for example, catalyst cracking, regeneration of the catalyst is a "must" and is achieved by burning off the coke under controlled combustion conditions. The resulting flue gases may contain catalyst dust, hydrocarbons, and other impurities originating in the charge stock, together with the products of combustion.

The dust problem in the regeneration of moving-bed-type catalysts requires control by water scrubbers and cyclones, cyclones and electrostatic precipitators, or high-efficiency cyclones, depending on the type of catalyst, the process, and the regenerator conditions. Hydrocarbons, carbon monoxide, ammonia, and organic acids can be controlled effectively by incineration in carbon monoxide waste-heat boilers. The waste-boiler offers a secondary control feature for plumes emitted from fluid catalyst cracking units. Other processes in refining operations employ liquid or solid catalysts. Regenerating some of these catalysts at the unit is feasible. Other catalysts are consumed or require special treatment by their manufacturer. Where regeneration is possible, a closed system can be applied to minimize the release of any air contaminants by venting the regenerator effluent to the firebox of the heater.

Effluent-Waste Disposal

Waste water, spent acids, spent caustic, and other waste liquid materials are generated by refining operations and present disposal problems. The waste water is processed through clarification units or gravity separators. Unless adequate control measures are applied, hydrocarbons contained in the waste water are released to the atmosphere. Acceptable control is achieved by venting the clarifier to vapor recovery and enclosing the separator with a floating roof or a vapor-tight cover. In the latter case, the vapor section should be gas blanketed to prevent explosive mixtures and fires. Spent waste materials can be recovered as acids or phenolic compounds or hauled to an acceptable disposal site (ocean or desert).

Processing Pumps and Compressors

Processing pumps and compressors required to move or transport liquids and gases in the refinery can leak product at the point of contact between the rotating shaft and stationary casing at the packing gland. Properly maintained packing glands or mechanical seals minimize the emissions from pumps. Compressor glands can be vented to a vapor recovery system or smokeless flare.

The internal combustion engines normally used to drive the compressors are fueled by natural gas or refinery process gas. Even with relatively high combustion efficiency and steady load conditions, some fuel can still pass through the engine unburned. Nitrogen oxides, aldehydes, and sulfur oxides can also be found in the exhaust gases. Control methods for reducing these contaminants continue to be studied.

Air-blowing Operations

Venting the air used for "brightening" and agitating petroleum products or oxidation of asphalt results in a discharge of entrained hydrocarbons, as mists and vapors, and malodorous compounds. Mechanical agitators that replace air agitation can reduce the volumes of these emissions. For the fumes from asphalt oxidation, incineration provides effective control.

Pipeline Valves and Flanges, Blind Changing, Process Drains

Liquid and vapor leaks can develop at valve stems as a result of heat, pressure, friction, corrosion, and vibration. Regular equipment inspections followed by adequate maintenance can keep losses at a minimum. Leaks at flanged connections are negligible if the connections are properly installed and maintained. Installation and removal of pipeline blinds can result in spillage of product. A certain amount of this spilled product evaporates regardless of drainage and flushing facilities. Special pipeline blinds have, however, been developed to reduce the amount of spillage.

In refinery and other plant operations, condensate water and flushing water must be drained from process equipment. Such drains also remove liquid leakage or spills used to cool pump glands. Modern refining and processing plant designs provide waste water-effluent systems with running-liquid-sealed traps and liquid-sealed and covered junction boxes. These seals keep the amount of liquid hydrocarbons exposed to the air to a minimum and thereby reduce hydrocarbon losses.

Cooling Towers

The large amount of water used for cooling is conserved by recooling the water in cooling towers. Cooling is accomplished by evaporating a part of the incoming water. Any hydrocarbons that might be entrained or dissolved in the water as a result of leakage from heat exchangers or other equipment are readily discharged to the atmosphere. Proper design and maintenance of heat exchanger equipment can minimize these losses. The new fin-fan cooling equipment has also replaced the need for the conventional cooling tower in many instances. A word of caution: process water that has come in contact with a hydrocarbon stream or has otherwise been contaminated with odorous materials should not be piped to a cooling tower.

Vacuum Jets and Barometric Condensers

In the CPI some processing equipment is operated at less than atmospheric pressure. Steam-driven vacuum jets and barometric condensers are used to obtain the desired vacuum. The lighter hydrocarbons that are not condensed are discharged to the atmosphere unless controlled. These can be completely controlled by incinerating the discharge. The barometric hot well can also be enclosed and vented to a vapor disposal system. The water from the hot well should not be returned to the cooling tower.

Effective Air Pollution Control Measures

As we have seen before, control of air contaminants can be achieved by process change, installation of control equipment, improved housekeeping,

TABLE 2.2. Some Control Measures for Reduction of Air Contaminants

Source	Control
Storage vessels	Vapor recovery systems, floating-roof tanks, pressure tanks, vapor balance, painting tanks white
Catalyst regenerators	Cyclones-precipitator-CO boiler, cyclones-water scrubber, multiple cyclones
Accumulator vents	Vapor recovery, vapor incineration
Blowdown systems	Smokeless flares-gas recovery
Pumps and compressors	Mechanical seals, vapor recovery, sealing glands by oil pressure, maintenance
Vacuum jets	Vapor incineration
Equipment valves	Inspection and maintenance
Pressure relief valves	Vapor recovery, vapor incineration, rupture discs, inspection and maintenance
Effluent-waste disposal	Enclosing separators, covering sewer boxes and using liquid seal, liquid seals on drains
Bulk-loading facilities	Vapor collection with recovery or incineration, submerged or bottom loading
Acid treating	Continuous-type agitators with mechanical mixing, replace with catalytic hydrogenation units, incinerate all vented cases, stop sludge burning
Acid sludge storage shipping	Caustic scrubbing, incineration, vapor return system, disposal at sea
Spent caustic handling	Incineration, scrubbing
Doctor treating	Steam strip spent doctor solution to hydrocarbon recovery before air regeneration, replace treating unit with other less objectionable units
Sour-water treating	Use sour-water oxidizers and gas incineration, conversion to ammonium sulfate
Mercaptan disposal	Conversion to disulfides, adding to catalytic cracking charge stock, incineration, using material in organic synthesis
Asphalt blowing	Incineration, water scrubbing (nonrecirculating type)
Shutdowns, turnarounds	Depressure and purge to vapor recovery

and better equipment maintenance through preventative maintenance programs. Some combination of these can often prove the most effective solution. These techniques are also applicable to the petrochemical and associated industries. Table 2.2 lists various methods for controlling most air pollution sources in the CPI and oil refineries.

Waste Gas Disposal

Large volumes of hydrocarbon gases are produced in modern refinery and petrochemical plants. Generally, these gases are used as fuel or as raw material for further processing. In the past, however, large quantities of these gases were considered waste gases and, along with waste liquids, were dumped into open pits and burned, producing large volumes of thick, black smoke. With the modernization of processing techniques and units, this method of waste gas disposal, even for emergency gas releases, has become less acceptable to the industry. Moreover, many local governments have adopted or are contemplating ordinances limiting the opacity of smoke from combustion processing.

Nevertheless, industries are still faced with the problem of safe disposal of volatile liquids and gases resulting from scheduled shutdowns and sudden and/or expected upsets in process units. Operational emergencies that can cause the sudden venting of excessive amounts of gases and vapors include fires, compressor failures, overpressure in process vessels, line breaks, and power failures. Uncontrolled releases of large volumes of gases also constitute a serious safety hazard to workers and equipment.

Typical Waste Disposal System

A system for the disposal of emergency and waste refinery gases consists of a manifolded pressure-relieving or blowdown system, and a blowdown recovery system or a system of flares for the combustion of the excess gases, or both. In addition to disposing of emergency and excess gas flows, these systems are used in the evacuation of units during shutdown and turnarounds. Normally, a unit is shut down by depressuring into a fuel gas or vapor recovery system, with further depressuring to essentially atmospheric pressures by venting to a low-pressure flare system. Thus, overall emissions of hydrocarbons are substantially reduced (11).

A blowdown or pressure-relieving system consists of relief valves, safety valves, manual bypass valves, blowdown headers, knockout drums, and holding tanks. A blowdown recovery system also includes compressors and vapor surge vessels such as gas holders or vapor spheres. Flares are usually considered as part of the blowdown system. Blowdown systems are usually segregated according to operating pressure. For instance, there can be a high-pressure system for equipment operating at 100 psig and over, and another for operating pressures below 100 psig.

3

PLANT LAYOUT AND CLASSIFICATION OF HAZARDOUS AREAS

3.1. INTRODUCTION

In this chapter our purpose is to describe the steps that are taken in the
design stages of a refinery or petrochemical plant to ensure worker safety
and health. Today these industries are dealing with more flammable and
potentially explosive products than ever before, and the drafting board
stage is the battleground to mitigate these problems before they become
reality. We have a potent combination: more and more plant areas with
potentially explosive atmospheres, and more and more electrical equipment, control instrumentation, lighting fixtures, and so on, that must operate safely within these areas.

3.2. PLANT LAYOUT

Preliminary Plot Plan

When the process flowsheet and data are released to the designer, plot plan
orientation can be started. The most important task is to establish a preliminary plot plan of buildings and major equipment indoors and outdoors.
For this the basic proportions of the equipment items are established from
flowsheet data and integrated into the arrangement. A number of alternative
schemes are made and reviewed by the planning group in collaboration with
the engineering groups.

The optimum plot plan is selected to suit the plant design and physical
constraints of the site. The firm design is agreed upon and all requirements of civil, chemical, electrical, and mechanical engineering are coordinated into the final layout.

Classification of Process Areas

Within the plot plan, the classification of areas is covered in detail. This
classification of areas is determined by reference to the National Electrical
Code (NEC) and the American Petroleum Institute (API) Standard RP 500,
bearing the title "API Recommended Practice for Classification of Areas
for Electrical Installations in Petroleum Refineries." As outlined in its
foreword, the API standard refers to petroleum refineries only and does
not provide a basis for classifying other areas where petroleum or its
products are handled. However, the standard is used widely as a guide in
the Chemical process industries (CPI) for hazardous liquids, gases, and
vapors.

The NEC is considered the definitive classification tool, so far as it
goes. Insurance companies and their inspectors generally insist that hazardous areas contain only electrical equipment listed and approved by
Underwriter's Laboratories (UL) under this code. Most state, municipalities, and public service companies also use the NEC as a standard. See
McPartland, J. (1979).

Electrical Safety—Hazardous Areas

The plant layout carefully segregates hazardous areas from nonhazardous
areas for classification purposes and for the use of electrical equipment
such as switchgear, motors, controls, etc. See LeVine, R. Y. (1972).
General purpose electrical equipment can cause explosions in areas
where flammable liquids, gases, or dusts are present. These areas require equipment suitable for the following precautions: (1) explosion proofing (of gases and vapors), (2) dust-ignition proofing, (3) spark prevention
(in ventilated areas), (4) purging and pressurization, and (5) making areas
intrinsically safe.

Flammable Gases, Vapors, and Liquids

Every flammable gas or vapor has a range of concentration in air within
which ignition and explosion can occur. This is known as the explosion
range. If the concentration (percent by volume of gas or vapor in air) is
outside the explosive range, the mixture is too lean to burn. The lower
limit of the range is known as the lower limit of explosibility (LEL), and
the upper limit is called the upper limit of explosibility (UEL). See Hickes,
W. F. (1972) and Hettig, S. B. (1966).
Properties of primary interest from the ignition point of view are
(1) vapor density, (2) LEL, (3) volatility, (4) flash point, (5) ignition temperature, and (6) ignition energy (see Table 3.1).

TABLE 3.1. Properties of Some Flammable Liquids and Gases

Material	Explosive range (% vol. in air) Lower	Upper	Vapor density (air = 1)	Flash point	Boiling point	Auto ignition
Acetone	2.6	12.8	2.0	0	134	1000
Acetylene	2.5	80	0.9	Gas	-118	571
Ammonia	16	27	0.6	Gas	-28	1204
Carbon disulfide	1.3	44	2.6	-22	115	212
Ethylene	2.8	28.6	1.0	Gas	-155	914
Ethylene oxide	3.6	100	1.5	<0	51	804
Ethyl ether	1.9	48.5	2.6	-49	95	356
Gasoline	1.3	7	3.0	-45	100–400	536
Hydrogen	4.0	74.2	0.1	Gas	-22	1035
Methanol	6.7	36.5	1.1	52	147	725
Propylene oxide	2.8	37	2.0	-35	95	—
Vinyl chloride	3.6	33	2.2	Gas	7	882

Temperature (°F) spans Flash point, Boiling point, Auto ignition columns.

TABLE 3.2. National Fire Protection Association Classifications of
Liquids

Type	Flash point	Boiling point
Flammable liquids		
1a	Below 73°F	Below 100°F
1b	Below 73°F	At or above 100°F
1c	At 73°F and below 100°F	
II	At 100°F and below 140°F	
Combustible liquids		
IIa	At 140°F and below 200°F	
IIIb	At or above 200°F	

Note: NFPA pamphlet No. 30, "Flammable and Combustible Liquids
Code," uses boiling point for comparing the volatility of flammable liquids.

Enrichment with oxygen widens the explosive range. In a pure-oxygen
atmosphere many materials not ordinarily flammable will burn vigorously.
Electrical equipment that is safe in fuel and air mixtures will not necessarily be safe in mixtures of fuel and oxygen-enriched air. Table 3.1
gives the explosive limits as well as a number of other fire and explosion properties.

Theoretically, a flammable liquid is not as hazardous as a flammable
gas or vapor. When a flammable liquid is spilled, the area in which the
spill has occurred does not become hazardous until enough of it has evaporated for the vapor concentration to reach the LEL. When, however, a
flammable gas or vapor is released, the area of this action becomes hazardous. The more volatile the liquid, the sooner the vapor concentration
will reach the LEL. The flash point of a flammable liquid is the temperature at which the liquid gives off enough vapors to form an ignitable mixture. This corresponds to the LEL. The more volatile a liquid and the
lower its flash point, the more closely it approximates a flammable gas or
vapor.

A combustible liquid with a flash point above 200°F is not considered
very hazardous. However, if handled at a temperature above its flash
point, its vapors will be flammable. Ordinarily, special electrical equipment is not required for code Class IIIb combustible liquids (see Table 3.2).
All gases and vapors have a tendency to disperse into the atmosphere and
become mixed with air and diluted. A lighter-than-air gas such as hydrogen diffuses into the atmosphere so readily that, except in enclosed spaces,
it usually does not produce hazardous mixtures.

Heavier gases with molecular weights greater than that of air (molecular weight of 29) are less likely to disperse in quiet areas. Carbon

disulfide and ethyl ether tend to creep along floors and surfaces. However, due to rotating and moving machinery and equipment and worker traffic within a room together with convection currents, mixing takes place. If the mixture reaches a source of ignition, such as a sparking electric motor or even an electric water cooler or telephone, a fire or explosion will result.

Mechanism of Ignition

The ignition temperature is that to which a fuel-air mixture needs to be heated for the mixture to ignite spontaneously, without the introduction of a flame or spark. For a hot surface to serve as an ignition source, it has to be large and hot enough to heat a fuel-air mixture to its point of ignition. If the surface area is large enough in relation to the volume of the fuel-air mixture, ignition will take place faster and the surface temperature can be lower than that for a smaller surface area. Let's take for example the air space within an electric motor. This is small in relation to the area of the hot metal surface of the armature or motor windings. Therefore, when a flammable mixture fills the air space, it will readily ignite if the surface temperature is at or above the autoignition temperature (see Table 3.1).

A much better source of ignition is a spark. Because of its concentration and high temperature, a small spark can be capable of heating a fuel-air mixture to its ignition temperature at the interface. Then, once ignition takes place, flames propagate rapidly throughout the mass. If the spark is involved with a volatile liquid and the heat is below its flash point, the spark must endure long enough to volatilize some of the liquid and then ignite its vapors. Then all it takes is the heat of the initial flame to sustain the combustion. Stoichiometric mixtures of fuel and air require the least spark energy due to the absence of the diluting effect of the air or fuel. Experiments tell that most flammable gases and vapors can be ignited by spark energies of 10 mJ or less.

Flammable Dusts

Flammable dusts that have properties of primary interest from an ignition point of view are those of particle size, minimum explosive concentration, dust-layer ignition temperature, and dust-cloud ignition energy. A dust explosion is the rapid combustion of dust particles in the air, accompanied by a rise in pressure in the surrounding air and gaseous products of combustion energy. Most large dust explosions are multiple explosions, with settled dust thrown into the air providing fuel for secondary, often more violent, explosions. See Hartman, I. (1947).

Generally, the finer the dust, the greater the chance of explosion. The most explosive dust is that finer than 200 mesh. Dust larger than 100 mesh is usually not hazardous. However, any dust finer than 60 mesh can be thrown into suspension by the turbulence ahead of an explosion flame, and so propagate a dust explosion.

Dust Explosion Pressures

There is a minimum concentration of dust below which an explosion will not occur. Explosions are most violent when the concentration of dust slightly exceeds that required for stoichiometric reaction with oxygen in an atmosphere. They are least violent at the minimum explosive concentration.

TABLE 3.3. Maximum Dust Explosion Pressures

Type of dust	Maximum dust explosion pressure
Coal dust	48 psig
Grain dust	46
Starches	47
Sugars	45
Woods	44
Sulfur	32
Hard rubber	37
Cork	40
Metal dusts	72
Fertilizers	51
Milk powders	42
Cocoa	23
Flours	42
Meals	42
Spices	43
Drugs	43
Resins, waxes, soaps	42
Shellac, rosin, gums	58
Phenolic resins	41
Cellulose acetates	68
Ground cotton floc	67
Ground wood flour	62
Asbestos, mica	Present no explosion hazard

Source: Data based on tests made in the dust-explosion laboratory of the Bureau of Mines, U.S. Department of Agriculture, Pittsburgh, Pennsylvania, report of investigation No. 3751.

Turbulence that intimately mixes the dust and air greatly increases the violence. Metallic dusts present a special problem because of their conductivity. They cause tracking, shorting, and arcing in ordinary electrical devices, in effect creating their own source of ignition.

The minimum ignition temperatures of dust layers of certain dusts are important. For a layer of wood flour it is 500°F, and for a cloud of wood flour it is 860°F. Wood flour if left in a layer at high temperature, will heat and eventually ignite. The flaming layer then becomes a source of ignition for the cloud. For this reason, the surface temperatures of electrical equipment upon which layers of dust can collect (such as motors) must be carefully controlled. The ignition temperature range of dust clouds is about the same as that of clouds of vapors and gases (482-1112°F). Thus, some flammable vapors and dusts can be ignited by the normally hot surfaces of electrical equipment.

Table 3.3 lists maximum explosion pressures attained by various dusts as determined by the U.S. Bureau of Mines.

3.3. THE NATIONAL ELECTRICAL CODE

Electrical equipment such as switch gear, circuit breakers, motor starters, pushbutton stations, and receptacles can produce arcs or sparks when contacts are opened and closed. Somewhat less hazardous is equipment that produces heat, such as lighting fixtures and motors. But surface temperatures of even these can exceed the ignition temperatures of some flammable atmospheres. A loose bulb in a fixture socket presents a double hazard, as it may combine arcing with the production of heat.

Many parts of an electrical system, including wiring connections— especially splices—transformers, impedance coils, solenoids, and other low-temperature equipment without contacts may become sources of ignition when insulation fails. To keep electrical installations from becoming a major source of ignition in areas where there may be explosive concentrations of gases, vapors, or dusts, there are special rules in Article 500 of the National Electrical Code that deal with electrical equipment in hazardous locations. As previously indicated, the code has been widely adopted by local and state governments, insurance companies, and industry. Recently, it was made a part of the safety standards of the Occupational Safety and Health Act (OSHA). The Federal Register of February 16, 1972, officially adopted the 1971 NEC as an OSHA standard. The Guide to OSHA Fire Protection Regulations has been published in cooperation with the OSHA administration by the National Fire Protection Association (NFPA) at 60 Batterymarch Street, Boston, Massachusetts 02110.

Article 500 defines three classes of hazardous locations:

Class I: locations made hazardous by flammable gases or vapors.
Class II: locations made hazardous by combustible dusts.

Class III: locations made hazardous by ignitable fibers or flyings. (This class is of little interest to the CPI.)

Class I Areas

Class I locations are divided into two divisions, with the first covering more hazardous locations than the second.

Class I, Division 1 locations are those (1) where hazardous concentrations of flammable vapors or gases exist continuously, intermittently, or periodically under normal conditions of operation and maintenance and with normal leakage; and (2) where the breakdown or faulty operation of process equipment could release explosive concentrations of fuels and cause a simultaneous failure of electrical equipment.

Class I, Division 2 locations are those (1) adjacent to division 1 locations which may occasionally be reached by hazardous concentrations; (2) where flammable volatile liquids or gases are handled, processed, or used but where concentrations are not normally hazardous because the liquids or gases are in closed systems; and (3) where hazardous concentrations are normally prevented by positive pressure ventilation. All these locations become hazardous only when vessels or piping are accidentally ruptured or when positive ventilation systems fail.

Precautions for Class I, Division 1 Locations

The entry of gases or vapors into unpressured electrical equipment cannot be prevented by even the tightest of gaskets. Accordingly, if electrical equipment operates long enough within an explosive atmosphere, and if there is a strong enough spark or a sufficiently hot surface, an explosion will eventually occur inside the equipment. To prevent such an occurrence from being extensive, the equipment's case must be strong enough to contain the explosion, and the casing's joints must be long enough and clearances small enough so that flame cannot propagate to the outside. In addition, the equipment's external temperature must be such that it will not ignite the atmosphere. This equipment is known in the industry as being explosion proof.

Explosion-proof Equipment

Explosion-proof equipment designed for one type of atmosphere is not necessarily acceptable for all atmospheres. This is so because each gas and vapor has specific explosion and flame-propagation properties, as well as specific ignition temperatures.

The NEC and UL take cognizance of the difference in the characteristics of gases and vapors by grouping chemicals according to their characteristics and by approving electrical equipment for specific groups (A, B, C,

and D). Prior to 1968 the list of chemicals in each group for which electrical equipment was approved was not enlarged. Most of the chemicals
produced and used in the CPI were not included.

In 1968, 15 widely used chemicals were added as the result of a research project suggested by the NFPA Sectional Committee on Electrical
Equipment in Chemical Atmospheres and carried out by the UL. Financial
support for the project was approved by the Manufacturing Chemists Association, American Petroleum Institute, American Insurance Association,
and the National Electrical Manufacturers Association. The test equipment
used to make the determinations is still available, and for a fee UL will
determine the electrical classification for any material submitted. One
important correlation was established by the project: there is no direct
relationship between explosion properties and ignition temperature; consequently, the two should be considered independent. Prior to the project,
electrical equipment for a particular group was designed to not only meet
the most stringent explosion requirements of any material in the group but
also the lowest ignition temperature.

NEC Code Groupings

Table 3.4 shows the comparison of the properties of the materials used by
UL for testing electrical equipment in the four groups. Obviously, there
is no correlation between ignition temperature and explosion properties or
ignition temperature and flame propagation properties. We can see, however, an obvious correlation between the explosion and flame-propagation
properties.

For all practical purposes, the equipment in groups A, B, and D was
designed to operate at a maximum temperature of 536°F, and that in
group C at a maximum of 356°F. It was found necessary, therefore, to use
group C equipment with any chemicals having a low ignition temperature,
even though the explosion and flame-propagation resistance properties of
group D equipment would have been adequate. Conversely, with chemicals
requiring the explosion and flame-propagation resistance properties of
group C equipment, it was found necessary to pay for the low-temperature
design requirements even though the ignition temperature was above 356°F.

NEC Code Markings

The NFPA Sectional Committee recommended that changes be made, and
the 1971-1972 NEC code now requires all heat-producing electrical equipment to be marked with its operating temperature range, as well as the
class and group for which it is approved. Now explosion-proof electrical
equipment can be selected from a particular group that will have the safe
maximum temperature necessary for a specific chemical.

TABLE 3.4. Chemicals by Groups

Chemical	Minimum ignition temperature (°F)
Group A atmospheres	
Acetylene	571
Group B atmospheres	
Butadiene[a]	788
Ethylene oxide[b]	804
Hydrogen	752
Manufactured gases containing more than 30% hydrogen by volume	752
Propylene oxide[b]	840
Group C atmospheres	
Acetaldehyde	347
Cyclopropane	932
Diethyl ether	320
Ethylene	914
Isoprene	428
Unsymmetrical dimethyl hydrazine	480
Group D atmospheres	
Acetone	869
Acrylonitrile	898
Ammonia	1204
Benzene	1040
Butane	761
1-Butanol	689
2-Butanol	761
n-Butyl acetate	797
Isobutyl acetate	790
Ethane	959
Ethanol	689
Ethyl acetate	800
Ethylene dichloride	775[f]
Gasoline	536
Heptanes	419[c]
Hexanes	437[c]
Methane (natural gas)	1004

TABLE 3.4. (Continued)

Chemical	Minimum ignition temperature (°F)
Group D atmospheres (cont.)	
Methanol	725
3-Methyl-1-butanol	662
Methyl ethyl ketone	960
Methyl isobutyl ketone	860
2-Methyl-1-propanol	800
2-Methyl-2-propanol	896
Petroleum naphtha[d]	550
Octanes	428[c]
Pentanes	500[c]
1-Pentanol	572
Propane	842
1-Propanol	824
2-Propanol	750[e]
Propylene	860
Styrene	914
Toluene	896
Vinyl acetate	800
Vinyl chloride	882
Xylenes	869

[a] Group D equipment may be used for this atmosphere if such equipment is isolated in accordance with Section 501-5(a) by sealing all conduits 1/2 in. or larger.

[b] Group C equipment may be used for this atmosphere if such equipment is isolated in accordance with Section 501-5(a) by sealing all conduits 1/2 in. or larger.

[c] The ignition temperature given is for the normal compound; various isomers are known to have higher ignition temperatures.

[d] A saturated hydrocarbon mixture boiling in the range 68-275°F. Also known by the synonyms benzine, ligroin, petroleum ether, or naphtha.

[e] The ignition temperature given is for the ortho isomer form; the meta and para isomers have higher ignition temperatures.

[f] The ignition temperature is for 50-60 octane gasoline. Higher octane gasolines have higher ignition temperatures.

TABLE 3.5. New National Electrical Code Chemical Groups

Group	Chemical atmosphere	Maximum explosion pressure (psi)	Experimental maximum safe gap (in.)	Minimum ignition temperature (°F)	Explosive range (percent)
A	Acetylene	1140	0.003	572	2.50-80
B	Hydrogen	845	0.003	1085	4.00-74.2
C	Diethyl ether	200	0.027	356	1.85-36.5
D	Gasoline	160	0.029	536	1.30- 6.0

Source: McPartland, J., National Electrical Code Handbook, 16th ed.,
McGraw-Hill, New York (1979).

Table 3.5 shows the new code groupings. The minimum ignition temperature of each chemical was added to make using the table easier.
Table 3.6 gives the code identification numbers for various maximum temperatures. Existing equipment is assumed to be approved for the following temperatures: group A, 536°F; group B, 536°F; group C, 356°F; and group D, 536°F.

TABLE 3.6. Code Identification Numbers

Maximum temperature (°F)	Identification number
842	T1
572	T2
536	T2A
500	T2B
446	T2C
419	T2D
392	T3
356	T3A
329	T3B
320	T3C
275	T4
248	T4A
212	T5
185	T6

Source: McPartland, J., National Electrical Code Handbook, 16th ed., McGraw-Hill, New York (1979).

A nearly complete line of explosion-proof electrical equipment for groups C and D is listed by UL. Less equipment is available for group B, and still less for group A. It is not permissible to use class I, group D, equipment in group A and B atmospheres on the basis that class I, group D is the best available. Doing so could lead to a disastrous explosion, because group D equipment will neither withstand the pressure of an internal explosion of acetylene or hydrogen nor prevent flame propagation through joints and seals. Therefore, for these materials, and for any unlisted material whose properties are not well known, another approach should be used; an option is to use Division 2 equipment.

3.4. AREA LOCATIONS

Class 1, Division 2 Locations

We saw that Division 1 locations are those where explosive concentrations normally can be expected for extended periods of time, Division 2 locations are those where explosive concentrations occur only under abnormal conditions, and then only occasionally and for relatively short periods.

In Division 2 belongs ordinary, low-temperature equipment that is nonsparking or has its "make or break" contacts immersed in oil or hermetically sealed. When nonsparking equipment is not available, comparable explosion-proof equipment or equipment contained in explosion-proof housings is used.

Division 2 equipment can cause an explosion only if it breaks down at the same time that an explosion concentration occurs. The chances of this occurring are very slight. Even in a Division 1 area, the possibility of an explosive concentration lasting for a prolonged period throughout the entire area is unlikely because the ventilation necessary to enable workers to continue working prevents hazardous concentrations of vapors and gases. Explosive mixtures are likely to occur only in the immediate vicinity of the vapor or gas source. The allowable concentrations for industrial health are usually far below the LELs, sometimes by a factor of 1000, and even 10,000.

If due to a malfunction of equipment, flammable vapors and gases escape, the equipment should be redesigned, or the handling procedures modified, to ensure confinement. In addition, process buildings should be provided with interlocked, positive, mechanical ventilation so that vapors and gases cannot accumulate. Providing such preventive measures can convert a Division 1 area into a Division 2 area. Outdoor, freely ventilated process areas are considered to be within Division 2 guidelines. If buildings with restricted ventilation are avoided, there are only a few areas where Division 1 explosion-proof equipment will be required:

In open, below grade areas, such as pits, sumps, and trenches, and in all above-ground areas within dike walls where vapors may accumulate. Electrical equipment should be kept out of such areas or

should be of Division 1 construction, with seals to prevent vapors
from passing into otherwise safe locations.

In pump and compressor rooms or houses with restricted ventilation
and in which flammable liquids, vapors, or gases are handled. Because a continuous process cannot always be shut down immediately,
leakage from around seals, packing, and bearings can build up explosive concentrations suddenly. Division 1 equipment is desirable
in such areas. When solvent pumps and compressors are located
outside, Division 2 motors can be used. Mounting them on raised
foundations provides additional safety.

In process buildings where equipment must be opened frequently for
repairs or for the addition of materials to the process, in drum-
filling buildings, and in buildings where the release of vapors cannot
be avoided. Even with live and adequate ventilation, there should be
only Division 1 equipment in special areas of these buildings.

In buildings where the failure of process equipment is likely to release
flammable concentrations of vapor or gases simultaneously with an
electrical failure.

In areas immediately around flammable-liquid loading and unloading
racks and around storage and process-tank breather vents.

3.5. EXTENT OF HAZARDOUS AREAS

In laying out the plot plan for a processing unit, it is important to be able
to identify the extent of hazardous areas. Although Division 1 and Division
2 areas can be readily identified from the code definitions, establishing
how far such areas should be extended from sources of vapor or gas releases is more difficult. The extent of an area is influenced by the

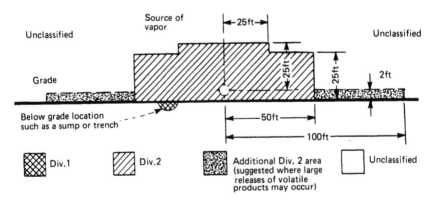

FIG. 3.1. Hazard in this typical refinery installation is located near grade
level in an adequately ventilated area. (From LeVine, R. Y., Electrical
Safety in Process Plants, Chemical Engineering, May 1, 1972).

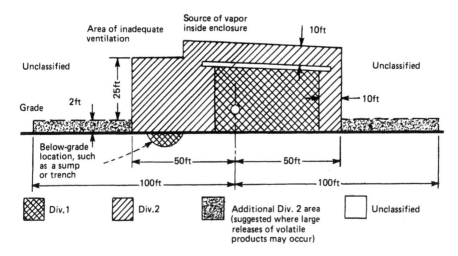

FIG. 3.2. Source of this typical installation is indicated inside an enclosure in an inadequately ventilated area. (From LeVine, R. Y., Electrical Safety in Process Plants, Chemical Engineering, May 1, 1972.

explosive limits and vapor density of the gas or vapor, the quantity of gas or vapor released, the type of ventilation, and the obstructions to the free movement of air or gas-air mixtures.

Figures 3.1 and 3.2 are examples of how API Standard RP500A classifies areas according to their distances from hazardous sources. These diagrams have found much use in process plant and oil refinery design and make it much simpler to decide whether an area should be classified Division 1, Division 2, or nonhazardous. NFPA standards Nos. 30, 33, 36, 50, 58 and 59, pertinent to the CPI, also provide useful information as to the extent of hazardous areas. As is typical of all guides, care must be exercised in their application since the information is based on "average" conditions.

Class II Areas

The NEC Code defines Class II, Division 1 areas as (1) those areas in which explosive dust concentrations are suspended in the air continuously, intermittently, or periodically under normal operating conditions; (2) those areas where abnormal operation of equipment and machinery can cause explosive dust concentrations and a source of ignition simultaneously; (3) those areas in which electrically conductive dusts may be present.

The Code defines Class II, Division 2 locations as those where combustible dusts will not normally be suspended in the air but where deposits of dust may interfere with the safe heat dissipation from electrical equipment and where deposits of dust may be ignited by electrical arcs, sparks, or burning material.

Confinement of Hazardous Areas

Providing adequate ventilation will not convert a Class II, Division 1 area into a Class II, Division 2 area. Adequate measures must be taken to provide dust collection and control equipment at the source (local exhaust) to prevent dust from becoming suspended in the air. A Division 1 area extends out from possible dust sources to a wall or a point beyond which there are no visible suspensions of dust cloud under normal operating conditions.

Division 2 areas are those where there are no visible dust clouds because the processing equipment is enclosed or source dust control is effective. Under abnormal conditions, however, such an area may occasionally have dust suspended in the air. A Division 2 area extends out from a Division 1 area, or from possible dust sources, to a wall or a point beyond which there will not be an appreciable accumulation of dust.

Equipment for Class II, Division 1 Areas

Equipment for Class I, Division 1 areas is known as dust-ignition proof. Its design is such that ignitable amounts of dust cannot get into it, so that arcs, sparks, or heat generated inside the electrical enclosure cannot ignite exterior accumulations or atmospheric suspensions.

Class II dust-ignition-proof equipment is grouped by the Code, and is approved and listed by UL, as follows:

Group E: atmospheres containing metal dust, including aluminum and magnesium, and their alloys, and other metals of similarly hazardous characteristics.

Group F: atmospheres containing carbon black, coal, or coke dust.

Group G: Atmospheres containing flour, starch, or grain dust.

Such dusts as sulfur, plastic, and rubber, which are important in the CPI, are not even listed. The expansion of the Class II list is long overdue; the Sectional Committee is working on it.

For practical reasons, when handling an unlisted dust whose dust-layer ignition temperature and electrical conductivity are not known, it is advisable to choose dust-ignition-proof equipment approved for groups F and G. There is much equipment that is approved for both groups. Surely, if the dust is metallic, group E equipment should be selected.

Equipment for Class II, Division 2 Areas

Equipment for this application may be dust-ignition proof or designed with enclosures to minimize deposits or entry of dusts and to prevent the escape of sparks or hot or burning material. Some open, cool, nonsparking equipment, such as motors, can be used if the dust is nonabrasive and nonconducting.

All equipment for Class II locations must function at full rating without developing surface temperatures high enough to cause excessive dehydration or gradual carbonization with the eventual spontaneous ignition of layered dusts. The maximum surface temperature of equipment not subject to overloading is limited to 329°F. For equipment such as motors and transformers, which may become overloaded, it is 248°F.

3.6. PURGED AND PRESSURIZED EQUIPMENT

Purged and Pressurized Enclosures

Purged and pressurized enclosures for electrical equipment are applicable to both Class I and Class II and Division 1 and Division 2 areas. NFPA Pamphlet No. 496, "Standard for Purged and Pressurized Equipment in Hazardous Locations," deals with three sizes of enclosures for Class I and Class II locations: small enclosures, such as those for instrumentation; larger enclosures, such as those for motors and other power equipment; and room enclosures, such as control rooms.

Purging of Enclosures

Purging used in Class I locations provides for the flow of clean outside air or inert gas, such as nitrogen, into an enclosure at a rate and pressure sufficient to reduce the initial concentration of flammable gas or vapor to a safe level. It also maintains this level by positive pressure with or without a continuing flow.

Types of Purging

There are three types of purging (X, Y, and Z). Which one is used, together with the safeguards that are required, will depend on the particular situation.

    Type X is required when an enclosure is in a Division 1 area and
        ordinary electrical equipment with sparking contacts is used with the
        enclosure.
    Type Y is required when an enclosure is in a Division 1 area, and
        Division 2 electrical equipment is used within the enclosure.
    Type Z is required when an enclosure is in a Division 2 area, and
        ordinary electrical equipment with sparking contacts is used within
        the enclosure.

Purging Practices

Because the loss of purging air to a type X enclosure creates a hazardous condition, the power to the equipment must be shut off automatically when flow and pressure are lost.

When this is not practical or desirable, type Y purging should be used. With this type of purging, it does not become necessary to shut off the power automatically, since it is not likely that an electrical failure will occur at the same time that an explosive concentration develops. However, an alarm should warn that purging has been lost, so that action to restore pressure can be taken.

With type Z purging, only an alarm is required, since there must be a purge failure simultaneous with an explosive concentration for an explosion to occur—a most unlikely event.

Pressurized enclosures are used in Class II locations. Pressuring is the practice of supplying an enclosure with clean outside air or inert gas at a rate and pressure sufficient to prevent the entrance of hazardous dusts with or without continuous flow. Atmospheres in enclosures made hazardous by dust, unlike those enclosures made hazardous by gases or vapors, cannot be reduced to a safe level solely by supplying a flow of clean outside air. The enclosure must also be opened and cleaned. With dust, however, the loss of pressure is not at once hazardous since it takes time for sufficient dust to filter into a normally tight enclosure to create a hazardous condition. It could take on the average from 1/2 to 1 hr to bring about the condition. Therefore, power to the enclosure need not be shut off at once when pressure fails, but an alarm should sound to warn of the malfunction, so that some action can be taken to correct the malfunction.

3.7. CONTROL ROOMS

Remotely controlled processes in the CPI and oil refinery, including petrochemicals, require the need for purged and pressurized control rooms. When so treated, the need for explosion-proof electrical equipment and controls is obviated. It is then possible to use general-purpose electrical equipment and control units.

It is not good practice to locate a control room in a Class I, Division 1 area, not only because of the threat to both personnel and continuity of production but also for purging reasons. A control room in this area would require type X purging, and the automatic cutting off of electricity would result in a precipitous shutdown, which could be just as dangerous as leaving the power source on. If locating a control room in a Division 1 area cannot be avoided, either Division 2 equipment should be installed in it so that type Y purging can be used or a pressurized building should be provided as hereinafter described in Chapter 9.

A control room is more properly located in a Division 2 area, where type Z purging can be used. Again, it is not necessary to shut off power

automatically but only to have an alarm sound. Because dust entering an
enclosure does not necessitate the immediate shutting down of electrical
equipment, a control house in a dust atmosphere does not present similar
problems.

Requirements for purging and pressurizing enclosures, including air
purity, pressure, flow, and metering of air, and alarms, controls, and
safeguards for restarting electrical equipment after an air failure are all
detailed in NFPA standard No. 496.

3.8. EXTENT OF HAZARDOUS AREAS

Experienced Practice

The practice of experienced electrical engineers in the CPI and petroleum
refining industries is to install explosion-proof equipment in all locations
in which flammable volatile liquids, highly flammable gases, and mixtures
of other highly flammable substances are manufactured, used, handled, or
stored because these flammable materials cannot be controlled after they
have escaped from their containing vessels. The standard in the industry
is to require that all electrical equipment, including service equipment
that is not explosion proof, be located not less than 50 ft from any building
in which highly flammable substances are handled. Also all service conduits in such areas must be underground. Figure 3.3 shows how the extent
of hazardous areas is determined. See Miller, E. E. (1963).

Size and shape of the building is considered in determining the minimum
safe distance where non-explosion-proof electrical equipment may be installed. Winds blowing in the direction indicated will disturb, but only
slightly, the air in the triangular areas. Should the air in these areas become charged with flammable gas or vapor, one can see that the natural
air movement will not be active enough to effect dilution of the mixture to
safe proportions and below the LEL.

Rough Rule

A rough rule for the positioning of equipment is that non-explosion-proof
electrical equipment should be located from the end of the building a distance not less than the building's width and from the side not less than the
building's length, but never less than 50 ft.

The conditions that exist when an explosion occurs from electrical
causes are usually

1. Gas in the immediate vicinity of electrical devices
2. Entrance of the gas into the device enclosure by breathing or
   otherwise
3. Ignition of the gas by arcing or sparking due to normal functioning
   of the device or by an insulation failure

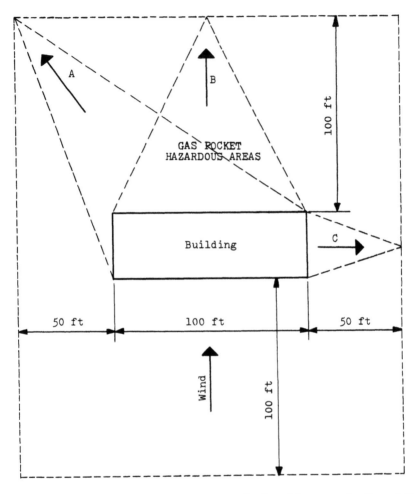

FIG. 3.3. Explosive gas mixtures may be found in areas A, B, and C when wind is in that direction.

4. Inability of the enclosure to restrain the explosion and prevent the escape of flames or hot gases.

The principal difference between non-explosion-proof and explosion-proof electrical devices is that the latter have the ability to restrain the explosion and prevent the escape of flames and dangerously hot gases.

   For plant and worker protection against fire and injuries, all explosion-proof equipment should be constructed in accordance with requirements of UL; also electrical equipment should be installed in accordance with the latest issue of the NEC. In this way protection is then assured at minimum cost and at the best the state of the art affords.

It takes the combined effort of all engineering disciplines in the design office to design, construct, and operate an oil refinery or chemical plant; civil engineering, chemical engineering, mechanical engineering, electrical engineering, and project engineering. All efforts must be coordinated throughout the project.

4

NATURAL VENTILATION

4.1. INTRODUCTION

The wind is the chief motive force utilized in the aeration of a building by natural means. It forces air in by way of certain openings, through the building, and out by other openings. In this chapter the effect of the wind and how and at what rates ventilation will take place without the need of mechanical ventilation will be discussed.

Aeration of Industrial Buildings

In the overall selection of industrial ventilation rates many considerations must be taken into account. Natural aeration of the building itself is

important. The forces of rotating equipment and traffic from workers all
help to stir up the air within the workplace and must be considered.

If the building is one in which heat is produced, and this is so in most
cases, the inside warmer air has a tendency to rise, due to its buoyancy,
thereby assisting in aeration. These two forces may aid or oppose each
other, and it is important that they be coordinated and controlled so that the
air is changed in the occupied zones if a building is to be successfully
aerated.

It is astonishing what great volumes of air can be moved into, through,
and out of a building by the forces of nature. However, it is not the great
volumes that are important as are the correct volumes, adequately
controlled.

Contrary to popular belief, the wind is reasonably consistent in its
direction and velocity. Weather reports show that for each locality in the
United States there is a prevailing wind whose direction holds constant for
many months at a stretch and for the same group of months year after
year. Its average velocity varies within comparatively small limits
throughout the year.

The buoyancy of warm air, that it rises and is replaced by cooler air,
or the reverse of this, that cold air falls and forces up the warm air which
is lighter, follows natural laws that have been known from time immemorial.
If there is a better understanding of the behavior of the wind, acting alone
or in combination with the flow created by temperature difference, then we
would be more cognizant of the vagaries of the wind that bring about some
of the peculiar things that happen in mechanical ventilation and heating systems when the wind is opposing or cooperating with the action of the mechanical systems.

Natural Ventilation of Spaces

General ventilation is nature's method, and nature does a rather neat job in
the summertime with wide-open buildings. To duplicate natural summertime ventilation, we would need air change rates through buildings of
60-600 air changes per hour, instead of the conventional mechanical ventilation rates of 6-60 air changes per hour. Experience shows that to provide
greater than 15 air changes per hour mechanically can become a tremendous
air handling problem.

Keep doors and windows closed and the prevailing wind no longer produces indoor air movements of several hundred feet per minute. Infiltration (doors and windows closed) may be as low as one-half air change per
hour. During the winter season, when the building is barricaded, the need
for special air-supply openings to introduce make-up air becomes apparent.
Table 4.1 gives air infiltration rates due to natural forces and traffic.

No matter how simple, flexible, or universal general ventilation may
seem at first glance, some industrial plants find that the great amount of
air required, overloading of the heating plant, and special equipment needed

TABLE 4.1. Air Infiltration Due to Natural Forces and Traffic

Type of space	Air changes per hour
Rooms	
1 side exposed	1
2 sides exposed	1-1/2
3 sides exposed	2
4 sides exposed	2
No windows or outside doors	1/2-3/4
Narrow room, windows in long wall, inside door	3/4-1
Narrow room, windows in short wall, inside door	1/2-3/4
Square room, windows in one wall, inside door	1-1-1/2
Room with windows in two walls, inside door	1-1/2-2
Room with windows in three walls, inside door	2-2-1/2
Office building lobby, swinging doors	2-6
Store or restaurant, many door openings per hour	3-5
Department store, swinging doors with vestibule	1/2-3
Factory building, modern tight construction, large floor area in proportion to wall area	1/4-1
Factory building, conventional construction	1/2-3
Factory building, large window area, poor construction	2-6
Normal factory building, masonry construction	1/2-1-1/2
Corrugated iron building, aluminum or asbestos	1-1/2-3
Shipping rooms	1/2-2-1/2
Single story garage	1/2-2-1/2
Ramp garage	1/2-3

Note: No mechanical ventilation, all windows and doors closed, no ridge vents, and no weather stripping or storm sash on windows or doors.

to introduce enough tempered air as makeup all combine to make general ventilation a costly procedure in cold climates. The best solution would be to design a compact local exhaust system that will remove an amount of space air small enough that the normal ventilation due to construction leakage (see Table 4.1) will accommodate the exhaust flow without going to an elaborate makeup air system.

Flow Due to the Wind

As we previously noted, the wind is not only a powerful motive force but also quite a consistent one. The average velocity and direction of the prevailing winds were obtained from Weather Bureau reports for every month at various typical localities in the United States. A survey of these data

quickly showed the general uniformity in the direction of the prevailing
wind and the small range of the average velocities of each locality.

Industrial buildings in which the processing takes place and produces
little heat must depend entirely on the wind for natural aeration. The
aeration is usually accomplished by the air blowing through the building,
coming in through openings in the side walls and going out through the open
windows and doors in the side walls and through openings in the roof. Also
in some cases air flows in through the roof openings and out through other
openings in the roof and side walls.

The wind forces air into the building usually through the openings on
the windward side. The pressure so developed usually pushes the air out
by way of openings in the leeward side, or even through openings on the
windward side of less pressure.

Air flow velocity through window openings, due to pressure effect of
the wind, depends upon and varies directly with wind speed. In all cases
velocity through a window opening will be less than wind speed, and under a
few conditions will be less than half wind speed, if there are adequate openings for outflow. Air flow volume depends on wind speed, its direction
with respect to the face of the openings, the number and size of openings,
and the resistance to flow built up by obstructions in the openings. Greatest flow will usually be obtained when the building is so oriented that the
prevailing wind blows directly flush against the wall having the most number of openings. The pressure built up and the resulting inflow varies
with the sine of the angle between the wind direction and the building face,
between 20° and 90°, or perpendicular to the building face.

Pull and Jump of Wind

The wind pulls air out of a building through openings in the leeward side and
through those openings near the windward side where there is a condition of
vacuum caused by the wind hitting the windward face and jumping out around
the adjacent side or up over the roof at that point. This jump of the wind
and suction area thereby developed holds true for flat-faced buildings.
There is a disadvantage to locating a monitor on the roof of a building parallel to the prevailing wind, since parallel flow of the wind does not create
a suction and there are suction openings only in the windward end of the
monitor under the jump. By running a monitor or ridge vent perpendicular
to the prevailing wind so that there will be openings under suction in the
leeward side, there will be a decided improvement. See Clarke, J. H.
(1967).

The suction created by the wind jump is more responsible than any
other factor for some buildings being aerated and other almost identical
buildings not being aerated. The greatest chance for aeration is created if
a building is designed and constructed to take advantage of the prevailing
wind direction to create suction where needed. In the design of a building
and its orientation, the designer must create a situation opposite that of a

ship builder. For the ship the design must be streamlined, for the building, there must be an absence of the effect of streamline flow. The length of the jump does not depend upon the velocity of the wind; that is, the suction area is independent of the vagaries of wind velocity. Suction intensity produced in the jump of the wind will vary with the square of the wind speed.

Motive Head Due to Temperature Difference

Almost everyone is familiar with the convection currents induced by the rise of warm air and the fall of cold air. The potential of this temperature difference for creating an air current is called the motive head to bring about flow. The motive head producing flow is directly proportional to both the difference in temperature and the vertical distance between inlet and outlet openings. See Koroff, W. G. (1966).

How to Figure Gravity Roof Venting

Despite the many attributes of mechanical ventilation, many industrial buildings are still provided with gravity ventilation, using the natural forces of the wind and convection to ventilate their interiors. In this respect the two most important factors are temperature difference between the inside and the outside and the flow produced by the wind. When considering temperature only these factors are dependent on (1) heat produced in the building, (2) vertical distance between inlet and outlet openings, and (3) area of inlet and outlet openings. It is accepted practice for summer ventilation design to assume a temperature difference of 10°F. The vertical distance above needs clarification and qualification. Vendors of roof vents recommend using the clear vertical height between openings only when flow openings are of unequal area and resistance.

   To compute the flow due to temperature difference, the following equation may be used:

$$Q = CA\sqrt{H(t_i - t_o)} + 30.83V \qquad (4.1)$$

where Q = air exhausted in cubic feet per minute, A = area of exhaust opening in square feet, C = coefficient of resistance, H = vertical clear distance between low and high openings in feet, t_i = average inside temperature in farenheit degrees, t_o = average or design outside temperature in farenheit degrees, and V = wind speed in miles per hour.

   For low-silhouette buildings, 10-15 ft in height, wind speed is the chief force in natural ventilation. As roof height increases, however, the thermal head, or temperature difference, becomes predominant. Buildings in which internal heat release is small (on the order of 3 Btu/hr/ft^3 of occupied space) must depend almost entirely on the wind effect. By using Eq. (4.1) one may predict the ventilation rate or use the values from Table 4.2. If the area of inlet openings exceeds the high exhaust openings (the usual

TABLE 4.2. Velocities (linear feet per minute) to Calculate Vent Area

Temperature difference (°F)	Vertical difference between openings (ft)	Wind speed (mph)						
		0	2	4	6	8	10	12
10	10	94	156	217	279	341	402	464
	20	133	195	256	318	380	441	503
	30	163	225	286	348	410	471	533
	40	188	250	311	373	435	496	558
	50	210	272	333	395	475	518	580
20	10	133	193	256	318	380	441	503
	20	188	250	311	373	435	496	558
	30	230	293	353	415	477	538	600
	40	266	328	389	451	513	574	636
	50	298	360	419	483	545	606	668
30	10	163	225	286	348	410	471	533
	20	230	293	353	415	477	538	600
	30	282	344	411	467	529	590	652
	40	326	388	449	511	573	534	696
	50	364	426	488	549	611	672	734
40	10	188	250	311	373	434	498	558
	20	268	330	391	453	512	578	638
	30	326	388	449	511	572	636	696
	40	376	438	499	561	622	686	746
	50	448	510	571	633	694	758	818

TABLE 4.3. Correction for Area Difference

Ratio of low inlet to outlet, or vice versa	Increase in air flow (percent)
1.0	0
1.25	11.0
1.5	17.7
2.0	27.0
2.5	31.5
3.0	34.0
3.5	36.0
4.0	37.0
4.5	37.5
5.0	37.7
5.5	38.0
6.0	38.0

case), or visa versa, the calculated air flow (or table values) should be increased by a percentage shown in Table 4.3. For maximum efficiency of natural ventilation, the height between these openings should be as great as possible.

Determining Roof Vent Area

Normally, the volume rate of air to be exhausted is already known, and the problem is to find the exhaust vent area A. Once it is found, the low-level intake area may be checked or selected, depending upon whether windows or louvered openings are used. To simplify the selection of roof opening areas, Table 4.2 was devised. Because roof openings are more expensive than wall openings or windows, our approach is to keep them at a minimum and to depend on larger low-positioned areas.

Table 4.2 is based on a C factor of 9.4 for normal internal space conditions such as warehouses and shops, 7.2 for cluttered process rooms and buildings, and 10.82 for free and clear areas. For conditions other than those that would use 9.4, multiply by direct proportion, that is, for C = 7.2, multiply by 7.2/9.4, or 0.77. Natural ventilation should always be designed on the basis of at least a 2-mph wind, but more often a 4-mph wind is considered. Other wind speeds can be used if actual conditions are reliably known.

In determining wind and temperature effects, remember that they are subject to the vagaries of the weather and that only approximate calculations can therefore be made. The effect of altitude is to decrease the density of the ambient air system, which will affect draft to a degree but can be ignored up to 5000 ft above sea level.

EXAMPLE 4.1. Consider a storage building 200 × 100 × 35 ft high. Its cubage is then 700,000 ft^3. The ventilation rate is to be 2 ft^3/min/ft^2 floor area. Temperature difference is 20°F. Convection or thermal head is 30 ft from louvered openings to ridge vent opening. Assume a 4-mph wind and a resistance coefficient of C = 9.4. Ratio of net louver area to vent area is 3.

SOLUTION   For these conditions, the velocity through the roof vent area is found from Table 4.2 to be 353 ft/min. The increase in air flow from Table 4.3 is 34%, and the new velocity results in (353)(1.34) = 473. The velocity through the net louvered area is 473/3 = 158 ft/min. Roof vent area = (200)(100)(2/473) = 85 ft^2.

Concept of the Neutral Zone

In order that there may be a flow of air due to temperature difference only, there must be a difference in height between inlet and outlet openings. While this fact is manifestly true, many building designs are found that depend for ventilation on getting air in at certain openings and out at other openings at just about the same level.

To compute the flow due to temperature difference, when inflow and outflow openings are of unequal area or resistance, there has been developed the important concept of the neutral zone. Every building has a neutral zone. If air will flow in at certain openings because atmospheric pressure is less, there is a point of equal atmospheric pressure somewhere between where the air will neither flow in nor flow out of an opening so situated. This explains why high-outflow openings and low-inflow openings are more effective than openings situated near midheight. The location of the neutral zone varies with the size and resistance of the inflow and outflow openings, and the location is found in somewhat the same way as the center of gravity of a section is obtained. This is covered by Prof. J. E. Emsweiler in a paper, "The Neutral Zone in Ventilation," published in the January 1926, issue of the Journal of the American Society of Heating and Ventilation Engineers [presently the American Society of Heating, Refrigeration, and Air Conditioning Engineers (ASHRAE).

Summer and Winter Ventilation Effects

In the summer advantage can usually be taken of the motive force of the wind, and large volumes of air can be brought in to reduce the temperature difference; but the effective head due to temperature difference becomes materially less. In the winter the story is different, and in general the head created by a temperature difference would be the chief motive force, since the inside air of an industrial building is considerably warmer than the outside air. This condition creates a sufficient head for all except the most extraordinary cases. Under winter conditions the pressure effect of the wind forcing air into a building would usually create too great a cooling effect and perhaps cause objectionable drafts.

The greatest flow in the summer will probably occur when all windows are open. The most effective flow, that is, through the breathing zone (5 ft above the floor), will usually occur when all except the high window openings on the windward side are open. In the winter, the best aerating conditions will occur when only the low openings on the windward side or leeward side and the high openings in the leeward side are opened. If opening the low sidewall windows should cause objectionable drafts or excessive cooling effects, then use higher openings for the inflow of air. This will reduce the excessive cooling effect that would occur with low incoming air streams. Then at the same time the decreased height between inlet and outlet openings will not decrease the head to such a degree that the air flow will not be adequate.

Factors that Control the Flow of Air

Since windows are most often used for natural ventilation, it is quite normal that more should be known about the influence of the different types of windows on the flow of air. In this respect two general conclusions have been established over a period of time.

1. The flow of air through a window opening does not depend on the type of window used. There is little to choose, for the same degree of opening, among windows with movable portions that are top hung, center pivoted, bottom hung, etc., and no one type has any mysterious and predominant advantage over any other.

2. The flow of air through a window opening varies with the area of the opening. For a pivoted window opening, the air flow varies with the angle of the opening, or more correctly, with the sine of the angle. In simpler terms, the first 15° of opening gives 25% of the total flow, the second 15°, 22%, the third 15°, 19%, the fourth 15°, 16%, the fifth 15°, 12%, and the last 15°, 6%. As you can see, the vertical height of the opening of a pivoted window is not a measure of the flow. One important matter should be recognized with a pivoted window: the operating devices usually limit the opening of top-hung pivoted windows to about 45°, whereas center-pivoted windows can normally be opened all the way to the 90° position.

Referring to Table 4.3, the size of the inlet and outlet openings should be about equal for the greatest flow per unit area of combined inlet and outlet area. There is an increased flow up to the point where the outlet area is twice the inlet area, and vice versa. Beyond that proportion there is correspondingly little to be gained, and the preponderance of the size of the outlet over the inlet (or the reverse) is of no real consequence. Some of the most inefficient uses of opening areas have been found where this simple fundamental rule has been violated.

Estimating Infiltration

The **ASHRAE Guide** publications are replete with tables and data to estimate infiltration through building construction of all types and should be used for that purpose. The "crack method" is definitive and should be applied wherever possible. The "air change" method may be used, and good approximations are shown in Table 4.1.

Buildings Must Breathe

Buildings must breathe to control condensation. Ventilation of some sort, by natural or mechanical means, is required for different reasons. The need may be to prevent carbon dioxide buildup, to eliminate odors, to dilute toxic or volatile gases, or more commonly, to maintain reasonable living temperature levels for human comfort during warm weather.

In parts of the country where winters are prolonged and outside temperatures reach 0°F or lower, condensation or moisture accumulation within walls or roof spaces has become a subject of considerable concern to plant managers and builders themselves.

Obviously, the question arises as to why we hear so much more about this condition now than we used to just a few years ago. The answer is relatively simple. During the last few years there has been a marked tendency by builders and plant owners to improve both their new and older buildings by increasing the comfort of the workers and decreasing operating costs and expenses. Prominent among these improvements are the increasing uses of storm sash, roof and wall insulation, weather stripping, caulking around windows and doors, and other means of decreasing heat losses and wind infiltration.

Effect of Higher Humidities

Because of the tighter construction, the normal humidity within a building so treated is higher than in buildings less tightly constructed. In older buildings with higher natural ventilation rates, moisture does not have a chance to build up. In addition, as a health and comfort measure the normal humidity is usually agumented by evaporating water from processing tanks or some other means of winter air conditioning. In industrial buildings, open tanks, and vats, processing of products can cause a buildup of water vapor within the building. Improvements that add to comfort and health are certainly worthwhile and are not to be discouraged, but it so happens that they introduce the unanticipated moisture problem just described.

Because of the trend to higher indoor humidities for health reasons, as well as comfort, and therefore high water vapor pressures indoors, there is a constant leakage of water vapor to the outside, the amount depending on the tightness of total construction. If doors and windows are loose, water vapor will readily pass to the outdoors, and if tight, to the outside will be minimized. However, attempts to protect buildings against high humidities have proved, for the most part, to be imperfect. The use of vapor barriers, vents in siding, or methods of ventilating the outer layers of the building walls is associated with many disadvantages. Water vapor can pass through wall and ceiling insulation and condense within the layers of insulation, reducing its insulating value and even icing up within the wall cavity itself.

Exhaust Ventilation Effective

How can the plant owner protect his insulation investment and still retain comfortable conditions? Ventilation from the interior outward by means of properly sized mechanical exhaust fans has proved itself in preventing moisture buildup. And, what's more, this ventilation can be less wasteful of heat than one can imagine. The rate of mechanical exhaust needed to dispel the water vapor (humidity) generated within a building depends upon the inside relative humidity to be maintained. The lower the relative humidity desired, the more air needs to be exhausted to remove the moisture generated. As indoor relative humidity is increased, less air needs to be exhausted to remove the same amount of moisture; thus less air needs to be removed as heat loss.

4.2. AIRTIGHT ENCLOSURES

Rate of Carbon Dioxide Buildup

To sustain life a building or enclosure must be able to breathe. Emergencies sometimes arise in which a person becomes trapped in an airtight enclosure with no outside air being supplied. A critical question in such cases is: How long will it take for the carbon dioxide concentration to build up to an unsafe level? This problem has relevance for fallout shelters, steel tanks (sometimes occupied for repairs), mines, and even buildings in the event of a breakdown of the ventilation system, plugging of intake screens and filters, etc.

Those involved with spaces where such emergencies could conceivably occur should ask the question: If there is no air supply, how long can we last? We now propose a quick way of determining the answer.

A space becomes uninhabitable when there is a negligible amount of air or no air entering the space through natural or mechanical means. Atmosphere containing less than 12% oxygen or more than 5% carbon dioxide by volume is considered dangerous to occupants. For safety reasons, a carbon dioxide concentration of 3% is often taken as the practical limit. The following formula, used by the U.S. Navy, is a good yardstick for determining time for carbon dioxide to build up to 3%:

$$T = 0.04V/P \tag{4.2}$$

where

  T = time to vitiate the air within the enclosure, hr
  V = net volume of air within the space, ft^3
  P = number of people occupying the space

The formula is based on the condition of minimum activity of the occupants and no generation of equipment fumes. Increased activity, such as that caused by panic, will use up oxygen quickly and will reduce the time by as much as three-quarters.

EXAMPLE 4.2. A fallout shelter with 40 occupants and a net volume of 4000 ft^3 has no outside air supply. How long will it take to make the shelter uninhabitable, assuming no panic?

SOLUTION $T = 0.04 (4,000/40) = 4$ hr. It would be wise to assume that the air will become stale after 1 hr or one-fourth of the calculated time.

EXAMPLE 4.3. Two repairmen become trapped in a steel tank having a net volume of 160 ft^3. If they are receiving no outside air, how long will it take for the carbon dioxide concentration to build up to the dangerous level?

SOLUTION $T = 0.04 (160/2) = 3.2$ hr, or 3 hr and 12 min. Again, the calculated value should be reduced to one-fourth, or 48 min, to play it safe.

4.3. GENERAL PRINCIPLES OF AERATION

Need for Openings

To aerate a building by natural means there must be openings and control. However, buildings vary greatly in their adaptability to good design along these lines. Each building is different and must be carefully studied to effect the best system. The number, size, location, and character of the openings is more or less individual with each building. Opening locations and their control is probably the paramount issue and usually receives less attention than the number, size, and character, perhaps because of the lack of authentic information along this line. Total inflow and outflow are not an index of good aeration, and it is apparent in many buildings that often a large proportion of the moving air was short circuited across or along a monitor and contributed little to the effective aeration and in some cases even jeopardized the aeration effort.

For example, in a large processing building ventilation was extremely poor despite numerous windows and monitors. The poor ventilation, upon investigation, was attributed to the opposition of the motive force of the wind to the head produced by temperature difference. The building was oriented parallel to the prevailing wind with processing equipment on the leeward end. The processing equipment gave a high heat release rate, together with a great deal of smoke. The jump of the wind created a vacuum and was strong enough to pull the heat and smoke the length of the building and out the monitor windows in the suction area at the windward end. Closing the monitor windows in the windward end and opening some low sidewall windows and the high monitor windows in the leeward end took the force of wind out of the picture and allowed the head due to temperature difference to do the work. Successful ventilation resulted and the environment cleared.

The general principles suggested below are offered simply for what they are worth, as a possible contribution to good construction and engineering.

1. Equal window openings, parallel and perpendicular to the longitudinal axis of the building.
2. Windows higher from the floor as they approach the center longitudinal axis. It may be desirable on account of the width of the building to have more than one axis.

The gains from following the application of these principles are:

1. There will always be openings, in the lee or jump of the wind, regardless of its direction, which can be opened for outflow, and always windows which are subjected to the pressure effect of the wind which can be used for inflow openings.
2. Air can be brought in at almost any desired point, using the pressure effect of the wind, carried through the zone of occupation, and forced out at other convenient points, providing an actual and controlled aeration.
3. The design lends itself to purely local control of the aeration at certain points, as well as mass control covering large floor areas.
4. The design lends itself to a wide range of air movement, ranging from relatively small to extremely large amounts, since the window opening area can be varied within wide limits.
5. The motive force of the wind and the head due to temperature differences can be coordinated for effective aeration.

The conservation of the human element and resources is a fertile field in the economics of industry. It is now quite generally accepted that those things which promote the general welfare and protect the health will favorably influence the morale, add to the satisfaction of workers, and in general increase their efficiency. Therefore, it seems feasible, since all the evidence to date would indicate that efficient ventilation fits in this picture very well, that there be incorporated in the design of industrial building adequate and correctly controlled aeration.

5

CONTROL BY MECHANICAL VENTILATION

5.1. INTRODUCTION

Emphasis in this chapter will be on general or dilution ventilation. In this system, contaminated air is exhausted to the outdoors, and large volumes of makeup air are introduced to dilute plant air contaminants to acceptable concentration levels. Experience shows that toxic and hazardous vapors and gases may be found in the in-plant atmospheres of processing buildings. If the processing system is normally closed, has minimum leakage, and is in safe operation, dilution with ventilation using outside air presents no problem, and the dilution method may be applied. Under such conditions, a minimum escape of gases and volatile vapors can be tolerated. Dilution air quantities determined herein are not recommended if the process piping and connections are not closed or if abnormal conditions prevail that permit the escape of excessive quantities of toxic and explosive materials into the work space. In such cases special ventilation measures, such as local capture and exhaust, will be required. The Occupational Safety and Health Act (OSHA) regulations do not prohibit the recirculation of air into the workspace. OSHA's primary requirement is that the contaminant concentration in plant air be less than the threshold limit value (TLV); the manner in which this quality is achieved is the responsibility of the plant. See Betz, G. M. (1977).

5.2. EXHAUST VENTILATION

Control by Ventilation

Exhaust ventilation design normally is dependent on a number of factors, including the physical state of the contaminant (dust, fume, smoke, mist, gas, or vapor), how it is generated, its release direction and velocity of release to the workspace, and its relative toxicity.

Index of Toxicity

The concept of maximum allowable concentration (MAC), now more commonly known as threshold limit value (TLV),expresses toxicity in numerical values. Measurement units may be expressed as parts of contaminant per million parts of air (ppm) for gases and vapors or as milligrams of contaminant per cubic meter of air (mg/m^3) for solids and mists. These

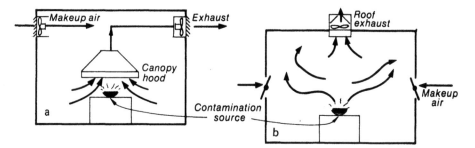

FIG. 5.1 a: Local ventilation removes contaminated air at the source via an exhaust hood. (From Power, February, 1976.) b: Dilution ventilation only dilutes air. (From Power, February, 1976.)

values, when used with understanding and caution, provide us with an index of concentration which a normal worker can safely tolerate for an 8-hr daily exposure for an indefinite length of time during a 5-day work week. These values must be applied with caution when calculating ventilation requirements and must never be used as absolute values. A list of TLVs is published annually by the American Conference of Governmental Industrial Hygienists (ACGIH).

The basic methods of ventilation are local exhaust ventilation and dilution (general) ventilation (Fig. 5.1a and b). See Hemeon, W. C. L. (1964).

Local Exhaust Ventilation

In local exhaust ventilation, the airborne contaminant is removed or captured from the environment at, or as close as possible to, the source before the contaminant enters the worker's breathing zone, or it is discharged into the general working environment. This type of system is preferred over dilution or general ventilation in most cases for the following reasons:

1. Less air needs to be exhausted to control the contaminant. This means that a smaller fan will be used and the power consumption will most likely be lower. Also, the makeup air required will necessarily be less, and in cold climates, or if air conditioning is used, this may be an important economic factor.
2. The contaminant is captured before it enters the worker's breathing zone and not after it has been generally distributed into the working room. With some highly toxic and radioactive substances, this is the only method of exhaust possible.
3. The contaminant is more highly concentrated in the conveying air stream. This is an important factor where the air will be cleaned either to salvage some valuable product or to prevent air pollution.

TABLE 5.1. Range of Capture Velocities

Condition of dispersion of contaminant	Examples	Capture velocity (fm)
Released, with practically no velocity, into quiet air	Evaporation from tanks, degreasing, etc.	50-100
Released at low velocity into moderately still air	Spray booths, intermittent container filling, low-speed conveyor transfers, welding, plating, pickling	100-200
Active generation into zone of rapid air motion	Spray painting in shallow booths, barrel filling, conveyor loading, crushers	200-500
Released at high initial velocity into zone of very rapid air motion	Grinding, abrasive blasting, tumbling	500-2000

Note: Capture velocities for specific operations are given in Industrial Ventilation—Manual of Recommended Practice, Committee on Industrial Ventilation, 11th ed.
Source: Chemical Engineering, August 10, 1970.

The disadvantages are that there is a high initial cost of installation and that an elaborate system of hoods and piping is frequently required that uses up valuable plant space. The basic principles and elements of local exhaust for design purposes must be understood before a design can be undertaken. Such information is available from standard texts and from the journals of the American Society of Heating, Refrigeration, and Air Conditioning Engineers (ASHRAE) (13).

Capture Velocities

The capture velocity is that velocity in front of the local exhaust hood that is necessary to overcome the dispersive forces and room currents so that the contaminant can be captured. Table 5.1 gives the range of capture velocities used in ventilation system design.

Exhaust Air Disposal

The disposal of air exhausted from local exhaust systems can present a problem in the case of toxic substances or substances that can create a nuisance, such as dusts and odors. Merely discharging the air outside the building may only serve to transfer the hazard to another area. Air currents may also carry the contaminants back into the very area from which they were removed or to other parts of the plant through windows or other openings. This situation can be lessened by discharging from stacks well above the building roof; however, this will contaminate the general atmosphere. In addition, the effluent may contain material of considerable recovery value. Systems have been developed to recover such materials.

Reducing the amount of ventilation air in a plant will usually bring substantial energy savings without hindering normal plant operations. But the air supply cannot be indiscriminately reduced. Providing sufficient air to maintain safety and worker health is more important than minimizing energy usage. The ventilation system must also be able to supply the recommended air change rates established by governmental agencies or industry groups.

Design Considerations

As previously discussed, the TLV is the maximum concentration of contaminants in the air that a healthy adult can encounter in a 40-hr work week without experiencing ill effects. TLVs for particulates range from less than 1 to 10 mg/m^3; for nontoxic or inert materials, the TLV is 10 mg/m^3, or 4.4 grains per 1000 ft^3. See also the listings in the latest publications of ACGIH.

Another method used to delineate relative toxicity is by the more general concepts of slightly toxic, moderately toxic, and highly toxic. Substances of unknown toxicity should be treated as highly toxic, until proven otherwise. Substances which carry numerical TLVs may also be classified in the above categories as shown in Table 5.2.

Need for Control

The need for control of a health hazard created by an industrial process as found in oil refineries and petrochemical plants must be determined by a

TABLE 5.2. Threshold Limit Values

Toxicity	ppm	mg/m^3	mppcf[a]
Slight	over 500	over 0.5	50
Moderate	101–500	0.101–0.5	20
High	0–100	0–0.1	5

[a] mppcf = million parts per cubic foot.
Source: Chemical Engineering, August 10, 1970.

trained industrial hygienist after careful evaluation and sampling of the in-plant environment. The air in the workplace must be analyzed chemically for contaminants. Their concentrations must be measured and rated as to toxicity. To determine the need for and the extent of ventilation control, in addition, length of the workday, working conditions, housekeeping practices, and time of the year are factors to be considered. See Clarke, J. H. (1959).

Operations that release highly toxic air contaminants alway require control; those releasing moderately toxic contaminants usually require control; and those releasing only slightly toxic contaminants only require control occasionally. Above all, the toxicity and concentration of con-taminants released into the atmosphere is the one most important factor in the determination of the need for control. See Sax, N. I. (1963).

General versus Local Exhaust

Control of hazardous contaminants by general or dilution ventilation is ac-complished by diluting the concentration of the contaminant before it reaches the worker's breathing zone with clean or uncontaminated air. Dilution ventilation does not reduce or eliminate the amount of hazardous material released into the workplace. On the other hand, the action of local exhaust ventilation is to control the contaminant at its source or point of generation, thus preventing contaminant release.

Normally, local exhaust ventilation is a better means for industrial hygiene control than dilution ventilation. Local exhaust has the advantage of requiring less air volume for effective control and of localizing the con-taminant. Less air is handled since the smaller volume of air at a higher concentration of the contaminant is removed rather than a larger volume at lower concentrations. This is an important consideration if the makeup air must be heated or cooled. In addition, localizing the contaminant has sev-eral other advantages:

1. It will eliminate nuisance complaints in the general area.
2. It will prevent the accumulation of particulates or condensable vapors which may create a housekeeping problem even through they are reduced to a hygienically safe concentration by dilution.

The difference between dilution and local exhaust ventilation cannot al-ways be determined with any degree of certainty. If the exhaust system is difficult to classify as one type or the other, the following criterion can be applied:

Dilution Ventilation System: concentration of the contaminant in the exhaust duct is not significantly higher than that in the general room air.

Local Exhaust System: concentration of the material in the exhaust duct is significantly higher than that in the general room air.

When to Use Dilution Ventilation

If the material of concern escapes into the air at a comparatively low rate and more or less uniformly throughout the work area—not at one or more isolated locations—dilution ventilation may be the most practical means of controlling the contaminant at the worker's breathing zone. However, if the process generates especially toxic or irritating substances, local exhaust should be used. The successful application of dilution ventilation depends upon the following conditions:

1. The contaminant generated can be diluted with a reasonable amount of air.
2. The distance between workers and point of generation of contaminant should be sufficient to assure that the workers will not be exposed to average concentrations in excess of the currently established TLVs.
3. The toxicity of the contaminant must be low (i.e., it must have a high TLV).
4. The contaminant should be generated at a reasonable uniform rate.

Dilution ventilation may be used with the greatest success when the rate of consumption can be determined with some degree of accuracy, by a materials balance or some other method, and when the volume of dilution air required can be calculated. It may well be that a health hazard does not exist due to dilution ventilation because of room construction and other features of the work area such as natural or mechanical ventilation. On the other hand, only a small amount of material is required to produce a hazardous condition in an air-tight room.

Dilution ventilation may be applied successfully to control the concentrations in workroom air of gases and organic vapors, with low toxic properties comparatively, such as heat and water vapor. Several reasons preclude the successful application of dilution ventilation for controlling the concentration of fumes and dusts. These are

1. The amount of material generated is usually too great, and reliable data on the rate of generation of fumes and dusts are very difficult to ascertain.
2. The material may be quite toxic and would require an excessive amount of dilution air.

Mixing Factor

Plant operators who must ventilate a contaminated space need an easy-to-follow method for estimating the necessary number of air changes. But first the true concentration must be measured. The method of determining the number of air changes outlined hereinafter will give a quick answer for purposes of reducing concentrations to acceptable levels in the work area.

Basic assumptions are that industrial hygiene personnel have identified the
contaminant and know the physiological effects of it. Judgment of whether
a contaminant is a hazard to health or well-being also requires evaluation of
the working environment. The initial concentration must be established;
well-known means are available.

Ventilation of contaminated air in a space would be simple if the outside
air could enter the enclosure in laminar-flow fashion without turbulence and
displace the contaminated air by a piston action. The air volume needed
would equal the enclosure volume; one air change would be required. In
practice, however, the theoretical piston action is not possible because the
introduced outside air continuously mixes with the contaminated air. Under
such conditions, after one air change a diluted mixture of fresh and contaminated air will remain.

Perfect Mixing

If mixing is perfect and continuous, then each air change reduces the contaminant concentration to about 36% of that at the start of the change. Perfect mixing is not always attained, however, and a mixing factor must be
applied in practical calculations of this type. The graph in Fig. 5.2 makes
use of the mixing factor, but first we should consider how the mixing factor
is related to the number of air changes. The equation for actual number of
air changes N in gross space volume of R ft^3 during elapsed time t min with
an air flow of f cfm is given by

$$N = \frac{f \times t}{R} \tag{5.1}$$

An equation often used by the industrial hygienists is

$$C = C_1 e^{-kN} \tag{5.2}$$

in which C is the contaminant concentration in parts per million at time t,
C_1 is the initial concentration at time t = 0 before dilution begins, e is the
napierian log base of 2.7183, N is the number of actual air changes, k is
the mixing factor, and kN is the number of effective air changes.

Mixing factor k is important for economy and safety. If k = 1 we have
the unattainable perfect displacement discussed above. Actual mixing factor
can vary from one-third to one-tenth, depending on contaminant toxicity,
uniformity of distribution in the work space, location of air inlets and outlets, enclosure geometry, and population.

Selection of Mixing Factor

Selection of mixing factor for any particular space is at best an estimate.
For small enclosures, such as fumigation booths and ovens, k values range
from one-third to one-fifth. An engineer not familiar with the efficiency of

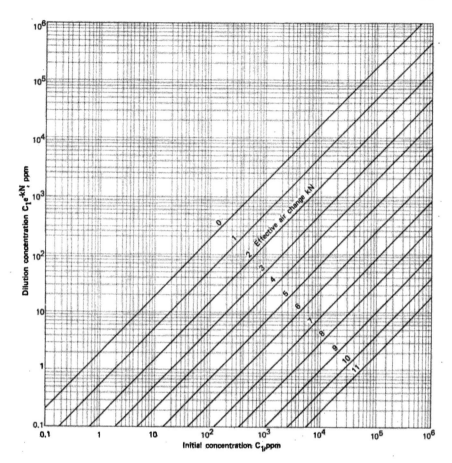

FIG. 5.2. Chart relates initial and final concentrations of contaminants.
(From Power, February, 1976).

air mixing within enclosures should use $k = 1/10$ to be on the safe side.
The more accurate the estimate of mixing factor, the more accurate will
be the calculation of concentration after N changes of the enclosure volume.

Determining Ventilation Needs

Here are suggested steps in determining ventilation needs:

1. Identify the contaminant and its toxicity.
2. Ascertain, calculate, or estimate the initial concentration of the
    contaminant.

TABLE 5.3.   Threshold Limit Value for Vapors

Vapor	TLV (ppm)	Vapor	TLV (ppm)
Acetone	1000	Ethyl alcohol	1000
Acrylonitrile	20	Gasoline	500
Ammonia	50	Methyl alcohol	200
Benzene	25	Naphtha (petroleum)	500
Carbon disulfide	20	Phenol	5
Carbon monoxide	50	Stoddard solvent	500
Carbon tetrachloride	10	Turpentine	100
Chlorine	1	Xylene	100

Source: Power, February, 1970.

3. Select a final safe concentration in the purged space. Base the selection on the TLV. Table 5.3 lists values for some common vapors. These values are taken from limits given by the ACGIH.
4. Use Fig. 5.2 to determine the effective air changes required to obtain the safe concentration.
5. Apply a mixing factor from one-third to one-tenth and select the ventilation rate. Add additional purge time if the enclosure contains absorbent materials.

EXAMPLE 5.1. Assume that a space contains 100 ppm phenol. If the mixing factor is estimated as one-fifth, what is the concentration in the space after 15 air changes have passed through the space?

SOLUTION: Effective air changes equal kN = 1/5(15) = 3. Enter Fig. 5.2 graph at 100 ppm at the bottom (initial concentration), and go up to kN = 3. At the left side, read 5 ppm as the final concentration, which Table 5.3 shows to be the TLV for phenol vapor in air.

Applying Dilution Ventilation

The greatest success in using dilution ventilation occurs when (1) the rate of consumption can be determined with some degree of accuracy by a materials balance or some other method, and (2) the volume of dilution air required can be calculated.

Dilution ventilation is applied most successfully in workroom air to control the concentrations of gases and organic vapors that have relatively low toxic properties. The technique is not recommended for controlling the concentration of fumes and dusts; the amount of material generated is usually too great, and reliable data on the rate of generation are not readily available. In addition, the material may be quite toxic and would require an excessive amount of dilution air. See Table 4.1 for the natural ventilation rates of rooms and buildings for air volumes that can feed outside air for dilution purposes when not using makeup air systems.

The K Factor

The formulas shown in Table 5.4 may be used for finding the amount of dilution air needed to bring room air down to safe limits for hazardous or toxic vapors. These formulas assume that the vapors act as ideal gases at normal room temperature and pressure (1 atm and 60°F) and that the contaminant is generated at a nearly uniform rate. Also, the formulas assume complete mixing of contaminated air with uncontaminated dilution air throughout the workspace.

The K factor is based on three primary considerations:

Estimating the efficiency of mixing and distribution of the makeup air and room air to reduce the contaminant concentration level to the desired level throughout the workspace.

Reducing the concentration of contaminant to some level at or below its TLV. This determination is based on the toxicological considerations used for the establishment of the TLV. These may include acute and/or chronic toxic effects, discomfort, irritation, and odor.

Estimating any additional variances the industrial hygienist determines to be important, based on his experience and the individual problem. Included in these criteria are such considerations as (1) seasonal changes in the amount of natural ventilation, (2) reduction in operating efficiency of mechanical air-moving devices, (3) duration of the process or operational cycle, (4) normal location of workers in relation to sources of contamination, and (5) location and number of points of contaminant generation in the workroom.

Effect of Distribution of Makeup Air

One of the most important factors in the design of dilution ventilation, and the one most frequently overlooked, is the need to supply sufficient and properly directed makeup air to replace the air exhausted (see Fig. 5.3). Ideally, the makeup air will be positively introduced and will be distributed in such a manner that the source of contamination is between the worker and the exhaust.

If this exhaust point is located as close as possible to the source of contamination, all the air will pass through the zone of contamination, and the contaminant will be diluted to design levels as soon as it is generated. Under such conditions, $K = 1$. Ideal conditions can never be assumed, however, and actual conditions will vary considerably (see Table 5.5).

The existence of the following factors results in average conditions:

Toxicity of the contaminant is moderate.
Exhaust fans are placed reasonably close to the vapor release points.
Makeup air is by infiltration through doors, windows, and walls, so a
    reasonable amount of dilution occurs as the contaminant is generated.

TABLE 5.4. Formulas for Finding Dilution-Ventilation Air Required, in
Cubic Feet per Minute

Formula 1 involves a knowledge of prevailing conditions during normal
    operations.

$$\text{cfm} = \frac{\text{concentration, ppm} \times \text{infiltration, cfm} \times \text{K}}{\text{TLV, ppm}} \quad (5.3)$$

This formula can be used only if tests can be made to determine actual
contaminant concentrations and the natural infiltration rate. These data
are difficult to obtain, however, and are subject to considerable error.

Formula 2 involves determining the actual evaporation rate by tests.

$$\text{cfm} = \frac{\substack{\text{specific gravity} \times \text{(pints of liquid evaporated/min)} \\ \times\ 403 \times 10^6 \times \text{K}}}{\text{molecular weight} \times \text{TLV}} \quad (5.4)$$

This is a more rational method; no guesswork here.

Formula 3 is used where the evaporation rate is expressed in pounds evap-
    orated each minute.

$$\text{cfm} = \frac{\text{(pounds evaporated/min)} \times 387 \times 10^6 \times \text{K}}{\text{molecular weight} \times \text{TLV}} \quad (5.5)$$

Finding the dilution ventilation rate for gases is much more difficult than
for liquids, but Formula 3 [Eq. (5.5)] is the most accurate where gases
require dilution. This is also the most accurate method for volatile
organic liquids.

Note: The above apply to vapors released by a single contaminant. Often,
dilution ventilation must be applied to vapors released by a mixture of volatile liquids. In the absence of more definitive information, dilution ventilation rates should be calculated for each component of a mixture and the
cubic feet per minute values so obtained added together to give the total
ventilation rate. For greater safety in handling unknown mixtures, assume
the entire mixture to be composed entirely of the component having the
highest rate requirement, and calculate the cubic feet per minute accordingly.
Source: Power, February 1976.

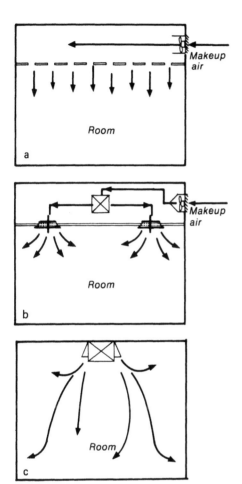

FIG. 5.3. a: Perforated ceiling. b: Diffusers. c: Duct header. (From Power, February, 1976.)

The worker is not too near the zone of concentrated contaminant release.

Under these conditions, K = 4, and the average concentration is about 25% of the TLV. The concentration in any part of the work space will probably not be higher than the TLV.

Selecting the K Factor

Since average distribution conditions are as elusive as ideal conditions, the need arises for a more rational basis for selecting the value of K to

TABLE 5.5.   K Ranges versus Distribution

K values	Distribution system
1.2-1.5	Perforated ceiling
1.5-2.0	Air diffusers
2.0-3.0	Duct headers along ceiling with branch jets pointing downward
3.0 and above	Window, wall fans, etc.

Source: Power, February 1976.

TABLE 5.6.   K Factors for Four Distribution Conditions versus Toxicity

Distribution condition	Toxicity		
	Slight	Moderate	High
Poor	7	8	11
Average	4	5	8
Good	3	4	7
Excellent	2	3	6

Source: Power, February 1976.

TABLE 5.7.   Comparison of Key Criteria for Common Toxic Solvents

Solvent	Molecular weight	Specific gravity	TLV (ppm)
Acetone	58	0.79	1000
Carbon tetrachloride	154	1.60	25
Chloroform	119	0.98	50
Ethyl acetate	88	0.90	400
Ethyl alcohol	46	0.79	1000
Methyl ethyl ketone	72	0.81	200
Toluol	92	0.87	200

Source: Power, February 1976.

reflect actual conditions—poor, average, good, or excellent (see Table 5.6). Poor distribution, for example, may be caused by a short-circuiting of makeup air, inadequacy of infiltration as a source of makeup air, or location of the worker in or directly downstream from the enveloping vapors. When these occur, an average K higher than 4 is required.

The TLV (or the relative toxicity) of the substance being controlled enters into the design directly, as the formulas show. Use TLVs promulgated by ACGIH (such as those in Table 5.7), plug them into the appropriate formula, and apply safety factors. For substances not listed by ACGIH, use these TLV guidelines: slightly toxic, 400 ppm; moderately toxic, 200 ppm; highly toxic, 50 ppm.

5.3. HOW TO APPLY DILUTION VENTILATION

Introduction

In industry, pump rooms and blower/compressor houses are subject to excess atmospheric contamination. Here's how these spaces can be safely ventilated. Table 5.8 lists ventilation needs for various areas and buildings that can form the composition of oil refineries, chemical plants, petrochemical plants, and general industry.

Ventilation of Potentially Hazardous Areas

The importance of ventilation for controlling atmospheric contamination in such potentially hazardous areas as pump rooms, blower houses, and compressor spaces is fully appreciated by industry. Studies indicate that dilution ventilation and general exhaust without ductwork produce acceptable air quality without sacrificing economy either in first cost or in operation. In this regard, field investigations have been conducted to obtain data on the following phenomena:

  Entrainment and jet-pump action of inlet louvers on dilution of vapors
  Effect of louver design on dilution of vapors
  Vapor dispersion by unit heaters
  Effect of exhaust-fan location on inlet-louver jet action
  Ventilation performance of pressurized rooms

Two Systems Compared

Two systems were compared in these investigations. In one, the rooms were ventilated by a system of intake louvers and fans (Fig. 5.4a). In the other, a form of positive ventilation, with fan, heater, and ductwork, was examined (Fig. 5.4b). For the Fig. 5.4a system, outside-air changes per hour, depending on space usage, were as follows: hot-fluid pump room, 50; cold-fluid pump room, 30; compressor house, 42; and blower house, 25.

TABLE 5.8. Ventilation Needs for Various Buildings and Areas
for the CPI (No Air Conditioning)

Building or area	Outside air changes per hour
Control house	
Control room	30
Access space	30
Locker room	5
Maintenance room	10
Office	2
Lavatory	10
Lab test area	15
Machinery room	20
Laboratory	10
Instrument shop	10
Electric shop	10
Switch house	15
Hot oil pump house	30
Cold oil pump house	20
Compressor house	20
Blower house	20
Analyzer house	2
Operator's shelter	2
Water pump house	20
Generator house	15
Boiler house	
Boiler room: 30 outside air changes exhaust; 30 supply	
Motor commutator house: use plant air purge 5-10 cfm at 1-2 in. water column	
Administration building (no air conditioning)	
Offices	2
Lobby	2
Hallway	2
Lavatory	10
Machinery room	20
Janitor closet	1
Telephone room	10
Shower room	10
Drafting room	10
Blue print room	10
Files and print storage	3
Conference room	10
Computer card storage	5
Computer room	10
Lunch room	5

TABLE 5.8. (Continued)

Building or area	Outside air changes per hour
Laboratory building	
Laboratory	20
Offices	2
Lobby	2
Shower	10
Toilet	10
Guard room	5
First aid	2
Nurse	2
Locker room	10
Cold room	1
Bottle wash	15
Mechanical equipment room	20
Reference fuels storage	10
Receiving room for fuels	10
Sample storage	5
Instrument shop	10
Electrical shop	10
Clock alley	—
Balance room	5
Knock test (hazardous)	20
Octane rating (hazardous)	20
Engine test (hazardous)	20
Personnel building	
Offices	2
Locker room	10
Guard house	5
First aid	2
Shower room	10
Dry room	5
Waiting	5
Storage	2
Machinery room	20
Janitor closet	1
Toilet	10
Maintenance shop	
Tool crib	5
Office	2
Shop area	12
Welding shop	15
Instrument shop	10
Electrical shop	10
Toilet	10

TABLE 5.8. (Continued)

Building or area	Outside air changes per hour
Maintenance shop (cont)	
Utility room	5
Battery room	15
Fire trucks	5
Garage (repair)	10
Welding area	10 (local exhaust)
Warehouse	5
Garage	10
Firehouse	5
Fire foam shed	2
Gate house	5
Weigh scale building	5
TEL building	
Toilet	10
Tank room	15
Control room	15
Dye room	15
Change house	
Locker area	5
Toilets	10
Shower	10
Dry room	5
Hang-up room	6 per locker
Manual labor locker room	10 + 7 cfm/locker
Heavy labor locker room	20 + 10 cfm/locker
Foreman's office	
Office	5
Waiting room	5
Toilet	10
Storage area	5
Chemical feed and mix building	10
Generator plants	12 exhaust; 30 supply
Brick storage	5
Urea bagged storage	5
Ammonium nitrate bagged storage	5
Urea bulk storage	8
Ammonium nitrate bulk storage	8
Engine test rooms	20

Note: Air-change quantities are for summer operation (natural or
mechanical) and may be reduced 50% for winter operation. For
positive pressure ventilation (all windows, doors, other openings
closed) increase quantities 50% using mechanical ventilation.
Interior toilets and lavatories use 50 cfm per water closet or
urinal. Air conditioned areas are to be given special treatment
in accordance with ASHRAE guidelines and industry practice.

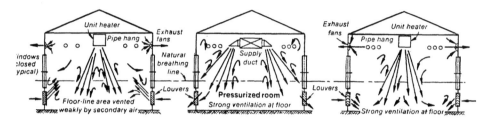

FIG. 5.4. a: Air supply at floor causes warm air to stratify above breathing line. b: Turbulence of air supply lowers effective breathing line to floor. c: Chevron-type louvers cause outside air to effectively sweep floor. (From Power, January 1975.)

For the Fig. 5.4b system, outside-air changes per hour were as follows: propane pump room, 20; oil pump room, 10; and control room, 10.

Process equipment and interconnecting piping were examined to ensure normal operation. Rooms were of brick construction and in good repair, with windows, doors, walls, and roofs structurally tight. In some cases, pipe sleeves were left open, permitting some uncontrolled leakage; however, this did not adversely affect ventilation efficiency except in pressurized rooms.

Test Results

For the types of rooms tested, the Fig. 5.4a system was found to meet normal requirements for year-round heating and ventilating. No perceptible stratification of gases at floor level was found in any test, nor were concentrations evident near or within the explosive range. Observations of chemical smoke (titanium tetrachloride) showed a definite upward-current component. Concentration gradients were nonexistent, as measured by explosimeter and test bombs.

Temperature gradients were definitely established, however, and made living conditions at the breathing line acceptable. These findings prove conclusively the desirability of removing air at high level and providing incoming air at the floor for dilution purposes—unlike conventional air distribution.

The inverted-chevron louver (Fig. 5.4c and Fig. 5.5) is a new departure in pump-house ventilation. It may be used to advantage, at no extra cost over the older design, in controlling concentrations of combustible gases and air. The considerations in arriving at the foregoing conclusions are outlined hereinafter.

Potential Hazards

The risk of explosion is ever-present in the confined areas of pump, blower, and compressor rooms in most segments of industry. Key criteria affecting the ignition of flammable, volatile liquids are the concentration of

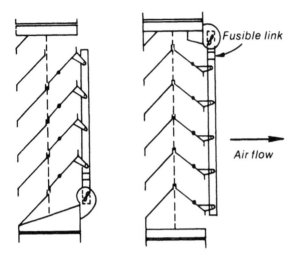

FIG. 5.5. Standard louver (left) and inverted chevron-type louver (right); both are provided with fusible linkage. (From Power, January 1975.)

their vapors in air and the temperature of the space, assuming atmospheric pressure. Vapors from hot, heavy oils may burn at concentrations as low as 0.4%, while those of propane, butane, or pentane, for example, may burn at concentrations as high as 8-9%. For natural gas, combustible limits are 5-15%.

These percentages are based on a thorough mixing with space air. If little mixing takes place, the danger of explosion increases in the zones between vapor and air. Higher temperatures also increase the danger of explosion. Flame propagation, size of containers holding the liquid, and ignition source are other factors.

From the standpoint of worker health and comfort, the maximum allowable concentration of gasoline vapors in air is 500 ppm by volume. Time of exposure is also important, but plays a minor role in pump, blower, and compressor rooms because occupancy is presumably of such short duration. See Schmidt, E. M. (1961).

Air Distribution

With dilution ventilation, distribution of air in confined spaces is critical. The primary effect of the distribution system is derived from the entrance of outside air into the space under the influence of a negative pressure created by an exhaust fan.

Figure 5.6 represents a room with an exhaust fan taking suction from the space at the rate of 1000 cfm. Under the influence of the fan, air enters

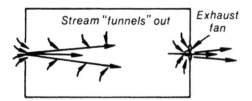

FIG. 5.6. Induced-air carry extends far into room via stream funnels created by fan. (From <u>Power</u>, January 1975.)

the room through an opening in an opposite wall. With no other openings, the effect is identical with the conditions prevailing in Fig. 5.7 in which a fan blows 1000 cfm into the room, the air escaping through an opening in the wall opposite.

Two significant groups of air currents are shown. One consists of those induced at the point of exit, whether or not an exhaust fan operates in the exit. The second consists of those entering the room through the single entrance orifice. The latter currents extend relatively greater distances into the room in roughly straight lines, whether under the influence of a forced-air fan or an exhaust fan in another wall. Distance from the inlet to the point beyond which velocities are insignificant (50 fpm or less) depends on the initial velocity and the opening area.

Air-entrainment Effects

Air-entrainment effects of such streams are so noticeable that it is virtually impossible to realize pure-air conditions in an outside air stream that passes through a space that contains contaminated air—except at a very short distance from the entrance. Total air movement created is up to seven times the primary air supplied at about 1200 fpm face velocity, or two times at 400 fpm face velocity.

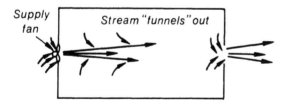

FIG. 5.7. Fan discharge extends far into room, creating air flow identical to Fig. 5.6. (From <u>Power</u>, January 1975.)

These projected air streams, however, provide the dilution characteristics so important to the proper functioning of dilution ventilation. In
spaces having numerous openings that have a large total area (permitting
infiltration from adjacent spaces at low velocities), the effect of entering
air currents in Figs. 5.6 and 5.7 may be lessened or entirely eliminated.
Secondary currents are also set up within spaces by such sources as hot
pump and turbine casings, hot piping, human traffic, air-cooled motors,
rotating pump and motor shafts, and flywheels. These currents create a
degree of turbulence which enhances dilution.

Product Escape

In most industrial processes, it is inevitable that some of the product escapes into the air. In this event, concentrations in the air will be gov-
erned by (1) the rate of product escape and (2) the rate of air movement
through the plant building, called the general ventilation rate. If only a
small amount of product is escaping, general ventilation is often enough to
keep atmospheric concentrations at safe levels.
    Frequently, atmospheric health hazards do not exist solely because of
general ventilation (natural or mechanical), because very little contaminant
may be required to produce an unsafe environment in air-tight spaces.
Obviously, therefore, boosting the general ventilation rate is a satisfactory
solution if the rate of contaminant production isn't excessive.

Other Considerations

Two modes of heat transfer are significant in confined spaces—radiation
and convection. Dilution ventilation will control convection heat transfer
in most cases. Radiant heating from hot piping and equipment can be controlled by means of shields and insulation. Ventilation is of little help,
although a worker's comfort may be enhanced by blowing cool air through
the area.
    The specific gravity of vapor-air mixtures might appear to encourage
a downward settling, leading to potentially hazardous conditions at the
breathing level and lower. This is not the case, however, except perhaps
quite close to where the mixtures emanate. Ventilation, cross currents,
turbulence from rotating machinery, convection currents, and heat all combine to dwarf into insignificance the effect of specific gravity. Central
ventilating systems were studied, but in most cases the presence of piping
and process equipment in confined spaces made the placement of cumbersome ductwork impractical if not impossible.

Testing Equipment

Air-flow measurements and test data were obtained with standard instruments and procedures. Flow rates were determined with a rotating-vane

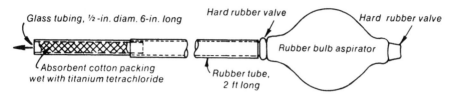

FIG. 5.8. Smoke generator is controlled manually to permit observation of air flow pattern. (From Power, January 1975.)

anemometer, averaging air velocity over a given cross-sectional area. Temperatures were read directly from standard mercury thermometers.

The behavior of convection currents was qualitatively analyzed with a chemical smoke generator; as a safety precaution, no flame or hot spot was used. Quantitative determinations were not made. The generator uses titanium tetrachloride, which hydrolyzes on contact with the moisture in air, forming dense white smoke. By means of this smoke tube (Fig. 5.8), the direction of convection currents was followed; the degree of air turbulence was also estimated.

A portable explosimeter of standard make, calibrated for propane-air mixtures, gave sufficiently accurate determinations of combustible vapor concentrations below the minimum explosive limit. To check for stratification, samples of room air were collected by test bombs, and densities were determined by the density-balance technique.

During the field investigations, a series of special tests were conducted to demonstrate the best application of dilution ventilation in pump, blower, and compressor rooms. The following sections highlight the results of these tests.

Entrainment, Jet-pump Action

When air is discharged from an opening into a large room, it will continue on its course for some distance. In this process, energy is lost due to friction between the relatively still air and the moving stream. This "drag" between moving and stationary air causes movement (called entrainment) in the form of eddy currents. Entrainment increases the cross-sectional area and reduces the velocity of the resulting air stream. The distance the jet will travel from the opening to a point at which air motion is reduced to 50 fpm is useful design information. The value of 50 fpm is normal room air velocity and is relatively quiet.

Louvers tested were like that shown in Fig. 5.5 left and were arranged with respect to the exhaust fans shown in Fig. 5.4c. With face velocities averaging 300 fpm, the throw, as determined by anemometer and smoke generator, was about 10 ft. Louvers placed on both sides of the room did not have good mixing at the floor lines. However, sampling of the air at

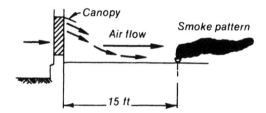

FIG. 5.9. Canopy effect on old-type louver leads to strong floor ventilation. (From Power, January 1975.)

the floor showed no evidence of the presence of a combustible mixture. Concentric dishes placed down the center aisle of the room showed some activity, but never any dead pockets.

Louver Design Versus Dilution

Deflection of the entering air stream downward at an angle of 45° greatly improved air distribution and dilution by getting at the source of contamination. A cardboard deflector was attached to the horizontal edge of a louver (canopy in Fig. 5.9), and swabs wet with titanium tetrachloride were placed at various distances from the louver face. The most effective distance was shown to be 15 ft at a louver-face velocity of 350 fpm.

Unit Heater Operation

The operation of a unit heater did not create sufficient turbulence at the floor line to be effective for vapor dispersion. Several tests were conducted at different mounting heights above the floor and at different temperatures of discharge. Under normal conditions, and as a result, it was concluded that unit heaters could not be relied upon for vapor dispersion unless specifically designed for that purpose.

Exhaust Fan Location

With all windows closed and louvers open, and all exhaust fans in operation, the air-distribution patterns were those shown in Fig. 5.10. Short-circuiting of the main jet was not observed when both the louver and exhaust fan

FIG. 5.10. Smoke pattern takes this shape in center aisle with dilution ventilation. (From Power, January 1975.)

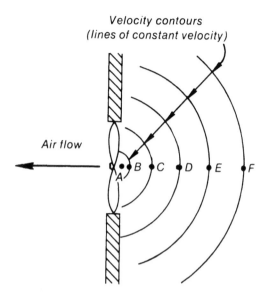

FIG. 5.11.   Induced flow at fan suction.   (From Power, January 1975.)

were in the same wall and vertically in line, as in Fig. 5.4a. Experimental
data on actual fan operation were collected during tests (Fig. 5.11; lettered
points indicate test positions).

Pressurized Rooms

A series of smoke tests reflected on a condition of much turbulence, instead of stratification, in rooms with Fig. 5.4b systems. Turbulence created by outlets in these spaces evened out the temperature and concentration
gradients. Warm air has a natural tendency to rise, creating livable temperatures at the breathing line (5-8 ft above the floor). If these natural
movements are disturbed, worker comfort is penalized, especially where
substantial heat gains, such as in hot-oil pump rooms, are involved. Smoke
tests proved that gases do not hug the floor, but permeate the entire room.
  Open pivoted-sash windows permitted room air to leave through the top
section and outside air to enter the room at the bottom section, as in
Fig. 5.12. Explosive concentrations of combustible vapors were not found
to exist. Windage from rotating shafts and flywheels, and discharges from
air-cooled motors, set up air currents that aided dilution. The normal outflow of air through exhaust louvers with windows closed was sluggish
(Fig. 5.13). Figure 5.14 shows a typical plan of exhaust fan and louvers
(chevron type) for dilution ventilation. Table 5.8 gives practical ventilation
needs for the CPI.

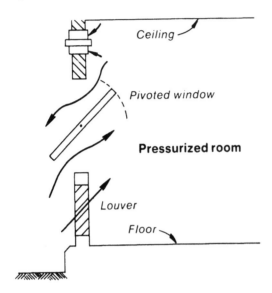

FIG. 5.12. Air entry and exit were tested in a pressurized room with this configuration. (From Power, January 1975.)

Importance of Specific Gravity

Considerable misapprehension appears to exist as to the importance of specific gravity in the design of ventilation systems. Most concentrated vapor-air mixtures usually do not have densities greater than 1.01 or 1.02 times that of air, and even densities of this order are not to be expected except within short distances from the emanating source. Solvent vapors do not usually collect near the floor in marked higher concentrations than at breathing level (5 ft). These observations are supported by investigations made by this author. Air samples from hot and cold pump rooms, where

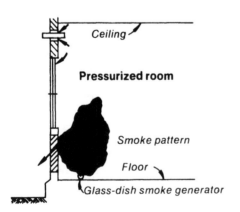

FIG. 5.13. Air escaping through pipe sleeves and window cracks causes louver flow to be sluggish in this pressurized room. (From Power, January 1975.)

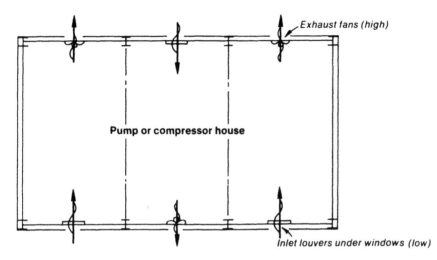

FIG. 5.14. Typical plan of exhaust fans and louvers for dilution ventilation. (From Power, January 1975.)

conditions can be hazardous, were found to have a density of 1.003 with respect to air (density = 1). Samples were taken at the floor line, in pits, and in trenches below the floor within the pump rooms.

Let us calculate, for example, the specific gravity of a gasoline vapor-air mixture. Assume a well-ventilated room with the vapor well-mixed with outside air in accordance with a Fig. 5.4c system. Gasoline has a TLV of 500 ppm and an approximate molecular weight of 120 and a LEL of 1.3%.

Specific gravity of air = 1.0

Specific gravity of gasoline vapor $= \dfrac{120}{29} = 4.14$

500 ppm = 0.05 part vapor to 99.95 parts air

0.0005(4.14) = 0.0021

0.9995(1.00) = 0.9995

0.0021 + 0.9995 = 1.0016 effective specific gravity of mixture, say
                              1.002

This is in line with the specific gravity determined by density balance during tests.

It is obvious that compared to clean air the vapor-air mixture would have a small tendency to hug the floor, expressed by the ratio of 100.2 to 100 and not by the ratio of 4.14 to 1.00 as is frequently implied. Thus, the effects of mechanical ventilation, window ventilation, cross currents, traffic, rotating machinery (pumps, compressors, etc.), convection currents, and heat can dwarf into insignificance the effect of specific gravity.

Considering the effective specific gravity on the basis of the LEL of gasoline vapor of 1.3% by volume, or its equivalent of 13,000 ppm, the effective specific gravity may be calculated in the same way to be 1.04.

$$\frac{13,000}{500} \times 0.05 = 1.3 \text{ parts vapor to } 98.7 \text{ parts air}$$

$$(0.0013)(4.14) = 0.005382$$

$$(0.0987)(1.00) = 0.098700$$

$$0.005382 + 0.098700 = 1.04 \text{ effective specific gravity}$$

A comparison of the two specific gravities calculated shows that an atmosphere meeting requirements adopted by ACGIH would definitely be below the LEL and would be safe. The TLV of 500 ppm for gasoline would be equivalent to 3.8% of the LEL, well below the accepted operating standard of 25% of the LEL.

Supply the Dilution Air or Exhaust

There is no hard and fast rule as to whether a dilution ventilating system should provide air only, exhaust air only, or use a combination of both. Each and every design situation must be carefully analyzed for the best system arrangement. Here are some suggestions to help arrive at a well-balanced system:

1. When providing an exhaust system, it must be supplied with outside makeup air.
2. The makeup air must be tempered to prevent drafts in cold weather.
3. Place the supply-air outlets to avoid short circuiting and to promote intimate mixing with contaminated air.
4. If only exhaust is used, check against Table 4.1 for natural infiltration flow to satisfy the exhaust-air needs. Otherwise, a makeup air system must be provided.
5. A well-designed air supply system will provide better dilution and lower operator exposure than an exhaust system. Thorough dilution and mixing are the watchwords.
6. To protect adjoining occupied areas against contamination, provide an excess of exhaust over supply air. If this is not a problem, provide a slight positive pressure that will encourage exfiltration. Check room function carefully before making your decision.
7. The ventilation air rate is the difference between supply and exhaust air flows. It is the excess of one over the other.
8. Avoid drafts from makeup air supply outlets by adequate tempering and supply outlet velocities. Do not attempt to "throw" the supply

    air long distances at high velocity; keep "throws" short and dis-
    charge outlets high. Provide discharge grille outlets with hori-
    zontal and vertical adjustment mechanisms.
9. Local exhaust hoods have a definite capture pattern which must
    not be disturbed by the turbulent air streams from supply outlets.
10. Review pertinent sections of this chapter for mixing factors.

As a final reminder, although local exhaust will be more effective and require that less air is handled, dilution ventilation can be most effective in
controlling minor and scattered sources of contamination.

    Methods of duct design and fan selection are similar to those for local
exhaust systems and are well established in the literature and in industry.
Thus, the details will not be included here. Please refer to the bibliography and reference sections at the end of this book.

Ventilation Rates for Machinery Rooms

Design experience shows that toxic and hazardous vapors and gases may be
found in the atmospheres of processing buildings. If a system is closed
and operationally safe, dilution by ventilation with outside air presents no
problem, and the method suggested herein may be applied. Under these
conditions, a minimum escape of gases and volatile vapors can be tolerated
without injury to the worker.

    The air quantities tabulated hereinafter are not recommended if the
processing system is not closed or if abnormal conditions prevail that permit the escape of excessive quantities of toxic and explosive materials into
the workspace. In such instances, special ventilation measures, such as
local exhaust or floor fans, are used or required.

    The heat generated by machinery and processing equipment may be
readily calculated, and the outside air requirements may be determined
from the formula

$$Q = \frac{H}{1.08\Delta t} \qquad\qquad (5.6)$$

where

    Q = ventilation air, cfm
    H = heat liberated by equipment and piping, Btuh
    t = arithmetic temperature difference between outside and desired in-
        side dry bulb temperatures, °F

In practice it has been found that the calculation of Q is cumbersome and
time consuming, and in most cases it is a downright guess. The air change
method (see Table 5.8) is often used in normal practice, but the recommended values can vary widely. In addition, excessive air flows may be
handled when not required.

TABLE 5.9. Centrifugal Pumps—Turbine Drive

Driver horsepower	Pumping temperature over 100°F (cfm)	Pumping temperature 100°F and under (cfm)
15	750	250
25	850	260
50	1100	400
75	1350	500
100	1550	600
125	1700	650
150	1850	700
175	1950	750
200	2050	810
225	2150	850
250	2250	900
275	2315	950
300	2400	965
325	2450	1000
350	2500	1015
375	2550	1050
400	2600	1060

TABLE 5.10. Centrifugal Pumps—Electric Drive

Driver horsepower	Pumping temperature over 100°F (cfm)	Pumping temperature 100°F and under (cfm)
15	550	200
25	655	250
50	950	350
75	1125	400
100	1260	500
125	1400	550
150	1500	600
175	1600	640
200	1660	660
225	1750	700
250	1800	725
275	1850	750
300	1900	775
325	1950	800
350	2000	805
375	2050	810
400	2060	815

TABLE 5.11. Reciprocating Pumps

Pump capacity (gpm)	Pumping temperature over 100°F (cfm)	Pumping temperature 100°F and under (cfm)
25	240	120
50	280	140
75	310	160
100	340	180
125	380	190
150	410	210
175	440	222
200	480	240
225	510	260
250	540	280
275	580	300
300	620	320
325	650	340
350	690	360
375	730	380
400	770	400
425	805	420
450	845	430
475	880	450
500	930	470
525	970	500
550	1020	520
575	1060	540
600	1100	560
625	1150	580
650	1200	600
700	1300	640

A unique alternative method used in industry to ventilate pump rooms, compressor rooms, and blower rooms is given in Tables 5.9 to 5.13. The quantities for present and future machinery are also obtained from these tables. The amounts of ventilation air for standby units are to be reduced 25% below the operating quantities. Quantities for unoccupied areas of the room (exclusive of space required for future machinery), is 5 cfm/ft^2 of floor area in hot oil pump rooms, 3 cfm/ft^2 in cold oil pump rooms, and 2 cfm/ft^2 in compressor and blower rooms. Quantities for other equipment are to be based on heat dissipation and the dilution of toxic and flammable gases and vapors. In Tables 5.9 to 5.13, quantities are for single units, including the drivers, and are to be applied to the floor area occupied

TABLE 5.12. Reciprocating Compressors

Driver horsepower	Gas and steam engine driven (cfm)	Electric motor driven (cfm)
100	850	750
150	1100	1000
200	1350	1175
250	1525	1350
300	1700	1500
350	1875	1650
400	2025	1775
450	2150	1900
500	2300	2025
550	2400	2150
600	2500	2250
650	2600	2350
700	2700	2450
750	2800	2525
800	2875	2600
850	2950	2700
900	3025	2750
950	3100	2850
1000	3175	2950

TABLE 5.13. Turbo Blowers

Driver horsepower	Cfm
500	750
1000	950
1500	1150
2000	1400
2500	1625
3000	1850
3500	2100
4000	2350

Note: Interpolate or extrapolate as required.

by the machine and the surrounding minimum aisle spaces. Use the plot plan, equipment layout, and electrical data for needed information. Interpolate and extrapolate as required.

Definitions

Air projection (throw): the distance an air stream travels from an outlet to a position at which air motion along the axis reduces to a velocity of 50 fpm.

Breathing line: level for normal occupancy; taken at 5 ft above the floor.

Central system: consists of a fan, heating coil, and ductwork for ventilation.

Cold oil pump room: room that houses pumps with drivers and piping. The average pumping temperature 150°F.

Convection: the motion in a fluid resulting from the difference in density and the action of gravity.

Density balance: an instrument for determining relative densities of a sample by comparing it directly with air by weighing.

Entrainment ratio: a ratio of the volume of room air entrained to the volume of primary air leaving a discharge outlet.

Exhaust fan: a wall-type fan arranged to draw air from a space and to discharge it to the atmosphere.

Hot oil pump room: a room that houses pumps and drivers with piping. The average pumping temperature is about 600°F.

Jet: a nozzle-shaped apparatus discharging an air stream at high velocity.

Local ventilation: Air movement that collects contaminated air in as concentrated a form as possible and conveys it to suitable disposal equipment.

Outside air change: one complete replacement of the air contained within a space by outside air.

Portable explosimeter: a device used for indicating the lower explosive limit (LEL) of a combustible-gas-air mixture. Any combustibles present in an air sample are burned upon contacting the hot platinum filament of the detector unit, thus increasing its temperature and in turn its resistance. This unbalances a bridge circuit in proportion to the concentration of combustible present in the sample and causes a deflection of the indicating needle to read a percentage of LEL.

Radiation, thermal heat: the transmission of energy by means of electromagnetic waves of very long wavelength. The radiant energy of any wavelength may, when adsorbed, become thermal energy and result in an increase in the temperature of the absorbing body.

Rotating vane anenometer: a device consisting of a propeller or revolving vane connected through a gear train to a set of recording dials that read the linear feet of air passing through in a measured length of time.

Test bomb: a portable steel chamber for collecting air samples. The chamber is evacuated and the sample is drawn in for testing later in the laboratory.

Unit heater: a fan and steam-condensing coil arrangement located at or near the ceiling for space heating.

Ventilation: a phenomenon dealing with air circulation. It implies supplying outside air and covers the exhausting of heat, dust, toxic fumes, and gases.

6

LOCAL EXHAUST VENTILATION

6.1. INTRODUCTION

In local exhaust ventilation, the airborne contaminant may be removed or captured from the workplace environment at or as close as possible to the source. It is the method of choice whenever contaminants are released or discharged from a definitive and narrowly circumscribed operation. Its basic advantages are that control can be positive and efficient, air volumes exhausted are comparatively low, and makeup air costs are a minimum. Its disadvantage is a high initial cost of installation; elaborate hood systems may be involved with ducting that uses up valuable plant space and relatively high power requirements. When installed in heavy process piping areas and workrooms, it can cause a problem when piping changes are required.

The technical literature is replete with design criteria for complete local exhaust systems, and the reader is referred to the literature for the details and ramifications of such systems. The reference list, Industrial Ventilation (1970), Alden, J. L. (1948), and the bibliography at the end of this book will be found most useful in pursuing this further.

6.2. LOCAL EXHAUST VENTILATION

General

A local exhaust system is made up of a pickup point, which may be a hood or a duct, that has its terminus in the form of a splayed section open at its end. An exhaust fan creates a suction pressure at the hood or splayed end by means of interconnecting ductwork. The air which is picked up by the suction point travels to the fan and is discharged to the outside or it is cleaned and recirculated.

The hood or other pickup section of duct located around, at, or near a source of atmospheric contamination prevents the escape of the contaminant by capturing it and conveying it away to the outside untreated, to the outside after being treated by an air cleaner or filter, or back to the workspace after being cleaned. The Occupational Safety and Health Act (OSHA) regulations do not prohibit the recirculation of air into the workspace, but its primary requirements are that the contaminant concentration in plant air be less than the threshold limit value (TLV). How this is achieved remains the responsibility of the plant.

Hoods

To repeat, the sole function of a local exhaust system is to protect the worker from exposure to hazardous contaminants which have been created in the workspace. The crux of the design of a local exhaust system is the hood or other pickup point, or orifice. Hood design is affected by a number of considerations: physical state of the contaminant, temperature of process, velocity and direction of contaminant discharge, nature of the operation discharging the contaminant, and the degree of operational control required of the process. The ideal situation would be to enclose the source of contamination completely and then provide the openings or configuration changes that may be required. The reader is referred to the literature and especially to the American Conference of Governmental Industrial Hygienists (ACGIH) publication "A Manual of Recommended Practice."

Ductwork

The connecting link between the hood and fan is the ductwork. It serves the dual function of controlling the rate of air flow and conveying the contaminant-laden air to the fan suction and away as heretofore mentioned. Duct design requires due consideration to aerodynamic principles so that resistance to air flow is kept at a minimum. For the details of duct design the reader is referred to the American Society of Heating, Refrigeration and Air Conditioning Engineers (ASHRAE) guide publications and the ACGIH "A Manual of Recommended Practice." See also the bibliography and reference listings at the end of this book.

Fans

Fans are the mechanical air-moving devices which make most industrial exhaust systems operate. Although the ventilation design engineer is not generally concerned with fan designs, he should know and understand enough of their theory and performance characteristics to be able to select, evaluate, and modify industrial exhaust fans.

For greatest effectiveness, any fan must increase the static pressure in the air being handled. Static pressure is potential energy and can be utilized to move the air stream. The increase in pressure developed in a fan arises from two sources: (1) the centrifugal force caused by the rotation of an enclosed volume of air and (2) the increased velocity in the direction of flow imparted to the air by the fan blades. The centrifugal force imparted to the air mass causes a compression of the gas or air. This is called static pressure and is dependent on the increase in the centrifugal component of the velocity of the air. The longer the fan blades, the greater will be the static pressure component. An increase in velocity in the direction of flow causes an increase in velocity pressure, which must be converted to static pressure to be useful. Total pressure is the sum of static and velocity pressure and is constant except for friction losses. Conversion of velocity pressure to static pressure can be made in both centrifugal and axial-flow fans by providing a constantly diverging discharge duct at the fan outlet.

TABLE 6.1. General Consideration of Fan Types

	Centrifugal fans			Axial-flow fans	
	Backwardly inclined	Radial blade	Forwardly curved	Vane-axial	Propeller and tube-axial
First cost[a]	High	Medium	Low	Low	Lowest
Efficiency	High	Medium	Medium	High	Lowest
Stability of operation	Good	Good	Poor	Good	Poor
Space required	Medium	Medium	Small	Small	Small
Tip speed (noise)	High	Medium	Low	Medium	High
Resistance to abrasion	Medium	Good	Poor	Medium	Medium
Ability to handle sticky materials	Medium	Good	Poor	Medium	Medium

[a] For normal duty applications, first cost essentially is the same for all three types of centrifugal fans. Heavy duty applications reflect the comparisons listed.

Fan Types

Types of axial-flow fans are propeller fans, tube-axial fans, and vane-axial fans. Centrifugal fans are most commonly used in industry for supply and exhaust systems, pneumatic conveying, or forced-draft applications. Axial-flow fans are made up of paddle-wheel fans, forward-curved blade fans, and backward-curved blade fans. Table 6.1 presents a general comparison of fan types used in ventilation work. For the details of fan types and their applications, the reader is referred to the literature.

Rating Point of a Fan

A fan manufacturer will guarantee a fan's performance at only one point on its performance curve. This is usually the point indicated on the client's specifications and has been determined by estimating friction loss and air flow rate of a designed system.

A fan running at a constant speed can operate at any volume-static pressure combination along its characteristic curve. The actual point at which it will operate is determined by the resistance of the ductwork to the air flow system, including the hood. The fan will operate at the intersection of the fan characteristic curve and the system curve due to resistance to air flow (see Fig. 6.1). The same fan develops its own curve at different constant speeds. Any question on fan selection and performance should be referred to the fan manufacturer.

Fan Selection

There are a number of fan types available to the designer, but the system requirements limit the type. The propeller fan is used principally for spray booths and such applications where large volumes of air are to be moved at relatively low pressures. The axial fan (vane or tubular) is somewhat similar but can generate higher pressures and is applied where higher pressures must be maintained and where an in-line fan is advantageous.

As for centrifugal fans, there are really three types and each has its own application. The forward curved fan is a relatively high-volume quiet fan with low space requirements. It is used principally to pump air at relatively low pressures for fume or mist handling. The paddle wheel fan is a pressure exhauster used for dust-handling systems. The backward curved or limit-load fan is an efficient, nonoverloading fan and is used to move clean air or air containing gases and vapors at moderate pressures; it can be used also for dust-handling systems when taking suction at the outlet side of a filter bank.

The specifications for a fan should be documented, and the fan manufacturers should be able to quote on a common basis. Selection is based on a set of manufacturer's rating tables, the fan laws, which are used to describe the change in cfm, pressure, horsepower, speed, and size of fan

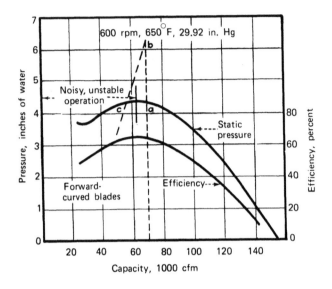

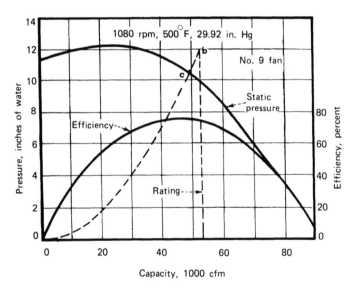

FIG. 6.1. Rating point of a fan. (From Power, August 1970.)

system. The fan laws permit the selection of a fan and the evaluation of
the adequacy of a fan on hand to be used for a new system. The effect of a
change in operating conditions on the duct system can also be evaluated.
See Cheremisenoff, P. N., and Young, R. A. (1974).

<u>Using the fan catalog</u> Once the fan specification has been established, refer to the proper fan catalog. Fan catalogs contain information on the performance, construction, dimensions, modifications, and accessories of one or more homologous series of different sizes of a type of fan. Performance data are most generally presented in the form of "multirating tables." Each table gives the rpm and horsepower required to move a given volume of air against a fan static pressure for one size of fan. The figures for points of maximum efficiency are sometimes underlined or in boldface type. The ideal fan size for a given task is the one where the point of highest efficiency coincides with the desired flow and static pressure. If this point falls between two fan sizes in a series, the smaller fan is usually selected, since it will cost less and will operate on a steeper sloped portion of its characteristic curve, where the operating stability is better. In most cases, interpolation between the points in the table will be necessary. A static pressure interpolation should be made first, followed by the volume interpolation. Arithmetic interpolations are usually satisfactory. Variations in the procedure required for conditions other than 70°F and 1 atm should be referred to the manufacturer. As a matter of good practice, all matters should be referred to the manufacturers, making them responsible for the selection once design conditions have been established.

Air Cleaning

Let us quickly review air cleaning, which is to be an integral part of an exhaust system. Each system must be designed to accommodate the filtration system and be compatible with all other system components. The design and size of an air cleaner will be dictated by the nature of the contaminant and the required degree of cleaning. Naturally, the effective resistance of the cleaning system will influence the type and horsepower of the fan. Air cleaning is a specialty in itself, and the designer should refer to the literature on the subject. See the bibliography and reference sections at the end of this book.

Makeup Air

Although the makeup air system will be discussed separately in a later chapter, and since it is one of the most important and least understood design considerations in exhaust system design, let us quickly review it here. If no makeup air is provided, all sorts of problems will develop in the plant, and the exhaust systems will not function properly. In addition, the air must be tempered in cold weather to avoid drafts. Nevertheless, its need is all too often overlooked, and natural ventilation is relied upon. This is all well and good, but natural ventilation flow must be evaluated by use of Table 4. 1. If more than the air that can be expected from natural infiltration sources is required, then a makeup system is a must. When using Table 4.1, know the building function and normal degree of tightness. Be sure that the building is not tight with insulation, weather stripping, and caulking. Otherwise incorporate a makeup air system.

Beside starving the exhaust system, the action of natural draft stacks will be negated and the backdraft of contaminants into the workspace will take place. Workers will also shut off exhaust fans to cut down on drafts, and high-velocity cross drafts can interfere with the efficient operation of exhaust hoods.

Recirculation

Energy conservation dictates consideration of the recirculation of work-room air after cleaning. Air discharged from an exhaust system may be completely or partly returned to the workroom after suitable cleaning, obviating the need for a costly makeup air system. Management is at-tracted by recirculation systems as a way to conserve fuel and to avoid expensive makeup air systems. Recently, the trend to install recircula-tion has been accelerated by the new sophisticated technologies to maintain the working environment to meet rigid temperature, humidity, and dust concentration specifications. Discharging the costly conditioned air im-poses a severe economic burden. In addition, increased emphasis on air pollution control is placing stricter requirements on the need for air-clean-ing devices where none was needed before. Furthermore, high-efficiency air cleaners are now needed more and more where cheaper collectors were acceptable before.

Where recirculation is permissible, it could be economically feasible to install high-efficiency air cleaning with recirculation where air pollution requirements would allow low-efficiency air cleaners and discharging to the outside. There are also cases where recirculation is mandatory when exhaust systems are so located that it is virtually impossible to run an exhaust pipe to the outdoors.

Although it is the ultimate responsibility of the plant management to decide the feasibility of recirculation, most state governments and others require prior approval for recirculation. It goes almost without saying that recirculation from systems handling highly toxic contaminants is al-most never granted because very efficient cleaning devices are not availa-ble to do the job. Whenever a highly toxic contaminant is being handled, it behooves the designer to avoid recirculation in any case because of the po-tential hazard that could result from improper operation or neglectful maintenance of the air-cleaning system or a massive collector failure. For some compelling reasons, or if proper safeguards are provided, mod-erately toxic contaminants may be handled in systems provided with re-circulation from systems handling contaminants of little or no toxicity is becoming more and more acceptable.

Desirable Conditions for Recirculation

What are the desirable conditions for recirculation that must be considered and evaluated?

1. Air cleaning must be highly efficient so that the percentage is a fraction of the TLV in the recirculated air. The tested TLV should be not more than 20% of the TLV, and it should be lower if at all possible. The rated cleaning efficiency of collectors, expressed in percent by weight of the contaminant removed from the air stream, can be misleading, especially when choosing a collector for a recirculating system, since many TLVs are expressed in terms of parts per million of air stream or millions of particles of dust per cubic foot of air sample. A 99% collector efficiency by weight can be inadequate, and it may require a number of collectors in series.

2. Dilution ventilation practices should be followed for large workrooms that are provided with good ventilation so that odors, water vapor, and contaminants may be effectively diluted.

3. Complete recirculation (100%) should be avoided for large systems or for those handling moderately toxic contaminants. Provide the system with the ability to discharge room air to the outdoors, especially during mild weather or when room air supply is not tempered. Remember: recirculate but do not suffocate. Provide a T-connection adequately dampered to go either outdoors or to complete the recirculation. This arrangement will also function as a safety measure should there be a failure of the air cleaner unit. Under certain operating conditions it might be desirable to limit and control the flow and duration of the recirculation function as much as possible and still take advantage of the desirable features of recirculation to the fullest. This may be accomplished by a control system operating automatically through the use of a modulating damper controlled by a thermostat that will recirculate or discharge to the outdoors in varying amounts depending on the season: cold or mild weather.

4. As mentioned previously, be careful not to design the system so that high-velocity air streams are discharged into the workroom that will create noise and drafts.

System Testing

All systems installed should be tested at installation and at periodically scheduled times to ensure proper operation and performance. Design exhaust flows should be checked with flow meters for design effectiveness. Here are some evaluation checks:

   Air velocity into a hood
   Pitot tube velocity test in duct leaving a hood
   Static pressure measurement at the throat of a hood

Static pressure measurement at the inlet and discharge of a fan
Static pressure measurement at both sides of a collector
Fan rpm
Fan brake horsepower

Effectiveness of hood control must be made by chemical analysis for the
contaminant at the hood and within the workspace at the breathing zone.
Such chemical analyses need to be made for testing the effectiveness of a
dilution ventilation system and at the inlet and outlet of collectors.

Exhaust System Maintenance

Once an exhaust system has been installed, its maintenance for continuing
high efficiency is often neglected. Many things can happen to the system,
and a preventative maintenance schedule should be set up and followed.
The operation can be provided with a false sense of security if the system
is left to chance. After an exhaust system or any air-handling system has
been designed, installed, and tested, the hood suction and fan inlet suction
should be measured when the system is new and all performing data should
be documented and kept for operating records. A good way to keep an eye
on air flow is to provide pressure points at the fan inlet and outlet, at each
hood or pickup point, connected to suitable pressure-indicating devices with
the proper pressure posted at each point. Alarms can be used in conjunction with pressure-indicating devices to give aural or visual indication of
pressure loss below the critical level. The exhaust fan should be provided
with an audible failure alarm. Under some circumstances, it may be necessary to provide automatic shutdown devices if the flow drops off too much.
However, a better way is to keep the system in operation at all times and
periodically check the pressure. See Perry, R. E. (1976).

Specifics of Design

The specifics of design relating to hoods and the specifics of industrial
processes are too numerous to be covered in this book, and the reader is
referred to the technical literature, most of which is listed in the bibliography and reference sections of this book. See also Cheremisenoff, P. N.,
and Cheremisenoff, N. P. (1976).

Precautions for Safety

In all calculations and in the selection of fans, good judgment and the intelligent use of safety factors must be exercised. It must be realized that occupational illnesses are caused by repeated daily exposures to low concentrations of toxic fumes. These concentrations are often so low that workers
are not aware of their existence.

There are great differences from individual to individual in regard to their vapor or gas absorption. Some can stand higher concentration while others will become ill at concentrations below the maximum allowable level (TLV). Therefore, it is highly recommended that periodic examinations be made of all workers exposed to toxic materials. It is also advisable to make periodic air-sampling tests in workrooms subject to toxic material emanation and around machinery which is suspect. There are good instruments available which permit gas and vapor sampling and the determination of vapor concentrations in a practical and simple way. The Mine Safety Appliances Company, Pittsburgh, Pennsylvania, and the Davis Emergency Equipment Company, Newark, New Jersey, for instance, are making gas analyzers and vapor testers practical for plant use. Industrial Hygiene News, published by Rimbach Publishing Company, Pittsburgh, Pennsylvania, is most helpful in this area. It is circulated without charge in the United States and its territories to persons responsible for worker health in all industries and at all levels of government upon receipt of information provided by these individuals.

One safety measure which should not be overlooked is the introduction of air-flow switches in the exhaust stacks. These instruments are adjustable to a certain air flow; they can be connected to an alarm or a safety switch which will stop the processing equipment if any change occurs in the amount of exhaust air after the dampers for air flow are once set. The air-flow switch will indicate any change in the exhaust system which may occur due to motor failures on exhaust fans, belt slippage on fan drives, plugging up of exhaust ducts, incorrect setting of dampers, or an accidental change in damper settings. On very important and expensive equipment, or in factory areas with high occupancy, it may be advisable to have explosion or gas-test instruments permanently installed that produce a record or will otherwise indicate a dangerous situation. It is also good practice to specify spark-proof fans of aluminum or other metal with spark-proof characteristics for any application where explosion hazards are present.

Inside any equipment where explosion hazards exist, only explosion-proof switches, lighting fixtures, and motors should be installed. Outside of equipment where great quantities of air are moved on account of toxicity hazards, explosion-proof equipment may not be necessary.

6.3. ESTIMATING EXHAUST AIR REQUIREMENTS FOR PROCESSES

General

In many process applications, you can calculate the correct flow of air for inplant contamination control by using the proper exhaust criteria. The need to meet higher standards for contaminant control in chemical processing plants, oil refineries, and petrochemical plants has placed many new responsibilities on the design engineer. More and better mechanical-exhaust systems are needed for the removal of fumes, odors, fog, dust, and heat. These systems must be installed close to the source of generation to prevent contamination of the total environment and to keep makeup air flows down to a minimum. Some dusts and vapors may be nontoxic, but their control is deemed necessary to ensure an acceptable inplant working environment for the individual worker.

Importance of Control

From the standpoint of production and quality control, products manufactured or processed in a contaminated area may be affected because of poor environmental control. Then, corrosive vapors and gases may be loosed into the area. If left uncontrolled, these can shorten the life of the structure, and even the processing and manufacturing equipment.

Of considerable importance is the control of dust, fumes, vapors, and gases to minimize fire and explosion. Lack of environmental control may disqualify the plant owner for insurance coverage.

Because of pressures being brought to bear on processing and manufacturing plants, control of atmospheric pollution is of paramount concern to management in the area of public relations. In addition, contaminated air may be harmful to workers and the manufactured product, and costly to plant operations. Thus it is essential that control be effective and economic. In the design of a control system (assuming that contaminants cannot be eliminated and that less toxic or less obnoxious chemicals cannot be used in the process), the first step is to see what can be done to contain the contaminants to minimize ventilation requirements and heating costs for makeup air.

When ceilings are high and the contaminant is primarily heat, the dilution method of control is recommended. In such a system, powered roof fans are used to dispel heat to the outdoors. However, the preferred method is by local exhaust, collecting the contaminants at their point of leaving a vessel. The dilution method may be used as an auxiliary arrangement (in addition to local exhaust required by insurance writers) in case of an emergency or accidental spill.

Air Quantities for Local Exhaust

The air quantities required for local exhaust systems are based on a number of design factors—especially capture velocities (see Chapter 5). In the chemical process industries (CPI), most applications will require capture velocities ranging from 50 to 200 fpm at a point in the system where the contaminant will tend to escape into the workroom. The lower value is used to control contaminants released at low speed in relatively quiet air. The higher values are used to control contaminants released at high rates or released to an atmosphere fraught with disturbing cross currents. Other factors that affect air exhaust flows are the area of the openings and the capture distance.

Much of the exhaust-air load in both typical and atypical chemical plants is obvious. There are hoods or enclosures of many types at the sources of possible environmental contamination. These are usually connected by ductwork to fans or exhausters discharging to scrubbers, collectors, or bag filters, depending on the nature of the contaminant.

Every cubic foot of air that is exhausted from a building must be replaced to keep the building from operating under a negative pressure. And in winter the incoming air must be warmed up (or tempered) by a makeup air system before being distributed inside the processing area. Without sufficient air, exhaust and ventilating systems cannot work properly.

Estimates for Replacement Air

There is no real problem where replacement air can be determined easily, such as in paint-spray booths. Here the volume of replacement air is the same as that of the spray-booth exhauster plus 10% to create a negative pressure within the enclosure.

To check an existing plant operation or to design for an adequate makeup air system, the data in the accompanying Table 6.2 provide specific exhaust criteria. These data may also be used to help determine if a plant is "air starved" and in need of a makeup air system.

In the planning of hooded systems, the value of using standard equipment should be appreciated from the standpoint of economy. Manufacturers' representatives are in a position to provide valuable information for the solution of problems in equipment selection and performance. These representatives should be called in to help select proper hoods from which the chemical engineer can determine the needed configurations.

However, the chemical (or other) engineer should become acquainted with the type of material used and with the capture velocities needed for this application. This should be done before undertaking a search of equipment catalogs and trade literature, or before calling a vendor's representative or an in-house environmental specialist.

Typical Plant Problems

EXAMPLE 6.1. An enclosed hood is to be provided over a conveyor belt system as shown in Fig. 6.2. The belt speed varies from 175 to 250 fpm, the belt width is 24 in., and the total opening area is 14 in. above the belt and 4 in. below the belt's return. What volume rate of air exhaust is required so that no product is emitted?

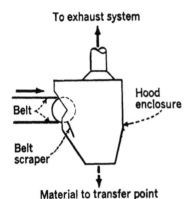

To exhaust system

Hood
enclosure

Belt

Belt
scraper

Material to transfer point

FIG. 6.2. Hood enclosure over conveyor belt dump point. (From Chemical
Engineering, August 10, 1970.)

SOLUTION: Obtain the capture velocities from Table 6.2. Since
belt speed is over 200 fpm, the capture velocity is 500 fpm.
Total opening area is

$$\frac{14}{12} \ \frac{24}{12} \ + \ \frac{4}{12} \ \frac{24}{12} \ = \ 3.00 \ \text{ft}^2$$

Use 3 ft^2 for the opening. On the basis of belt width, the exhaust volume is $(500)(24/12) = 1000$ cfm. Check as directed in
Table 6.2: $(200)(3) = 600$ cfm. Use 1000 cfm.

EXAMPLE 6.2. Determine exhaust cfm needed for the bag-filling
operation shown in Fig. 6.3. The slot is 6 in. wide, and the
filling funnel is 18 in. in diameter. The dust is nontoxic, so that
the capture velocity to use is 500 fpm.

SOLUTION:

$$\text{Slot area} = \pi \ \frac{18}{12} \ \frac{5}{12} \ = \ 2.36 \ \text{ft}^2$$

$$\text{Exhaust volume} = (2.36)(500) = 1180 \ \text{cfm}$$

If the dust is toxic, the recommended capture velocity is 1000
fpm, and the new exhaust volume rate is $(1000)(2.36) = 2360$ cfm.

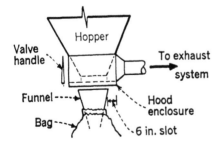

Valve
handle

Hopper

To exhaust
system

Funnel

Hood
enclosure

Bag

6 in. slot

FIG. 6.3. Hood enclosure over bag-
filling operation. (From Chemical
Engineering, August 10, 1970.)

TABLE 6.2. Estimates of Exhaust-Air Requirements

System	Design criteria
1. Drying, baking, curing ovens	100 scfm/ft^2 of booth cross-section
2. Fully hooded, stationary melting pot	200-300 scfm/ft^2 of space between top of tank and canopy
3. Pickling or cleaning tank with canopy hood	150 scfm/ft2 door opening, or 200 scfm/^{2} of hood face
4. Canopy for door opening of a continuous washer, dryer, or oven	150 scfm/ft^2 door opening, or 200 scfm/ft^2 of hood face
5. Hooded bag or drum filter from pulverizer	130-150 scfm/ft^2 of hood face opening
6. Fully hooded continuous vacuum filter	120 scfm/ft^2 open hood face
7. Slotted hood for plastic molding machines	150 scfm/ft^2 of areas between platens
8. Booth-type hood enclosure of pressure filter	100 scfm/ft^2 hood enclosure opening
9. Hood over horizontal enclosed leaf filter	100 scfm/ft^2 hood enclosure opening
10. Slotted hood over large vertical closed filter	200 scfm/ft^2 slotted opening
11. Hood for cleaning filter housing between batches	100 scfm/ft^2 hooded face opening
12. Hood for pressure-filter assembly cleaning	100 scfm/ft^2 hood face opening
13. Hood enclosure over pressure-filter assembly	100 scfm/ft^2 hood face opening
14. Hood enclosure for bag packing	125 scfm/ft^2 hood face opening
15. Hood enclosure for small-drum dumping	125 scfm/ft^2 hood face opening
16. Hood enclosure for manual feeding of material to sifter, mill, etc.	125 scfm/ft^2 hood face opening
17. Flat-deck screens	200 scfm/ft^2 opening, but not less than 50 scfm/ft^2 gross screen area

TABLE 6.2. (Continued)

System	Design criteria
18. Barrel-filling hood	100 scfm/ft^2 barrel top, minimum
19. Bag filling	450–500 scfm/ft^2 of pouring slot
20. Conveyor belt systems	Enclose as much as possible. Belt speeds under 200 fpm use 350 scfm/ft^2 of width, at least 150 fpm through openings. Belt speeds over 200 fpm use 500 scfm/ft of belt width, at least 200 fpm through openings.
21. Bin and hopper ventilation (manual loading)	150 scfm/ft^2 face area of hood
22. Retractable hood exhaust over operating door in process vessel	500 fpm through slotted opening between door opening and hood
23. Hood enclosure over centrifuges	100 fpm control velocity across openings
24. Hood over fluidized packer	125 scfm/ft^2 hood area
25. Hood over bag packing from belt packer	125 scfm/ft^2 hood area
26. Hood enclosure over drum dump of highly toxic or irritating material	125 scfm/ft^2 face area of hood
27. Hood enclosure over drum dump of solids; hood opening diameter 6 in. larger than drum	125 fpm control velocity across opening
28. Hood enclosure over empty bag flattening and tie up operation to control residual dust	100 scfm/ft^2 area of hood
29. Hood enclosure over open-top jacketed kettle; hood diameter 4 in. less than kettle diameter; aqua regia at 300°F	225 fpm control velocity across perimeter opening

TABLE 6.2.   (Continued)

System	Design criteria
30. Banbury mixer	200–300 scfm/ft^2 open face area; 500 scfm/ft of belt-width belt feeder

Source: Chemical Engineering, August 10, 1970.

EXAMPLE 6.3. A steam-jacketed precious-metal stripping
kettle is to be provided with an exhaust hood to carry off aqua
regia fumes used in the stripping process. Since condensation
drip is a problem, prevent dripping on the floor by using the type
of inboard hood shown in Fig. 6.4. Determine the exhaust volume necessary to effect capture. The top of the kettle is 4 ft in
diameter.

SOLUTION: Refer to Fig. 6.4 and use a slot capture velocity of
225 fpm as given for item 29 in Table 6.2.

$$\text{Slot area} = 4\pi \ \frac{4}{12} \ = \ 4.2 \ ft^2$$

$$\text{Volume rate} = (4.2)(225) = 945 \ cfm$$

Use 1000 cfm.

EXAMPLE 6.4. A processing building of corrugated-asbestos
siding and roofing has a gross volume of 100,000 ft^3. Under
normal conditions of ventilation with the building occupied, infiltration takes place at a rate equivalent to three outside air

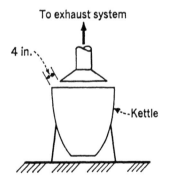

To exhaust system

4 in.

--Kettle

FIG. 6.4. Hood over processing kettle.
(From Chemical Engineering, August 10,
1970.)

changes per hour. The total contamination exhaust is 10,000 cfm. Determine the makeup air heating-steam requirements for plant steam balance charged to the exhaust. Assume that the inside is to be maintained at 60°F when the outside temperature is +10°F.

SOLUTION: The total air to be made up is that due to normal in-filtration and process. The amount due to infiltration is

$$100,000 \ \frac{3}{60} \ = \ 5000 \ \text{cfm}$$

The amount due to exhaust is 10,000 cfm. The total makeup air requirement is

$$5000 \ + \ 10,000 \ = \ 15,000 \ \text{cfm}$$

For pressure design, the makeup air should be filtered. The heat required for exhaust makeup is

$$(10,000)(1.08)(60 - 10) \ = \ 540,000 \ \text{Btuh}$$

Building and process heating are not included and require separate calculations. This amount of heat is equivalent to 540,000/1000, or 540 lb/hr of steam. The heat of condensation of steam is assumed to be 1000 Btu/lb in round figures and is sufficiently accurate for the steam balance.

In the summertime, building ventilation systems (roof fans) would also be operating. This exhaust rate would have to be included in sizing the makeup air units to keep the building pressurized and also to keep dust out. If a dust-free atmosphere is not a strict requirement, then the makeup air system needed should be sized for winter operation only. In this case, doors and windows may be left open for atmospheric makeup.

EXAMPLE 6.5. A 2 lb cylinder of chlorine gas fell off a lab table and broke, permitting the gas to escape into a closed room of 50 X 27 X 15 ft in size. (1) Calculate the concentration in ppm. The barometric pressure is 760 mmHg and the temperature is 22°C. (2) On the basis of the current TLVs, would it be dangerous to remain in this room for 3 hr? The room volume is 20,250 ft^3.

SOLUTION:

$$1. \ \text{ppm} \ = \ \frac{(\text{weight}) \ (22.4 \ \text{liters})(760/P)[273 + T°C)/(273)](10^6)}{(\text{mol. wt.}) \ (\text{g mol}) \ (\text{volume})}$$

$$= \ \frac{(2 \ \text{lb}) \ (454 \ \text{g}) \ (22.4 \ \text{liters})}{[(70.9 \ \text{g})/(\text{g mol})] \ (\text{lb}) \ (\text{g mol})}$$

$$\times \ \frac{(760/760) \ (295/273) \ (10^6)}{(20,250) \ (1 \ \text{liter}/0.035 \ \text{ft}^3)} \ = \ 536 \ \text{ppm}$$

2. The TLV for chlorine gas is 1. Therefore, it would be very dangerous to remain in the room any length of time.

EXAMPLE 6.6. In a test set-up, assuming standard temperature and pressure, a concentration of benzol (benzene) is desired at the TLV. What volume of liquid benzol must be vaporized to give this average concentration in a room of 1440 ft^3? Benzol TLV is 25 ppm.

SOLUTION:

$$ml = \frac{(ppm)\ (g)\ (volume)\ (28.3\ liters)}{(22.4)\ (g\ mol)\ (specific\ gravity)\ (ft^3)\ (10^6)}$$

$$= \frac{(25)\ (78)\ (10)\ (12)\ (10)\ (28.3)}{(22.4)\ (10^6)\ (0.879)} = 3.36\ ml$$

EXAMPLE 6.7. A surge tank, used for line storage of a liquid at room temperature in a manufacturing process, is located in an occupied building separate from the process. The tank breathes through a vent in the top, and during a 10-hr filling cycle fills at a rate of 15 gpm. Liquid vapor pressure at room temperature is 84.50 mmHg. The barometer reads 760 mmHg. What concentration of the vapor might be expected in the tank? Express the answer in percent and ppm.

SOLUTION: Saturation concentration in the tank = (84.5/760) $\times$ 100 = 11.12%.

$$[84.50/(760 - 84.50)] \times 10^6\ ppm = 125,091\ ppm$$

6.4. VAPOR DENSITY EFFECT OF EXHAUST SYSTEM DESIGN

General

The storage and handling of volatile combustible liquids presents a problem in ventilation with which engineers are confronted. The question of resulting vapor density (or specific gravity) often determines ventilation techniques, but confusion results as to when to use floor ventilation (local exhaust) instead of ceiling ventilation. What are the factors to look for in such a design problem, and which of the two systems is more effective in a particular case?

Heavier or Lighter than Air

Ventilation may be either natural or mechanical. Natural ventilation has the advantage of being in continuous operation, but is affected by the vagaries of the wind direction and intensity. It is independent of power source. Pivoted windows with roof ventilators (gravity type) is a desirable type of ventilation system. Mechanical ventilation is more positive and should be used in most cases, and particularly where plant operations are extensive.

In considering flammable gases and vapors, one important point to remember is whether they are heavier or lighter than air, and by how much. The belief that vapors of volatile combustible liquids of high molecular weight sink rapidly to the floor or another adjacent low point and accumulate there in high concentration sometimes results in the practice of exhausting air near the floor level in the belief that the vapors are thus more effectively removed. If such inlet openings are located close to the source of contamination (local exhaust), or if a quantity of air sufficiently great to dilute the vapors is drawn across the source of contamination, there is no objection to this practice. Serious error is likely to result, however, if an insufficient flow of air is provided to control the vapors by either of the two above-mentioned methods.

When large quantities of air must be withdrawn for effective dilution, it may be desirable to exhaust it at points near the floor to minimize heating difficulties during cold weather. On the other hand, if exhaust inlets located at higher levels can be made to entrain appreciable quantities of vapor by local exhaust, then the amounts of air handled are reduced, with attendant reduction of heating problems and the possible elimination of the need of a makeup air system. It may be noted that whenever the amount of air to be removed is in excess of three space airchanges per hour, then a tempered makeup air supply should be provided for best results. See Table 4.1 for air changes due to natural ventilation.

Dilution Forces

In Chapter 5 we discussed the effect of adequate mixing of vapor and air to provide specific gravity results close to air alone. Air motion is created in the vicinity of vapor-generating processes by many forces not subject to direct evaluation. Motion or energy effects fundamental to the machine or process itself causes dispersion of the gas or vapor. The fan action of rotating wheels and pulsating displacement of air by reciprocating machines or tools all play a part in preventing stratification. Forces incidental to the operation of the machine or process, such as air blast from a poorly located exhaust port on a pneumatic tool, air blast from totally enclosed fan-cooled electric motors, vibration of machinery, natural convection currents, motion of nearby machinery, and room traffic, all contribute in this respect.

Gas escaping from a pipe or tank and vapor given off by a liquid, such as gasoline, tend to diffuse in the surrounding air in about the same way that a drop of ink in a glass of water diffuses. Some gases, and also vapors, diffuse slowly, while others diffuse rapidly. It will be noted from Table 6.3

TABLE 6.3. Rates of Vapor Diffusion

Gas or vapor	Specific gravity (air = 1)	Diffusion rate (air = 1)
Acetone	2.0	0.69
Acetylene	0.9	1.05
Ethyl alcohol	1.6	0.79
Ammonia	0.59	1.3
Benzene	3.0	0.58
Butane	2.0	0.71
Carbon disulfide	2.6	0.62
Carbon dioxide	1.5	0.82
Carbon monoxide	0.97	1.02
Ether (ether)	2.60	0.62
Ethylene	0.97	1.02
Gasoline	3.5	0.53
Hydrogen	0.069	3.81
Hydrogen sulfide	1.17	0.92
Illuminating gas	0.65	1.25
Kerosene	4.5	0.47
Methane	0.55	1.35
Methyl alcohol	1.1	0.95
Methyl chloride	1.7	0.76
Propane	1.5	0.82
Sulfur dioxide	2.2	0.67
Turpentine	4.7	0.46

Source: Chemical Engineering, August 10, 1970.

that ammonia gas diffuses in air about twice as fast as carbon disulfide, and that the lighter the gas the faster it diffuses. Hydrogen, the lightest of all gases, diffuses about 3.5 times as fast as carbon monoxide.

Dispersion by Air Currents

Air motion is created near vapor-generating processes by many forces not subject to direct evaluation. The characteristics of an individual machine can be determined only by studying its operation. It is helpful, however, to consider the four common sources of motion around vapor-generating machines:

1. Motion or energy effects fundamental to the machine or process it-
    self. Examples: fan action of a rotating wheel and pulsating dis-
    placement of air by reciprocating machinery or tools.

2. Forces incidental to the operation of the machine or process.
   Examples: air blast from poorly placed exhaust port on a pneumatic tool, air blast from totally enclosed fan-cooled electric
   motors, and vibration from machinery.
3. Drag of air by large particles dynamically projected from their
   source. Example: stream of sparks thrown off by a grinding
   wheel creates an air current which carries along vapor.
4. Miscellaneous external forces. Examples: natural convection currents, motion of nearby machinery, and traffic within the workspace.

6.5. FAN PERFORMANCE CORRECTIONS

Corrections for Temperature, Moisture, and Elevation

Fan tables, exhaust volume requirements, and air flow resistance charts
assume standard atmospheric conditions. These assumptions fix the air
density at close to 0.075 lb/bt^3. Where appreciable variation occurs, the
change in air density must be considered. Factors for increased temperatures and increased elevation are listed in the literature.

Corrections for temperatures between 40 and 100°F and/or elevations
between -1000 ft and +1000 ft are seldom required with the permissible
variations in usual exhaust system design. It is helpful to keep in mind
that a centrifugal exhaust fan connected to a given system will exhaust the
same volume regardless of air density. The weight rate in pounds of air
moved, however, will be a function of the density, as will the pressure
developed and the horsepower consumed.

Variable Temperature and/or Different
Elevation—Normal Moisture

Assume an exhaust fan connected to a given system and capable of moving
10,000 cfm of air at standard conditions through that system. If the standard air entering the exhaust hoods is subsequently heated to 600°F before
entering the exhauster, the volume would be 10,000 cfm at 600°F. The volume at this temperature would contract to 5000 cfm at 70°F, reducing the
inflow of air to the hoods of 50% of the original volume.

In a similar manner, move the exhaust system handling standard air
to an elevation of 5500 ft above sea level. The fan will still handle
10,000 cfm, but the pound rate of air will be reduced to 81% of the weight
of standard air.

Where high temperatures or elevations are encountered in design work,
corrections from standard air data can be made as follows:

Increase exhaust volumes by the reciprocal of the density factor to
keep the number of pounds of air moving into the hood the same as
those for standard conditions in order to prevent dust or heat from
escaping into the room.

Size the main and branch ducts, calculate the pressure losses, and
select the exhaust fan as if corrected volumes were for standard
air. This procedure will arrive at the correct size of fan and motor
and the correct rpm.

Horsepower and pressure losses throughout the system will decrease
directly with the density factor.

High-moisture-content air must be given special treatment. When air
temperature is under 100°F, no correction for humidity is necessary.
However, when air temperature exceeds 100°F and moisture content is
greater than 0.02 lb water (140 grains) per pound of dry air, correction is
required to determine fan operating rpm and horsepower. Correction
factors must be read from the psychrometric charts in the literature.

EXAMPLE 6.8. A fan is to deliver 6000 cfm measured at a temperature of 125°F and a barometric pressure of 27.4 in. Hg
against a static pressure of 1.0 in. w.g. (inches of water). Determine the standard static pressure and brake horsepower required in order to select the proper fan.

SOLUTION: Fan tables are based on air of standard density (70°F
and 29.92 in. Hg; density 0.075 lb/ft^3). When a fan is required
to handle air at conditions other than standard, a correction must
be made in the static pressure, and the horsepower must be corrected. A fan is essentially a constant-volume machine, and at
a given speed on a given system, the volume in cfm will not change
regardless of density. The static pressure, however, changes
directly with the density. Care must be exercised to see that the
static pressure is correctly calculated for the specified conditions. All friction tables and charts on ducts, filters, coils,
etc., are based on the standard air. For actual friction at conditions other than standard, multiply the calculated friction,
using actual air volume, by the density correction factor. The
density correction factor is

$$\frac{460 + 70}{460 + 125} \times \frac{27.4}{29.92} = 0.832$$

$$\frac{1 \text{ in. specified static}}{0.832} = 1.2 \text{ in. w.g.}$$

Fan selection tables for a given fan show a standard air brake
horsepower requirement of 2.11 at 6000 cfm and 1.2 in. w.g.
static pressure. This brake horsepower must be corrected to
read

Corrected hp = 2.11 × 0.832 = 1.76

If the fan will, at times, be required to handle denser air, a
motor sufficiently large to handle the requirements at the greater
density should be selected.

7

MAKEUP AIR SYSTEMS

7.1. INTRODUCTION

All too frequently the need for makeup air to replace the air exhausted is overlooked, and natural ventilation is relied on. In some cases, natural ventilation will be able to compensate, particularly where exhaust volumes are low and plant heating capacity is adequate. However, such an approach can produce adverse effects, particularly in a new "tight" building which will not allow enough outside air to infiltrate.

In this chapter, we will discuss makeup air systems to satisfy the needs of workroom air exhausted where natural ventilation air changes are insufficient. Requirements are outlined and design criteria are discussed.

7.2. PROVISIONS FOR MAKEUP AIR

General Requirements

When the amount of air exhausted from a work room or building exceeds three times the cubical contents per hour of such a room or building,

consideration should be given to provide clean, outside air through a fan
and duct system to make up the difference between the amount exhausted
and at least three times the cubical contents exhausted for maintaining a
slight positive pressure inside the building. Means should also be provided to heat the makeup air to maintain the proper temperature within the
building spaces. During warm weather these conditions may be ignored by
leaving doors and windows open to permit makeup air to enter the building
through these openings.

When exhaust systems are in operation and when there is air conditioning or a high degree of air cleanliness is required, the amount of outside makeup air to be supplied should be at least 10% greater than the air
exhausted, and means should be provided for cleaning the makeup air so
that it is consistent with the degree of cleanliness required.

Makeup air distribution points should be carefully considered so as not
to disturb the normal patterns around hoods and other points of exhaust. In
addition, to keep disturbing drafts to a minimum, makeup air outlets should
be located close to the vicinity of the process being exhausted. The air
stream motion caused by the air discharge into the workspace should not be
in excess of 100 fpm within 8 ft of the floor line. The air stream should not
blow directly on the workers.

Depending upon the application, makeup air may or may not need to be
filtered. In many applications of dilution ventilation in oil refineries and
chemical plants in the chemical process industries (CPI), air filtration is
not a strict requirement. In a later chapter we will discuss quantitatively
a method for determining economically the amount of outside air needed for
pressurization.

7.3. DESIGNING THE MAKEUP AIR SYSTEM

Why Make Up Air?

For each cubic foot of workroom air exhausted, at least 1 ft^3 of outside
air, tempered and/or filtered, must be supplied. Without a balanced air
condition existing in a plant, the very reason for exhausting air in the first
place is neutralized. If air is exhausted to remove harmful processing
tank fumes and makeup air is not added, you cause the exhaust system to
work against a vacuum created by its own operation. Table 7.1 provides a
pictorial representation of the effects of negative pressure on the working
environment, and Table 7.2 shows a comparison of fan-type performance
as the result of negative pressure in a plant.

If air is not made up, the exhaust system will not work or perform its
original design duty, and fumes will permeate the workspace. Heating
bills will also increase. Here are some benefits of good makeup air
conditions:

Proper operation of fume ventilation equipment
No danger of spill-back of hazardous fumes or gases

TABLE 7.1. Effects of Negative Pressure on Working Environment

Air pressure in building (in. w.g.)	Effects
-0.01	Drafts on workers and interference with exhaust hoods
-0.02	Reduced or reversed natural ventilation through roof vents or monitors
-0.03	CO hazard—backdraft short, low temperature flues (water heaters, unit heaters, furnaces)
-0.04 to -0.22	Reduced ventilation from propeller fans
-0.25	Reduced ventilation from local exhaust systems; doors difficult to open or close

No positive infiltration of dirt-laden outside air
Maximum fan efficiency which saves horsepower and electricity
Product protection from cold drafts and dirty outside air
Fuel savings due to improved fuel combustion
No longer necessary to overheat inner bays to drive heat to outer bays
More production from properly heated workers and machines
Less housekeeping and maintenance because air can be filtered clean
    instead of leaking unfiltered through window and door cracks, etc.
No danger of carbon monoxide from the heating plant being sucked back
    into plant area when the plant is under a positive pressure

TABLE 7.2. Effect of Negative Pressure on Fan Performance

Negative pressure in plant (in. w.g.)	Approximate reduction in air handled (percent)			
	Propeller roof fan	Propeller fans	Centrifugal roof ventilators	Centrifugal fan
0	0	0	0	0
-0.05	-3	-2.5	-2	-1
-0.10	-5.5	-4.0	-2.6	-1.5
-0.15	-8.0	-6.0	-5.0	-2.0
-0.20	-12.0	-8.0	-7.0	-2.5
-0.25	-15.0	-12.0	-9.0	-3.0
-0.30	-18.0	-15.0	-12.0	-5.0
-0.35	-22.0	-18.0	-14.0	-7.0
-0.40	-26.0	-21.0	-17.0	-8.0

No danger of cracked walls due to excessive negative pressure
Maximum worker protection against poor operation of fume ventilation
  equipment
Protection of premium penalties for compensation insurance
Doors easier to open under positive pressure conditions
Positive odor control localized at source
Spread of nuisance odors throughout plant and offices avoided

Design Considerations for Makeup Air Systems

Here are a number of design considerations to keep in mind when designing
a makeup air system:

1. The makeup air installation should not be considered as part of the
building heating system. It should serve only to replace exhausted air and
to temper (heat) replacement air to room temperature. The system should
be designed for summer as well as winter use.

2. The makeup air system should be wired to operate from a simple
wall switch, or it should be electrically interlocked with the air exhaust
system fans.

3. Locate the system close to an outside wall so that duct runs can
be kept short.

4. Protect the outside air inlet with a 1/2 in. screen and hoods and
louvers. Filters may be located in the inlet duct when conditions warrant
their use. Install a back-draft damper in the inlet duct to open by gravity
or motor drive when a fan starts. This will prevent freezing of the outside
air heating coil and creating cold drafts that will enter the system when the
fan is not operating.

5. Size the fan to handle all makeup air cfm load plus any static
pressure developed in the air handling system (inlet duct, filters, distribution duct system, unit, etc.). System static loss is usually low and, in
most cases, can be handled by a relatively small horsepower motor and
drives run at low rpm.

6. Stainless steel tube heating coils are recommended against corrosion. This moisture of condensation that occurs inside the heat exchanger
tubes is highly corrosive. Corrosion is also promoted by the burners
cycling on and off when the entering air temperatures are less than 40°F;
thus, modulating control is necessary. Use these units in nonhazardous
plant areas only.

7. A duct furnace is recommended for makeup air systems. It has a
stainless steel heat exchanger with a modulating gas valve which regulates
and varies flame height and maintains a constant discharge makeup air
temperature.

8. At low firing rates, cold entering air chills the flue gases below
the temperature that is required for gravity venting of the flue gases.
These makeup air systems whould be provided with power-driven flue gas
exhausters.

9. The modulating valve controlling the gas flow for combustion should have its sensing element located in the discharge air stream so that an average discharge air stream is sensed. The element should be provided with a radiation shield or baffle to ward off radiation from the furnace. A room thermostat is not required.

10. To avoid interference with the building heating system, control of space temperature makeup air should be discharged into the workspace or building at or slightly below room temperature. The modulating gas valve is provided with a temperature control knob which may be adjusted for the desired discharge air temperature.

11. It is frequently possible to design supply systems to provide comfort ventilation at the occupied zone of the plant below the 8-10 ft level and thus obviate the need for heating air in unoccupied zones in high-ceilinged work spaces.

12. In some instances, untempered makeup air can be brought directly to the vicinity of an exhausted operation when there are no workers in that vicinity.

13. In hazardous plant areas requiring makeup air, the unit is provided with a nonfreeze steam coil instead of a duct furnace or other gas-fired heater.

14. The steam coil should be all stainless steel and fin construction.

15. Steam supply to the coil should be at a pressure of 15 psig steam dry and saturated with the pressure suffering a 10-lb drop through the throttling steam controller. This will provide a pressure of 5 psig inside the coil.

16. Locate the control valve sensing element in the discharge air stream. A room thermostat will not be required.

Every Building an Individual Problem

New or old, a building's makeup air problem is the same. The makeup air system design varies only with the building operation, the severity of seasonal changes in temperature, and the geographical location. Every building is an individual case and has problems peculiar to its modus operandi. Thus, an analysis of its operation must be made to justify the installation of a makeup air system for the safety, health, and comfort of the workers. Such systems must be economically sound.

Design Examples

Let's consider the problem of a building with individual spaces that require air exhaust. Because of the generation of heat, undesirable heat, or air contaminated by fumes, odors, or particulate matter, positive exhaust is required. Such an arrangement requires critical analysis for its proper solution because an exhaust system in one space may draw contaminated air from another space. Such an imbalance can cause unhealthy conditions for the worker or upset the production process.

As an example, an oil refinery workshop is provided with a wood-working facility located next to finishing areas. The wood-working shop is provided with an exhaust system to remove dust created there. The finishing area is also provided with a paint spray booth similarly exhausted. Should positive and clean makeup air not be provided for the main spray area, contaminated air could be drawn from the adjacent wood-working area and upset the system there.

Let's consider another example. A heated or air conditioned office area is located within a large warehouse. If the warehouse is provided with roof exhaust ventilation, its fans could pull conditioned air from the office spaces. This could upset the heating and air conditioning system and create other problems of air imbalance.

Areas with process furnaces are usually provided with large air exhaust systems, often at rates of 20 air changes per hour. Unless the building is solely used for the furnaces, makeup air may be drawn directly from the outdoors, unfiltered and unheated. However, if there are adjacent areas within the furnace building, the furnace room exhausters will draw replacement air from these adjacent spaces and can create a door-closing or door-opening problem. Also, too great a negative pressure can cause a reverse flow of stack gases back into the workspace.

Planning the Makeup Air System

Carefully analyze your makeup air problem needs before you start your design. Not only must the amount of air be determined but, in addition, the type of system you plan to use. Lay out your plan so that you will be able to determine the expected operation and how you can best fit the system into the building construction.

The first item to consider is the air-handling unit with its heat exchanger to temper the air. From here on the equipment and its arrangement is refined to meet the particular requirements of the operation it is to serve. The air handler continuously circulates the air, and the heat exchanger tempers the air stream. If cleaning the air is a requirement, then a filtering system must be added.

Now, for the air distribution needs of the installation, if the air handler is to be remotely located, then ductwork is required and air diffusers are to be added and properly situated to provide good air distribution so as not to interfere with the normal pattern of exhaust within the room. At this point in planning, the mechanical engineer must coordinate his design with the architect and civil engineer to provide the needed space for the air handler and the ductwork.

Heating control to temper the air can be designed to use indoor and outdoor conditions so as not to overheat. The heat exchanger should be selected on the basis of equipment cost, installation cost, operating and maintenance costs, replacement costs, availability of equipment and fuel, code requirements, and the like.

Sizing the Unit

Here are the various steps taken to select and size the equipment:

1. Determine the exhaust air requirements on need.
2. Evaluate the natural infiltration supply that can be expected by using Table 4.1 and correcting for weather stripping and caulking of doors and windows. One half of the window and door infiltration may be used if weather-stripping or caulked.
3. If natural infiltration is sufficient and is 10-15% higher than exhaust needs, then a makeup air system is not required. The decision must be made on the long term exhaust air needs.
4. If the decision is to go with a makeup air unit, the amount of make-up air should be somewhat greater than the amount exhausted to maintain a slight positive pressure in the space on the order of 0.1 in. w.g. (inches of water).
5. Base size selection on supplying makeup air into the space at 2-4°F above room temperature or temperatures of 75-80°F. If high heat loads are given off by the process, then makeup air supply temperature can be from 2 to 5°F below room temperature and supply air outlets discharging high into the heated air envelope at the ceiling.
6. Calculate the amount of heat required to do the job according to the formula

$$H = (cfm\ exhaust)(1.08)\ (temperature\ of\ supply\ air\ in\ °F$$
$$- temperature\ of\ outside\ air\ in\ °F)$$

EXAMPLE 7.1. A workroom is provided with an exhaust system for a furnace, exhausting 15,000 cfm. The average room temperature is 75°F and the outdoor temperature is -10°F design. Determine the capacity of the capacity of the makeup air unit and the heat rate for the unit in Btuh.

SOLUTION:

Fan capacity of the makeup air unit, assuming an overage of 10%, is (15,000)(1.10) = 16,500 cfm.

Maximum makeup air temperature discharge = 80°F, and outdoor temperature is -10°F.

Heat load on unit = (16,500)(1.08) [80 - (-10)] = 1,603,800 Btuh

Since the makeup air handler will be working against the unit resistance plus duct resistance plus a workspace pressure of +0.1 in. w.g., all must be taken into account when sizing for fan and fan horsepower.

Equipment Selection—Duct Furnace Units
(Nonhazardous Areas)

Direct-fired duct furnaces seem to offer several advantages over indirect-fired units. Equipment first cost is almost equivalent to indirect-fired heaters with their boilers, piping, and controls. As for installation costs, gas-fired duct furnaces usually cost less than the indirect-type units because it involves simple duct connections for the outside and discharge ends of the unit. There is only one pipe (gas) compared with two pipes for other systems. There is no pipe installation, traps, drains, vents, or fittings. If standby units are required, duct furnaces may be obtained with dual-fuel burners to operate on city gas or liquified petroleum gas (LPG). Flue gases must be vented directly to the outdoors.

Maintenance and Operating Costs

The maintenance and operating costs are quite favorable. Only occasional cleaning of heat exchanger surfaces and burners are required. Using a simple wire brush and scraper will do an acceptable job, requiring no real skill except for patience and thoroughness. During a shutdown there is no real lost time or loss of heating comfort. Air filters do require periodic cleaning to maintain design flow rate.

Operation and Control of System

Since the basic need for a makeup air system is to supply replacement air to a space, they need to operate only when needed, when exhaust systems are in use. However, in newer buildings a makeup air system may be designed in such a way that it also may be used for building heating, through the use of automatic dampers for outside air, as well as recirculation. When makeup air is needed the damper arrangement can permit entrance of a maximum or minimum of outside air. The outside-air damper can be completely closed during unoccupied periods.

If the system is installed for supplying outside makeup air only, it can be controlled to operate only when the exhaust system is operating. If the system is designed with filters, it should operate also during the summertime as well as in winter to provide filtered air all year round. The cost to operate makeup air systems during the summer comes from fan horsepower operation. In winter the cost of fuel is added.

Without a makeup air system, depending solely on uncontrolled infiltration air, adds to the plant heating bill with attendant drafts and uncomfortable conditions during the heating season. The benefits obtained through the installation of a makeup air system are well worth the investment.

Typical Control Arrangement—
Direct-Fired Makeup Unit

A typical control arrangement for a direct-fired makeup air duct furnace
consists of the following items:

   On-off Switch   This can be either a manual (push-button or wall-type)
or automatic wired switch in parallel with the controls to the exhausting
fan devices.

   Blower   The blower operates continuously to maintain conditions
within the workspace. Air for replacement is drawn from a nonhazardous
and clean area outside the building. It may be required to locate the air
intake point above the top of the roof of the building, at least 10 ft above
grade and at least 15 ft from any discharge stacks.

   Automatic Interlock Valve   This provides a positive electrical interlock between the blower and heat exchanger and is actuated by the on-off
switch. For the exchanger to be fired, the blower must always be in
operation.

   Modulating Valve   This controls the gas-firing rate of the main burner
through the temperature sensing element remotely located in the discharge
air stream. It modulates the gas feed rate up or down to maintain a constant air discharge temperature. It works as follows: as the outside air
temperature increases, the valve modulates to a minimum gas input rate
of about 20% of full open, then snaps shut if the outside air temperature
continues to rise. Under certain loading conditions and when two makeup
air units are placed in series, the sensing element of the discharge unit

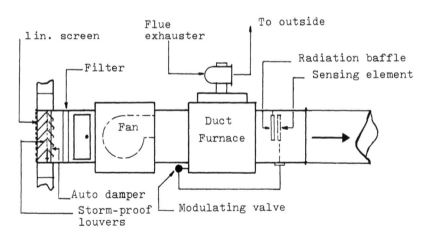

FIG. 7.1. Elements of a basic makeup air system-duct furnace unit.

should be set at the desired discharge air temperature, and the second sensing element for the upstream unit should be set 3 or 4°F lower so that the second heater will operate only when its additional capacity is required.

Limit Control Switch   This is wired in series with the automatic valve. Should the air flow through the unit be restricted or interrupted, the limit control will break the circuit to the automatic valve and will then shut off gas flow to the burners until adequate air flow is reestablished. Unless this limit control is provided, the continued burning of gas at the exchanger will overheat and burn out the exchanger.

Safety Pilot Switch   This is also wired in series with the automatic valve and, in the event of pilot failure, the automatic valve circuit will be broken and gas flow to the main burners will be interrupted until the pilot circuit is reestablished.

Regulator   The regulator controls gas pressure at line conditions to within operating pressures of about 3.5 in. w.g.

Safety Controls   These should meet the requirements of Factory Mutual Engineering standards.

Figure 7.1 shows a typical makeup air system. The air distribution system is not shown, but it is a very important part of the total system, as heretofore mentioned. Note that duct furnaces are provided with a mechanical exhauster for positive removal of products of combustion.

The use of these heaters is limited in the CPI because of the hazards involved. The closed stream or hot water coil units are most commonly used. Such units are similar to the unit shown in Fig. 7.1, except that the duct furnace is replaced with an extended surface coil unit controlled by a sensing element controlling a modulating steam or hot water valve. No room thermostat is required. See Hama, G. N. (1962).

8

DUST CONTROL IN THE WORKPLACE

8.1. INTRODUCTION

The potential hazard of inplant dust can be reduced by unit and central collector systems. When considering any system of dust collection, the plant engineer should be able to distinguish between the roles of both kinds of systems and should take pains to closely investigate and evaluate the quality and performance of the equipment involved. In this chapter we will consider points in selecting the optimum dust control system that will maximize the overall result.

8.2. OSHA REQUIREMENTS

The generation of dust in the workplace creates a potential health hazard. The Occupational Safety and Health Act (OSHA) requires that in-plant dust be controlled. OSHA states:

> Wherever dry grinding, dry polishing, or buffing is performed,
> and the employee exposure, without regard to the use of
> respirators, exceeds permissible exposure limits prescribed [by

OSHA], a local exhaust ventilation should be provided and used to maintain employee exposure within the prescribed limits

OSHA says that more than hoods and ventilation systems are required. OSHA's regulations further state that "all exhaust systems shall be provided with suitable dust collectors." If the local exhaust system discharges to the outdoors, it must meet Environmental Protection Agency (EPA) standards as well. If a company wants to recirculate, a dust collection system is required.

In the chemical process industries (CPI) and in oil refineries, practice dust generation is minimal. However, in chemical and fertilizer plant operations, the presence of dust can become a problem, and dust collection systems are important as part of plant operations. See Marchello, J. M., and Kelly, J. J. (1975).

8.3. BASIC TYPES OF DUST COLLECTION SYSTEMS

Two Basic Types

There are two basic types of dust control systems: (1) systems that vent the dust-laden workroom air to a central dust collector, and (2) systems that vent to small unit collectors close to the dust-generating equipment. These are known as the central system concept and the unit collector concept. Each of the systems plays a definite role within the plant, and it behooves the plant engineer to investigate and understand the quality and performance of the entailed equipment. There can be any number of arrangements that can befit the need, and manufacturers need to be explored for their specifics of equipment and arrangements.

Some plants use central systems with long runs of ductwork that have been a standard for many years. Central systems offer certain advantages:

They utilize less floor space than unit systems.
They can be located at long distances from the control point or even outside the plant itself. If floor space is at a premium, as it often is, a central system is desirable.
Dust can pile up in one location, thus making it less costly to install an automated dust-disposal system.

However, central systems have their disadvantages:

At better than $25 per running foot, the long runs of ductwork are expensive
Air horsepower requirements mount up.
Special duct design is required for elbows and inlets where abrasion is present at changes in air flow direction.
The system as a whole must operate even if only a few pickup points are needed and in operation.
Should the system malfunction, the entire process system is out of operation.

Dusts with various combustible and toxic properties can accumulate in one system and can present the danger of explosion.

Since changes in ductwork cannot be made without affecting performance, they must remain fixed.

In the unit collector concept, dust feeds from a number of dust generating points into an adjacent unit collector; this is a more flexible system. Should one of them malfunction, a replacement is usually readily available for installation. Long lengths of ductwork are not required with attendant large horsepower requirements. Then, too, maintenance is minimal because each unit is small, and a problem in one does not affect the other.

Exhaust Volumes

Both systems need to maintain specific exhaust volumes to protect the worker. Each unit is designed specifically for the service required by the equipment being served. See the American Conference of Government Industrial Hygienists (ACGIH) publication Industrial Ventilation, a Manual of Recommended Practice, latest edition. OSHA has adopted these guidelines as regulations. A copy of this manual should be at the desk of every engineer whose responsibility it is to design and operate environmental control systems. See Licht, W. (1980).

System Costing

Total costs of both systems should be determined, especially for ductwork, installation costs of the ductwork, air horsepower required, and system maintenance must all be taken into account. The cost of a set of unit collectors is usually greater than the cost of a single collector and its central system. However, with unit collectors, less, and in most cases lighter thickness, ductwork can be used than in the central system. As we can well appreciate, a unit collector installation is often less expensive overall.

Cost of ductwork installed can vary widely, but Table 8.1 provides some costs. These are based on U.S. standard gauge 22, from 8 to 18 in., and on 18 gauge for larger diameters. Where dusts are highly abrasive, heavier gauges may be required.

Designing for Explosion Protection

All ignition sources should be eliminated from equipment containing flammable dusts and from the areas surrounding such equipment. Open flames or smoking, the use of electric welding equipment, and gas cutting must be carefully avoided in dusty areas. All machinery capable of producing sparks from static electricity should be grounded, and even fan belts should be avoided by using direct-connected fan drives or installing static conducting belts. Dust-proof wiring and switches should be used in accordance with the National Electrical Code (NEC) rules and regulations. Electromagnetic separators to prevent the entrance of ferrous metals to dust-grinding mills and the use of nonferrous fan blades to guard against sparking in systems which handle dusty air should be enforced.

Buildings should be designed in such a way as to avoid the collection of dust on roof beams and ledges and other overhead surfaces. Good house-keeping practices should be administered and adhered to, and vacuum cleaning used predominantly to clear these surfaces. Detached building units should be used to store flammable dusts, and substantial fire walls should be built within building areas to separate hazardous dusty areas. Equipment should be of dust-free-type construction.

Vents, in the form of hinged windows, panels, or light wall construction in work rooms, and the use of adequate release diaphrams and vents in equipment when properly designed, proportioned, and distributed, will release explosion pressures with no resultant structural damage. Recommended venting areas range from 1 ft^2 per 15 ft^3 of room volume to 1 ft^2 per 80 ft^3 or more, depending on operating factors. Proper areas for venting depend on several factors, such as structural strength or equipment strength, pressures, and the rates of pressure rise developed in dust explosions. See Hartman, I. (1947).

Dust collectors should be located outdoors or in detached work areas that are provided with adequate explosion vents. Grinding and conveying equipment may be protected by purging with an inert gas such as nitrogen that will reduce the normal oxygen content below the explosive limit. The inert gas may be obtained from inert gas generators, nitrogen bottle systems, or carbon dioxide storage systems. Refer to Table 3.2 for a listing of dust explosion pressures. Maximum allowable oxygen percentages in dusty environments may be obtained from the National Fire Protection Association (NFPA) publications.

TABLE 8.1   Cost of Installed Ductwork (Average)

Duct diameter (in.)	100 ft straight run ($)	90° elbow ($)	30° entry ($)
6	730	25	66
8	775	40	86
10	935	75	102
12	1060	85	121
14	1310	120	142
16	1510	225	165
18	1650	255	178
20	1790	275	196
24	1940	300	217

Exhaust from
   other units

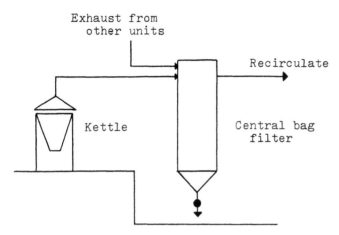

FIG. 8.1. Recirculation of filtered air after bag filter.

EXAMPLE 8.1 An open-top batch processing tank used for mixing
a powder and ethyl alcohol is to be provided with a local exhaust
system. A decision must be made whether to provide a separate
system and bag filter or to discharge the alcohol-laden dusty air
to a central bag filter and, after dust removal, to recirculate the
cleaned air to the work room as a conservation measure. The
air discharge from the separate system would be expelled to the
atmosphere.

Requirement Calculate the exhaust-air flow to adequately ventilate the tank and the alcohol vapor concentration in the effluent
air stream as required by law. Design the hood arrangement,
taking into account an acceptable capture velocity at the hood
entrance. What are the chances of alcohol vapors condensing in
the air stream and plugging the air filter fabric? See Figs. 8.1
and 8.2 for schemes to be considered.

   Tank: Open top, 18 in. diameter
   Work room-process room dimensions: 20 X 30 X 15 ft high
   Room natural ventilation rate: 1-1/2 air changes per hour
   Rate of alcohol vaporation: 0.110 lb/hr/ft^2 tank top surface
   Range of explosibility alcohol: lower limit (LEL) = 3.3% by
      volume in air; upper limit (UEL) = 19% by volume in air
   Threshold limit value (TLV) allowed in processing areas for
      an 8-hr exposure = 1000 ppm
   Vapor-dust capture velocity = 200 fpm
   Room temperature = 60°F
   Molecular weight of air = 29
   Molecular weight of alcohol = 46

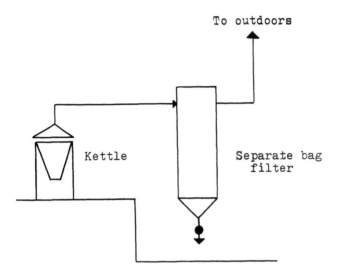

FIG. 8.2. Discharge to atmosphere after filter.

Specific weight of air = 0.075 lb/ft^3
Volume of 1 lb-mol of air at standard conditions = 379 ft^3
Atmospheric pressure = 14.7 psia

SOLUTION: Determine the alcohol vapors generated and to be captured.

$$\frac{0.110}{60} \ x \ \frac{379}{46} \ (0.7854) \ x \ \frac{18^2}{12} = 0.027 \ cfm \ vapors$$

Determine the exhaust air flow.

$$Tank \ perimeter = \pi \ X \frac{18}{12} \ = \ 4.7 \ ft$$

$$Perimeter \ slot \ for \ air \ flow = 4.7 \ X \ \frac{6}{12} \ = \ 2.35 \ ft^2$$

(2.35)(200) capture velocity = 470 cfm exhaust air needed

Determine the alcohol vapor concentration in exhaust air.

$$\frac{0.027}{470} \ X \ (100) \ = \ 0.0057\% \ by \ volume, \ or \ 57 \ ppm$$

This is below the allowable TLV of 1000 ppm, which is not a problem. This is also the concentration inside the exhaust duct.

Determine the concentration of alcohol vapor inside the work room. Air circulates inside the room due to natural causes at

1-1/2 air changes per hr = $(20)(30)(15) \times \dfrac{1.5}{60} = 225$ cfm

The concentration of vapors inside the work room is

$\dfrac{0.027}{470 + 225} \times (100) = 0.0039\%$ by volume or, therefore, conditions are safe. Compare these conditions with those at LEL.

$\dfrac{3.3}{100} \times (1)(10)^6 = 3.3 (10)^4 = 33{,}000$ ppm at LEL

39 ppm versus 33,000 ppm

Determine the dew point of the vapor mixture inside the duct and collector. Using the humidity ratio where the partial pressure of alcohol is represented by pp. al.

$\dfrac{\text{pp. al}}{14.7 - \text{pp. al.}} \times \dfrac{46}{29} =$ lb vapor/min/lb air/min

lb vapor $= 0.027 \times \dfrac{46}{379} = 0.003277$ lb/min

lb air $= (470)(0.075) = 35.25$ lb/min

$\dfrac{\text{pp. al.}}{14.7 - \text{pp. al.}} \times \dfrac{46}{29} = \dfrac{0.003277}{35.25} = 0.0000930$

$\dfrac{\text{pp. al.}}{14.7 - 11.\text{ al.}} = \dfrac{0.0000930}{1.59} = 0.000058$

pp. al. $= (0.000058)(14.7 - \text{pp. al.})$

From which

pp. al. $= \dfrac{0.00085}{1.000058} = 0.00084$ psia

Expressed in mm

$\dfrac{0.00084}{14.7} (760) = 0.0434$ mmHg

This corresponds to a dew point of about 60°C or 76°F. The chances of ethyl alcohol vapors condensing inside the duct and inside the collector are nil. The dewpoint of -76°F is well below room temperature, and odor is not objectionable. Finally, choose scheme A, which is safe, conserving of energy and heat, and less costly, since only one bag collector will be necessary. See Fig. 8.3 for the hood design.

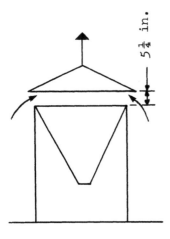

$5\frac{1}{4}$ in.

FIG. 8.3. Dust mixing kettle-batch
operation.

Avoiding Combustible Dust Mixtures

Unit collector grouping practice provides for handling dusts that can be
safely mixed. In this way, combustible dust mixtures can be avoided and
the danger of explosions can be eliminated. Reusable and spark-generating
dusts can be isolated in this way. In any event, care should be exercised
to protect the unit collector's fabric elements from sparks that might develop. A simple spark trap will do the job.

As we have indicated before, OSHA permits cleaned air to be recirculated to the workplace so long as the TLV for dusts is not reached in workroom breathing zones.

A central collector system simplifies recirculation, but additional fan
horsepower is required for moving the air through extensive ductwork, as
compared with the unit system. Then if the central collector is located
outdoors, recirculating air can be higher or lower than room temperature.
Under these conditions, additional heating or cooling of the recirculated air
would be necessary, with the attendant increase in capital and operating
costs. The advantage of the unit collector, in this case, is that air can be
recirculated directly into the workroom with no further heating or cooling.

In the last analysis, the final selection of a dust collection system is
affected by plant layout changes that can take place over a period of time.
Where such flexibility is required, unit collectors may be the best answer
because they are often small enough to be moved easily and need not be
bolted down.

Methods of Cleaning Air

We will not attempt to provide design details but will discuss general principles and design features to be used only as a guide for the selection of

suitable air-cleaning equipment. In most cases, such equipment is purchased and not built by plant personnel because all types of equipment are
now commercially available. Manufacturers' representatives can furnish
valuable assistance and guidance and, most importantly, provide guaranteed
performance standards to meet requirements of the law. See Friedlander,
S. K., et al. (1952).

The job of removing contaminants from an air or gas stream can be
simple and straightforward or complicated and difficult, depending on the
number, nature, and concentration of the contaminants that are to be removed. Air cleaning mechanisms are preferential to certain kinds of contaminants. Some are effective and some are ineffective. The selection of
air cleaning devices to remove a given contaminant or combinations of contaminants must be based on a thorough evaluation of the air stream components to be removed and equipment efficiency to do the job.

Air cleaning devices are usually required for one or more of the following reasons:

1. To meet the requirements of air pollution control ordinances
2. To reclaim or classify product material
3. To prevent a nuisance or property damage
4. To be used in recirculating air systems for the workplace

Dust Collector Data Sheet

Table 8.2 is a data sheet for a dust collector provided with cloth bags.
Such a collector is one of the most efficient and widely used for removing
dry particulate matter from an air stream. It is also known as a bag filter.
Any fibrous, woven, or felted material can be used as the filter medium.
Usually, tubes made up of the cloth are used, with the dust-laden air stream
impinging on one side of the cloth and leaving the other side as clean air.
In most commercial designs, the fabric bags are mounted on a suitable
framework within a steel housing. Air enters from below after passing
through a settling plenum which separates the larger particles first. These
collect in the base of the unit, which is cone-shaped, and are removed from
the unit from time to time. To dislodge adhering material from the upstream side of the bag, a manual or motorized shaking mechanism is used
to periodically shake the fabric. The dust so removed falls into the same
hopper bottom of the unit and is removed at intervals. At the start of the
filtration process, filtering efficiency is poor until such time as a buildup
of particles provides the real filtering process.

The material most commonly used as filter medium is cotton or wool
sateen or felt. The operating temperature is usually the determining factor
in medium selection. Cotton may be used with temperatures up to 180°F.
Wool is acceptable for temperatures of 200°F, and synthetics such as acryl-
ics are available for temperatures up to 350°F and higher. Glass fiber and
asbestos fabrics have been used for applications up to 650° F, but the fragile
natures of the fabrics cause their failure after a few shakings.

TABLE 8.2. Dust Collector Data Sheet

Service Conditions
Type of Collector_____
Gas Characteristics:
    Material_____
    Capacity_____
    Pressure_____ Temperature_____
    Density_____ Relative Humidity_____
    Dust Loading_____
Dust Characteristics:
    Material_____
    True Density_____ Bag Density_____
    Size Range_____
Design Data:
    Cloth Material_____
    Air-to-Cloth Ratio_____ Total Surface_____
    Size and Shape of Elements_____

    _____
    Draft Loss_____
    Collector Housing_____

    _____
    Inlet Size_____ Outlet Size_____
    Cleaning Cycle_____
    Mechanical Shakers_____
    Blowback System_____
    Blowers (Refer to Blower Data Sheets)_____

    _____
    Discharge Lock or Conveyor_____
    Support Steel_____
    Ductwork_____
    Type, Size and Speed of Drivers_____

    _____
    Type of Drive_____ Drive Base_____
    Total Weight of Complete Unit_____
    Remarks:_____

    _____
    _____

Other details of equipment selection such as filter size, resistance to
air flow, and flow velocity should be considered. Good design will call for
a 3:1 ratio, i.e., a filtering velocity of 3 linear fpm (cfm to cloth area
ratio of 3:1).

The shaking mechanism and cycle is an important design feature. It is
very important not to permit the buildup of particulates to get beyond a certain point that will slow down air flow below a critical minimum, especially
if specific exhaust volume rates are to be maintained. This shaking can
take place at predetermined intervals, such as during plant shutdowns, at
lunch time, or at the day's end. Interlocks between fan and shaker mechanism will provide the required cycle so that when the fan is shut down the
shaker mechanism is actuated. When abnormal dust loading is encountered
and continuous filtration is required, multicompartment collectors may be
used that are provided with separate shaking mechanisms. When one com-
partment is down, only two-thirds of the total filtering area is available,
but this presents no problem.

EXAMPLE 8.2. A fabric dust collector handles 400 cfm with a
dust loading of 10 gr/ft^3. Its initial resistance is 1 in. w.g. At
the end of 6 hr it reaches the maximum permissible resistance of
5 in. w.g. How soon would 5 in. w.g. be reached for

1. A dust loading of 20 gr/ft^3 and a flow rate of 400 cfm?
2. A dust loading of 10 gr/ft^3 and a flow rate of 800 cfm?

SOLUTION:

1. Resistance builds up at the rate of 4 in. over 6 hr or
    2/3 in./hr. Since flow through the bags is in a stream-
    line condition, resistance is proportional to flow rate. If
    there is twice as much dust, the given resistance will be
    attained in one-half the time. Thus,

    $$6 \text{ hr} \times 1/2 = 3 \text{ hr}$$

2. Initial resistance is doubled to 2 in., leaving 3 in. for
    buildup. Twice the dust is caught per minute, doubling
    the buildup rate. Twice the flow doubles the buildup rate.

    $$\frac{3 \text{ in. w.g.}}{2/3 \text{ in. w.g./hr (2)(2)}} = 9/8 = 1.13 \text{ hr}$$

Choosing a Dust Collector

In three out of every ten dust collector cleaning systems, experience has
shown that the collector itself has been overautomated where; and it appears that perhaps only half of them really needed automated features at all.
Adding the automated feature to clean continuously can easily increase the

initial cost of the collector by 25-50%. Plants that do not require auto-matic cleaning and yet install them are paying a penalty in excessive initial costs, maintenance, and downtime.

There is a clear-cut difference between automatic, continuously cleaned collectors and intermittently cleaned collectors. Take the continu-ous unit first. Accumulated dust is automatically cleared from the col-lector's filter tubes while the unit is in operation. In the intermittent col-lector, the dust-control system is shut down at scheduled intervals—about every 4-8 hr—while the dust-laden tubes are mechanically shaken and cleared of dust.

There are two basic designs of automatic, continuously cleaned filter-tube collectors commonly used in industry: the shaker type and the com-pressed-air-cleaned type. The shaker-type units are continuously cleaned by use of multiple-compartment housings. While the tubes in one com-partment are shut down and mechanically shaken to free the accumulated dust, the other compartments are kept in operation. This cycle is repeated at predetermined intervals in each compartment, so we see that the dust control system is never really shut down.

The compressed-air-cleaned collector uses a pulsed jet of compressed air that travels across a group of tubes and dislodges trapped dust. This action is repeated as the jet of air moves over the next section of tubes. Since the operation of cleaning is a continuous one, eventually all tubes are cleaned. The tube-cleaning sequence is repeated without the need for a shutdown.

Criteria for Selection

Before deciding on which type of dust collector to install, some key ques-tions must be answered as to the actual needs of the plant or the manufac-turing process.

1. Is there a real need for continuous operation?
2. Are shutdowns intolerable?
3. Are there enough normal interruptions in the process such as coffee breaks, shift changes, process changes, etc., to allow time for the intermittent cleaning of the collector?
4. Can dust control be dispensed with to safely permit shutdown for several minutes for collector cleaning?

Other Considerations

A thorough familiarity with your plant's processing system is a definite re-quirement for the person who will be responsible for the selection of a dust control system. The nature of the dust generated in the process can dictate the type of collector required. Stringy and fibrous particles can cause a cleaning problem in air-cleaned units because of the reluctance of such particles to break away from the filter bag.

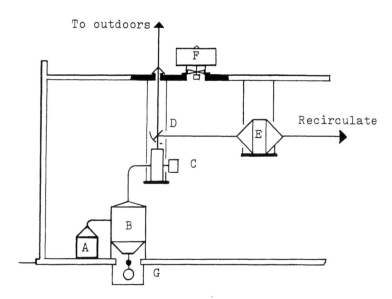

FIG. 8.4. Local capture, clean, and recirculate system. System returns filtered air to the work space or can exhaust air directly to the outdoors by opening the bypass damper. A, dust source; B, dust collector; C, exhaust fan; D, bypass damper; E, high-efficiency filter; F, roof exhaust fan; G, pneumatic conveying system for dust.

Collectors of the continuous cleaning type may require special housing partitions, valved inlets and outlets, extra wiring, and a compressed air system. All such items will boost equipment and maintenance costs.

The person responsible must also be aware (or be made aware) of any future plant expansion plans. Surely, these considerations will influence the choice of a dust collector. Although power requirements differ only slightly for the continuous-type versus the intermittent-type collector, any additional power needs can affect facilities planning. This is especially true in areas that can experience power shortages.

Then there is always the possibility that an intermittent collector will need to be upgraded to a continuous type sometime in the future. It behooves the person to select equipment that can be easily modified to suit conditions if they change. See Cowie, D. (1976).

Local Capture, Clean, and Recirculate Vent Systems

Local capture, clean, and recirculate vent systems are similar to local exhaust systems, but they pass air through a dust collector for contaminant removal (Fig. 8.4). Clean air is then recirculated through the plant instead of being exhausted. Dust collectors are less than 100% efficient, and thus introduce a secondary source of contamination into the plant outside air. Because local capture and recirculate systems do not retain all the dust generated, they must be augmented with dilution or general ventilation systems.

9

DESIGNING FOR PRESSURE VENTILATION

9.1. INTRODUCTION

The preferred method of explosion-proofing buildings in hazardous process areas is to pressurize them with safe air. This has proven to be
economical, as well as safe. This chapter includes data and sample calculations and a design procedure for pressurizing control rooms. The same
technique may be used to pressurize other buildings located in hazardous
areas and to protect electrical equipment and large motors against corrosion, explosion, and moisture.

9.2. CLASSIFICATION OF AREAS

A Potent Combination

Today, the chemical process industries (CPI) are dealing with more flammable and potentially explosive products than ever before; and the continued
growth of chemical and petrochemical processing indicates that the future
will see more of such products. At the same time, rapid advances in electrical and electronic technology have sharply increased the amount and
variety of this equipment used by the CPI. Thus we have a potent condition;
more and more plant areas with potentially explosive atmospheres, and
more and more electrical equipment, control instruments, lighting fixtures,
and so on, that must operate safely within those areas.

Where the atmosphere is hazardous, the installation of explosion-proof
electrical equipment and switch gear is mandatory. Rather than using such
equipment, it becomes more economical, and is considered good practice,
to exclude the hazardous atmosphere by housing general-purpose (nonexplo-
sion-proof) electrical equipment within pressurized buildings. If the enclosing building is adequately protected against the infiltration of outside
explosive vapors or gases by pressurization with uncontaminated ventilation air, general purpose equipment is permitted by the codes.

The classification of areas is covered in detail in the National Electrical
Code (NEC) and American Petroleum Institute (API) Standard RP 500, bearing the title "API Recommended Practice for Classification of Areas for
Electrical Installations in Petroleum Refineries." As outlined in its foreword, the API standard refers to petroleum refineries only, and does not
provide a basis for classifying other areas where petroleum or its products
are handled. However, it is used widely as a guide in the CPI for hazardous liquids and vapors. See McPartland, J. (1979).

The NEC is considered the definitive classification tool; however, it
does not cover all equipment and situations. Insurance companies and their

inspectors generally insist that hazardous areas contain only electrical equipment listed and approved by Underwriter's Laboratories (UL) under this code. Most states, municipalities, and public service companies also use the NEC as a standard for their inspectors. For a more detailed coverage of hazardous areas, refer to Chapter 3.

Designing for Pressure

To be adequately protected, a pressurized building must take its ventilating air from a point either high enough or far enough away to be considered nonhazardous. If the building is away from other structures, air intake can be through a stack extending 25 ft above grade, in accordance with the rules established by RP 500.

When the building to be pressurized is located in an area considered entirely hazardous, the air intake must be located far enough away to preclude contamination. This is done by using a fan to take in air at a safe location and ducting the air under pressure to the building. Air intakes must be free of adjacent structures or roof ridges, and this may require stack heights in excess of 25 ft.

It is accepted practice to pressurize to 0.1 in. of water, which is equivalent to an outdoor wind velocity of 20 mph. This velocity is assumed necessary for that disturbance which will prevent gases from accumulating in concentrations above their lower explosive limits (LEL). On the other hand, pressures in excess of 0.1 in. water tend to cause problems with the opening and closing of doors.

Air locks are not needed at the doors of pressurized buildings, nor should fixed window sashes be installed; it is important only to keep the doors and windows closed. A pressure switch and a factory-set time delay of 15 sec should be provided to actuate an alarm at each door (Fig. 9.1).

Ventilating Fans

Ventilating fans should be backward-curved (nonoverloading characteristic) to give the proper head-capacity relationship. The building should be equipped with adjustable check dampers (Fig. 9.2). Since the ventilating system is called on to purge the building initially, the fan motor should be explosion-proof and directly connected to the fan shaft. If a directly connected fan is not practical, a static-resisting belt drive should be used. Fan wheels should be made of aluminum or nonferrous metal to prevent sparks during operation.

How Much Air?

The quantity of air to be pumped into a pressurized building is a function not only of explosion hazards but also of the need for healthful ventilation and heat dissipation. If the requirements for occupancy by people (about

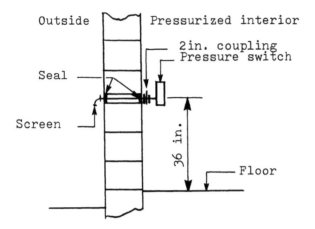

FIG. 9.1 Pressure alarm to guard against open doors. (From Chemical Engineering, September 20, 1971.)

15 cfm/person, minimum) or for heat dissipation are greater than the requirements for maintaining 0.1 in. water pressure, the excess air is relieved to the outdoors through a check-damper that has been sized for a net escape velocity of 500 fpm. Figure 9.2 shows a typical check-damper, equipped with an adjustable counter weight that may be slid forward or backward for sensitivity and backpressure.

The pressure within a building depends on the pressure drop through the different points of leakage, which have been classified (Table 9.1) for the convenience and ease of presenting a design approach. The data (Table 9.1) should not be considered complete, however, and further information may be found in the American Society of Heating, Refrigerating and Air-Conditioning Engineers (ASHRAE) guide and other such sources.

Since the ventilating requirements depend on the number of occupants, it is only necessary to seal enough of the leaks to provide the required pressure at the required air circulation rate. If the leakage is not enough for this, then check-dampers must be added to relieve and control backpressure.

From the point of view of economics, leak points should be sealed in the following order:

Door cracks
Window cracks
Wall openings
Flat-surface joints
Intersecting-surface cracks

EXAMPLE 9.1. Calculate the air required to pressure-ventilate the combined control room and laboratory shown in Fig. 9.3. The

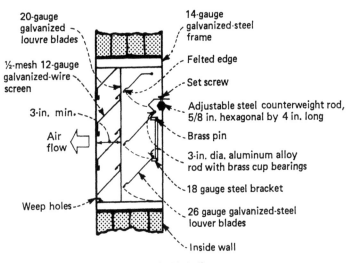

20-gauge
galvanized
louvre blades

14-gauge
galvanized-steel
frame

½-mesh 12-gauge
galvanized-wire
screen

Felted edge

Set screw

3-in. min.

Adjustable steel counterweight rod,
5/8 in. hexagonal by 4 in. long

Air
flow

Brass pin

3-in. dia. aluminum alloy
rod with brass cup bearings

18 gauge steel bracket

Weep holes

26 gauge galvanized-steel
louver blades

Inside wall

To position, loosen set screw and slide in line
with air flow so as to adjust length of mo-
ment arm and thus sensitivity; then tighten
set screw.

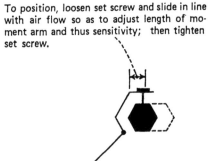

FIG. 9.2. Check dampers that permit ventilating air to escape against
adjustable inside pressure. (From Chemical Engineering, September 20,
1971.)

effective wall height may be taken as 10 ft. Windows are metal
trim, industrial-pivoted, with a crack length of 12 ft for each of
the 5 × 4 ft windows, and 10 ft for each of the 4 × 3 ft windows.
Doors are 7 × 3 ft and are weather-stripped. Wall construction
is concrete block with two coats of cement paint inside and out.
The roof is 2-in. concrete with roof membrane. There are two
check-dampers relieving air to the outdoors. The combined exhaust for the toilet and laboratory is 1500 cfm. How much air is
required to maintain the building at 0.1 in. water pressure?

SOLUTION: Since the building is of masonry, surface and inter-
secting-joint leakage are not included. The total outflow is then

TABLE 9.1. Leakage Rates for Unsealed Constructions

	Leakage rate $ft^3/min/ft^2$
Continuous surfaces	
13-in. plain brick	0.11
Brick, furring, lath and plaster	0.0064
Brick, 1 coat white lead and oil	0.11
Brick, 3 coats white lead and oil	0.082
Brick, 1 coat cold-water paint	0.05
Brick, plain	0.20
Brick, 8-1/2 in. plastered	0.0018
Concrete block, 2 coats cement paint inside and outside	0.067
Concrete, 2 in. slab, unfinished	0.002
Concrete, 4 in. slab, unfinished	Negligible
Concrete, 2 in. slab, finished with 2 coats rubber-base paint	Negligible

Flat-surface joints

Crack width, in.	0.020	0.040	0.083	0.111
$ft^3/min/ft$ of crack	0.5	2.0	6.1	9.5

Window cracks
Steel sach $2860 \ ft^3/min/1000$ ft of crack

Door cracks
Poorly fitting single-swing $3640 \ ft^3/min$ per 1000 ft of crack
wood door with no weather
stripping

Weather-stripped door
Single $100 \ ft^3/min$ per 1000 ft of crack
Double $150 \ ft^3/min$ per 1000 ft of crack

Wall openings
3/4-in. o.d. pipe in 1-1/4-in. $11.4 \ ft^3/min$
    diam. hole
1-1/2-in. o.d. pipe in 2-in. $19.0 \ ft^3/min$
    diam. hole
2-1/2-in. o.d. pipe in 3-in. $31.5 \ ft^3/min$
    diam. hole

Note: Air-leakage flowrates were obtained from ASHRAE infiltration rates applied in reverse fashion. Wind velocities of 15-20 mi./hr were assumed. Infiltration rates for flat-surface joints, intersecting-surface joints and wall openings were obtained from experience.
Source: Chemical Engineering, September 20, 1971.

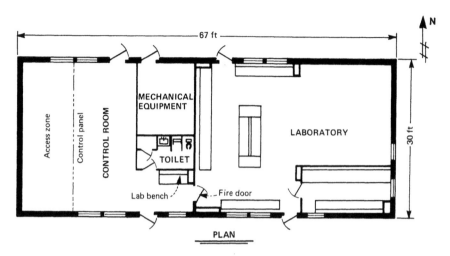

FIG. 9.3. Combined control room and laboratory to be pressurized.
(From Chemical Engineering, September 20, 1971.)

$$
\begin{aligned}
\text{Windows} &= 366 \text{ cfm} \\
\text{Doors} &= 10 \text{ cfm} \\
\text{Walls} &= 110 \text{ cfm} \\
\text{Roof} &= 4 \text{ cfm} \\
\text{Check dampers} &= 1000 \text{ cfm} \\
\text{Total} &= 1490 \text{ cfm}
\end{aligned}
$$

As a check, this figure is compared with an average leakage of
0.7 cfm/ft^2 floor area* which experience has shown to be greater
than the minimum allowance of 0.5. The floor area is 2010 ft^2;
and 2010 $(0.7) = 1407$, slightly less than that calculated. Also, if
the maximum occupancy is 20 people, the requirements for
ventilation are 20 $(15) = 300$ cfm, which is well within the leakage
rate. Accordingly, the total air requirements are

$$1490 + 1500 = 2990 \text{ cfm}$$

In summary, not only is pressure ventilation the most economical
way of explosion-proofing onsite buildings, it is also easy to design
such systems if one follows the established guidelines of good
practice.

---

*According to New Jersey Building Code NJAC 12-115, May 1, 1971,
p. 158, the minimum allowable is 0.5 cfm/ft^2 floor area; however, this
is not recommended for design.

Air Intake Locations

As we have previously discussed, but is worthwhile repeating, when all or
a part of a building is located in a hazardous area as indicated on the plot
plan, building pressurization and ventilation with uncontaminated air is a
must. Air for pressurization must be taken from nonhazardous areas
using the criteria shown in Figs. 3.1 and 3.2.

Generally, wall intake louvers may be used if located at least 50 ft
away from any source of vapor. Often, however, an air intake stack with
an intake hood 25 ft above grade becomes necessary. As seen in Figs. 3.1
and 3.2, a 25-ft high intake stack need only be 25 ft from any vapor source.
Many design engineers provide an air intake stack for any building located
in a hazardous area without exception even if wall louvers would work.
They are anticipating the possibility of future modifications in process
equipment and piping arrangements. Process buildings located directly below pipe racks with pipe lines carrying volatile products require intake
stacks with openings 25 ft above the pipe rack itself. If pipes are all of
welded, uninterrupted construction, and if valves in these lines are located
at least 25 ft from the buildings, measured horizontally in plan, then these
pipes in general are not considered a potential source of vapor escape and
may be disregarded when locating the intake point. In any event, the designer must consider all aspects, investigate all requirements, and establish the building design pressure in cooperation with the electrical engineer in charge.

Ventilation and Pressurization Air Needs

In retrospect, for maximum protection a tight building shell and continuous
pressurization are the key words. As for the degree of pressurization,
design experience has highlighted the fact that a positive building pressure
of 0.1 in w.g. is adequate, provided that the system is working 24 hr each
day and includes a properly controlled standby fan. Slightly higher pressures, up to 0.25 in w.g. (inches of water), are often used to include a
safety margin. And occasionally, pressures as high as 0.5 in. w.g. are
required by codes or by the client. This will increase the air intake needs
for pressurization. Data on infiltration leakage may be found in the latest
editions of the ASHRAE "Handbook of Fundamentals" and the "Carrier
Design Manual" published by McGraw-Hill Book Company, New York.

After building pressure is established, the volume of outside air supplied to the building can be calculated. The amount of outside air required
is equal to the amount of air required to maintain pressure. However, in
most non-air conditioned buildings containing electrical equipment, this
volume of air must be recalculated on the basis of heat removal needs.

Code Requirements for Pressurization

Here are sample short descriptions for building pressurization.

1. The NEC calls for an adequate positive pressure ventilation system but does not specify a minimum required building pressure or minimum air requirements.

2. The National Fire Protection Association (NFPA), in publication No. 496-1967, recommends a positive building pressure of 0.1 in. w.g. Ventilation requirements in air flow are as follows:

Control buildings require a "total ventilation system with sufficient capacity to maintain a minimum velocity of 60 fpm through all openings, considering all doors and windows open." In other words, 60 cfm is required for each square foot opening of exterior door and openable window area. Where most control buildings include year-round air conditioning, this high outside air requirement (1200 cfm for each standard 3 × 7 ft door) can adversely affect design and operation of the air conditioning system. In such cases an auxiliary supply fan complementing the air conditioning unit and operating during emergency conditions only may be included. During normal operation with all doors closed, ventilation and pressurization is provided by the air conditioning unit alone.

Switch gear buildings, substations, and similar buildings require sufficient air to adequately cool electrical equipment, depending on design conditions.

Local codes may supersede the NEC and other specifications and should be checked carefully. See McPartland, J. (1979) and Carrier (1965).

Pressurization Needs for Typed Buildings

The outside air needs to maintain building pressure depends on the required building pressure and on the air tightness of the building shell itself. Air tightness varies mainly with the type building, which may be divided into four groups:

1. Solid concrete buildings
2. Concrete block and similar masonry-type buildings
3. Prefabricated metal buildings
4. Steel frame with corrugated roofing and siding buildings

Concrete buildings   Blast-resistant buildings with solid poured-in-place concrete walls and roof are often used in hazardous refinery and chemical plant areas to provide physical protection against accidental explosions in surrounding process areas. These buildings have no windows, are virtually air tight, and the only air leakage takes place around doors. All doors must be close fitting, weather-stripped, and provided with automatic door closers.

Air leakage may be calculated from Table 9.1 for maintaining 0.1 in. w.g.; for 0.25 in. w.g., multiply the factors by 2.5. If exhaust fans are used to ventilate toilets, battery racks, etc., makeup air must be added to the pressurizing air for a grand total. In simply ventilated buildings, the outside air needed for equipment cooling and ventilation often exceeds the air required for pressurization and makeup. Under these conditions the excess air may be relieved from the building through counterweighted check dampers as in Fig. 9.2. These are set to open only when the building pressure exceeds design conditions.

Concrete block buildings   Pressurizing air requirements for concrete block buildings are higher than for concrete poured-in-place buildings because some air will exfiltrate through the wall masonry. See Table 9.1 for comparisons. Most masonry refinery buildings are built of 8 in. concrete block, and workmanship is generally good. Construction drawings and specifications should specify careful sealing of all walls and joints. Exfiltration through masonry walls with two coats of plaster on the inside face may be neglected. Similarly for concrete buildings, the air required for equipment cooling and ventilation normally exceeds the air required for pressurization.

Prefabricated metal buildings   The air tightness of prefabricated metal buildings with formed wall panels of various profiles may vary considerably, depending on building design and the care with which the building is erected and sealed in the field. Potential sources of air leaks are the many joints between the metal panels, the eave joints, the wall-to-floor joints, and the pipe and conduit penetrations. No published data are available as to the air tightness of these buildings. Roof and wall insulation with flat metal liner panels will greatly improve air tightness. Most building manufacturers include gaskets and sealing strips, matching the wall panel profile, for field installation.

In order to ensure fair results in the field, building plans and specifications should emphasize air tight sealing. Close supervision during erection is highly desirable. To maintain 0.1 in. w.g. pressure, an approximate outside air flow equal to one air change per hour is required for good quality sealed buildings with flat liner panels, and 1-1/2 air changes per hour is required for buildings without liner panels. From data in the ASHRAE "Handbook of Fundamentals" there appears to be a close liner relationship between building pressure and exfiltration. Based on these data, 2-1/2 air changes per hour would be needed to maintain a pressure of 0.25 in. w.g. in a building with liner panels.

When building erection is done by experienced and specialized contractors, it is often possible to purchase these buildings with a guaranteed maximum exfiltration rate at a specified building pressure.

<u>Steel frame buildings with corrugated roofing and siding</u> Corrugated
buildings are not recommended in hazardous areas where safety depends
on building pressurization. Corrugated buildings are sometimes used in
borderline areas when economic restrictions prohibit more expensive construction. With extensive caulking of the many joints and the use of matching sealing strips, a building pressure of 0.1 in. w.g. can be obtained with
approximately two air changes per hour. Again, workmanship and installation care in sealing is important and directly influences the outside air
needs.

Outside Air Needs for Ventilated Buildings

When buildings are not provided with air conditioning, sufficient outside air
must be supplied to remove solar heat and the heat dissipated by lighting
and electrical equipment installed inside the building so that the building
temperature can be maintained below a set maximum. Since outside air is
used as a cooling medium, the maximum allowable inside temperature
must necessarily be higher than the maximum anticipated outside temperature. Normally, the outside air required for cooling exceeds that required
to maintain the building at the specified pressure. A low temperature difference can result in prohibitive fan capacities as indicated by the following
formula relating heat rate, cfm, and temperature difference:

$$\text{cfm} = \frac{\text{heat release, btuh}}{1.08 \times \text{temperature difference}} \tag{9.1}$$

Most electrical equipment is designed for 40° C (104° F) allowable
ambient temperature. Electrical engineers allow an override on this temperature for short periods during peak afternoon hours. Refer to the
ASHRAE "Handbook of Fundamentals" for outdoor design temperatures
which are normally not exceeded for more than 1% of the 4 month period
of June through September. When we use these values against a 104°F allowable indoor temperature, the result in temperature difference values
can vary from 5 to 12°F for most locations within the United States. The
exceptions are those extremely hot areas where the 1% outdoor design temperature exceeds 100°F. Here air conditioning is strongly recommended
even when the electrical equipment used is suitable for operation in higher
ambient temperatures.

Since cooling is attained by recirculation of chilled air, the amount of
outside air is calculated to include air for pressurization, ventilation, and
makeup air.

Ventilated Buildings with Winter Heating

For heat conservation, outside air intake for heating buildings is, during
the heating season, normally limited to whatever air is required to maintain

the building pressure. Since this air flow is generally insufficient for equipment cooling during warm weather, some means of regulating outside air intake is needed. This is normally accomplished with motor-operated recirculation dampers and outside dampers which thermostatically control the outside air quality to provide minimum outside air during cold weather. Counterbalanced check dampers or motor-operated exhaust dampers regulate the disposal of excess air and the building pressure.

Air Conditioned Buildings

For buildings that are to be air conditioned, the outside air quantity is calculated on the basis of required building pressure only, subject to applicable codes and regulations.

To determine the outside air required for non-air conditioned buildings, both the solar load and the internal load must be calculated. Solar heat transmitted through sunlit roof and walls may be calculated by conventional methods. Since switch gear buildings, substations, and similar buildings are generally designed for indoor temperatures appreciably higher than 75°F, the heat dissipated from electrical equipment is part of the cooling load. Estimated and tabulated heat dissipation data for switch gear, transformers, circuit breakers, and other electrical equipment are shown in Table 9.2. In addition, heat dissipated by controls, lighting, and instrumentation must be included. The total building load is then the sum of the solar load plus the total electrical load. The required outside air quality for the non-air conditioned building is taken from Formula (9.1), which is modified to

$$\text{cfm} = \frac{\text{heat release, btuh}}{1.08 \times \text{temperature difference}} \tag{9.2}$$

where

   cfm = desired air quantity
   btuh = heat release plus total electrical load
   T.D. = indoor temperature minus outdoor temperature, °F

Note that the required air supply depends largely on the assigned T.D. value, or how much we allow the building temperature to rise above the outdoor temperature.

Table 9.3 shows ranges of equipment heat loads for various buildings and equipment.

Standby Pressurizing Fans and Alarms

API Standards and the NEC call for "adequate safeguards against ventilation failure" in pressurized buildings and enclosures. The possible causes of ventilation failure include breaking of belts, loose fan wheel-to-shaft connections, fan motor failure, debris-plugged air intakes, and electrical

TABLE 9.2. Internal Heat Loads from Motor Control Centers and
Electrical Equipment

Motor starters CB combination type
    (Size)   (Watts)
     1   35
     2   70
     3   120
     4   205
     5   370

Feeder circuit breakers—moulded case
    (Frame)   (Watts)
    100 A   60
    225 A   100
    400 A   200

Drawout-type air circuit breakers in L.V. metal clad gear
    (Frame)   (Watts)
    225 A   140
    600 A   215
    1600 A   460
    3000 A 1080
    4000 A   960

High-voltage interrupter switches
    (KV)   (Watts)
   5 or 15   100

Transformers—self-cooled
    all sizes   1-1/2% of nameplate capacity

Type	KVA	Full Load	3/4 Load	1/2 Load
Lighting transformer	3	154	99	61
	6	221	196	93
	9	250	167	108
	15	412	279	185
	20	500	338	223
Power transformer	30	962	638	406
	45	1,345	890	562
	75	2,317	1,475	840

Heat loss[a] (watts)

TABLE 9.2. (Continued)

Type	KVA	Full Load	3/4 Load	1/2 Load
			Heat loss[a] (watts)	
Power transformer	112-1/2	2,858	1,815	1.075
(cont)	150	3,625	2,260	1,300
	225	4,975	3,095	1,750
	300	5,760	3,620	2,110
	500	8,057	5,200	3,140
	750	9,800	6,630	4,330
	1000	12,000	8,435	5,858
	1500	16,000	11,200	7,750
	2000	20,000	14,100	9,880

Heat losses

Power rectifiers
    Silicon AC-DC conversion units   6.6% of rated kW output

Battery chargers
    Silicon-controlled, single-phase   66% of rated kW output
    Silicon-controlled, three-phase   11% of rated kW output
    Selenium battery chargers, unregulated   100% of rated kW output

Moulded-case circuit breakers

Breaker frame	Trip rating (amperes)	1 pole	3 pole
		Heat losses (watts)	
100 A, 240 V AC	15	0.7	2.1
and	20	1.0	3.0
100 A, 480 V AC	30	1.7	5.2
	40	2.4	7.2
	50	3.5	10.5
	70	4.1	12.3
	90	5.2	15.6
	100	5.6	17.0
100 A, 240 V AC	15		4
	20		4
	25		5

TABLE 9.2. (Continued)

Moulded-case circuit breakers (cont)

Breaker frame	Trip rating (amperes)	Heat losses (watts)	
		1 pole	3 pole
100 A, 240 V AC	30		5
(cont)	35		6
	40		7
	50		9
	60		9
	70		12
	90		17
	100		19
225 A, 600 V AC	125		19
	150		21
	175		23
	200		27
	225		29
400 A, 600 V AC	250		27
	300		31
	350		40
	400		44
800 A, 600 V AC	125		17
	150		22
	175		25
	200		23
	225		26
	250		28
	300		28
	350		30
	400		35
	450		36
	500		40
	550		44
	600		50
	700		63
	800		75

TABLE 9.2.   (Continued)

Air circuit breakers

Type	Trip rating (amperes)	Heat losses[b] (watts)	
		1 pole	3 pole
1MB 15, IMB 25	100		11
	125		13
	150		13
	200		15
	225		15
	300		24
	350		34
	400		45
	500		60
	600		87
IMB 50, IMB 75	100		10
	125		11
	150		10
	200		12
	225		11
	250		13
	300		15
	350		22
	400		23
	500		36
	600		52
	800		92
	1000		135
	1200		194
	1600		346
	2000		304
	3000		870

	Heat losses[c] (watts)
Switch gear 7-15 kV (indoor)	
1200 A breakers	1000 per cubicle plus space heaters
2000 A breakers	1500 per cubic plus space heaters
4.16 kV starters	
400 A starters	200

TABLE 9.2. (Continued)

	Heat losses (watts)
Low-voltage motor control (starter size)	
1	40
2	65
3	110
4	170
5	360
Metal clad	
Breaker compartment	1200
Auxiliary compartment	200
Limit amp	
Induction motor section	600
Synchronous motor section	1000
480 V MCC	
Incoming breaker (AK50)	500
Molded case breaker	
100 A	60
225 A	100
400 A	200
Combination starter (Size)	
1	15
2	35
3	100
4	170
5	300
Primary interrupter	100

[a] Based on total losses of dry-type transformers typically used in indoor installations (load centers are individually mounted). Losses for liquid-filled transformers are somewhat less. These values may vary as much as +10% among the various designs and manufacturers. Full load losses should normally be considered unless it is definitely known that the transformer will operate at less than rated load.

[b] Based on resistance for FPE breakers and 80% of rated current.

[c] Based on General Electric combination circuit breakers and starters. Considerable difference in heat losses exists among the various makes of starters, but these figures are believed to represent the maximum values.

Note: 1 W = 3.4 Btuh; 1 kW = 3400 Btuh.

TABLE 9.3. Equipment Heat Loads for Various Buildings

Description	Heat load (Btuh/ft^2 floor area)
Offices	5
Switch rooms	45
Laboratories	
R & D center	45
Physics	15
Chemistry	15-30
Special	30-70
Light load	15
Medium load	30
Heavy load	70
Machine shops	20-150
Manufacturing plants	20-150
Engine manufacturing	100
Precision parts manufacturing	150
Control rooms	10-45
Computers	
Digital	100-200
Analog	70-110
TV station—monitor room	120
Foundry furnace rooms	700
Power plant—operator floor	100
Gas turbo generator building	150

breakdowns, including interruption of the main power supply. A standby fan or blower, taking air from a nonhazardous area, must be installed to provide pressurization immediately after the primary fan fails. Under most conditions, the primary fan and its standby can utilize the same air intake stack with one-way check-dampers at each fan discharge to prevent backflow.

To assure operation of the standby fan during a power failure, it is suggested that this fan be connected to an emergency power supply system. Where such an arrangement is not possible, the normal power supply to the building should include a manual reset to allow the building interior to be checked for hazardous vapors before power is restored. Both primary and standby fans should be of explosion-proof construction to provide safe starting after interrupts to the ventilation system. For air conditioned buildings in Division 2 areas (see Chapter 3), the explosion-proof requirements for the primary fan are often waived; this permits building pressurization by use of the fan of a commercial air conditioning unit. A number of manufacturers of air conditioning units provide special explosion-proof air conditioners. Under such conditions the explosion-proof standby fan allows purging of the building interior before the main power supply to the building and the air conditioning unit are restored.

Energizing the Standby Fan

Energizing the standby fan may be accomplished in a number of ways.

1. Manually   If plant personnel is present 24 hr per day, such as in control rooms, manual starting is acceptable, provided a good alarm system is installed to warn the operator of the loss of building pressure or failure of the primary fan.

2. Electrical interlock   Direct-driven fans may be interlocked electrically by wiring a normally open auxiliary relay between the fans. This will allow automatic starting of the standby fan when the primary fan fails. This will not protect against the remote possibility of a loose fan wheel connection. Starting the standby fan through a flow switch circuit with the flow switch itself located in the discharge air stream can overcome this possibility. No matter what, an alarm should be installed to warn of building system pressure loss. Buildings in remote areas of the plant without full-time operating personnel should be provided with a warning alarm (sound or light) wired to a central control building or other location where full-time personnel presence is ensured.

3. Pressure switch   The safest way to start the standby fan is to tie it into a pressure switch that senses building pressure. As previously mentioned, a time-delay must be included to allow passage of plant personnel through outside doors. But the safest design is to have but one outside door so protected with all other outside doors locked. Since the outside air is used as the pressure reference point, the outside static pressure sensor must not be located in an area subject to pressure vagaries caused by the wind. Shielded roof-mounted pressure sensors do provide fairly accurate pressure response and should be used wherever possible. Sometimes the standby fan and the pressure-loss alarm are operated from the same pressure sensor to draw attention to primary fan failure.

General Design Considerations

Sealing of building construction is of utmost importance. This also includes the sealing of underground conduits entering the building.

Fan static pressure must include building static pressure to ensure fan performance. The fan static pressure included in the fan specifications is the sum of system static resistance plus building static pressure. Building pressure should not exceed 0.25 in. w.g., and 0.1 in. w.g. is recommended and accepted. Design experience has shown that building pressures in excess of 0.25 in. w.g. are quite difficult to maintain even when well-sealed masonry buildings are used. High building pressures may also cause some difficulties in the opening and closing of doors. A pressure differential between the inside and outside of 0.5 in w.g. is equal to 2.6 lb/ ft^2. This equates to a force of 54.6 lb on a standard 3 × 7 ft door. Half of this force, or about 27 lb, would be required to operate the door, which makes passage through frequently used doors inconvenient. Under such conditions double doors with an air interlock at an intermediate pressure should be considered. However, the use of 0.1 in. w.g. building pressure obviates the need for air locks.

Packaged Air Conditioning Units

Remember that each 1000 cfm of outside air required for ventilation through an air conditioning unit will add about 5 tons of refrigeration to the load. It thus behooves the designer to trim outside air needs to a minimum. Small buildings located in hazardous areas and requiring both pressurization and air conditioning often incorporate package-type air conditioning units.
When plant cooling water is available, a standard package unit with a water-cooled condenser may be used and located within the air conditioned building or room. Where no cooling water is available, and an air-cooled condenser is needed, the remote air-cooled condenser, located outdoors, must be of explosion-proof construction. Air-cooled condensers most often incorporate aluminum nonsparking fan wheels and are available with explosion-proof fan motors and static-conducting belts. The only modification required is to enclose or relocate the fan contactors and low-ambient controls. The main unit located indoors includes compressors, the evaporator section, and all the controls and can be of standard or special explosion-proof construction.
      Since package units normally do not include compressor capacity, control compressor cycling can be a serious problem when the outside air required for pressurization exceeds 15-20% of the total quantity of circulated air handled by the unit. Thus, the building must be kept tight against infiltration in order to keep the outside air required for pressurization to a minimum. An antirecycling relay can normally be supplied as part of the air conditioning unit to prevent the compressor from restarting in 5 min intervals.

Filters

If air filters are not normally included with the package unit, they should be included in each pressurization system. Standard fiberglass throwaway-type filters are acceptable in most cases. However, where buildings contain dust-sensitive equipment or instruments, or in areas where dust and sand storms are common, high-efficiency filters may be necessary. Where resistance to air flow is increased beyond that which the fan can handle, especially a package unit, a booster fan may be necessary with connecting ductwork.

Where buildings are located in process areas in which H_2S, SO_2, or other atmospheric contaminants are present, chemical filtration with special impregnated carbon filters may be required. This becomes an important consideration especially if the building houses delicate metal parts or contact points on computers, controls, or instrumentation.

9.3. HOW TO PRESSURE-VENTILATE LARGE MOTORS FOR CORROSION, EXPLOSION, AND MOISTURE PROTECTION

General

The CPI now deal with more corrosive flammable and potentially explosive products than ever. At the same time, there is an increasing need for large electric motors as power demands keep pace with industry changes. These motors are of the open type, thus, in addition to their normal requirements for cooling, they must be protected from flammable and corrosive vapors. The chemical engineer, both in the design office and the chemical plant, often must cope with this situation.

An accepted method of protecting large general-purpose induction and synchronous motors from corrosive and explosive atmospheres is to surround the motors with pressurized air drawn from a safe distance.

Classification of Areas

As we have seen previously (and is worth repeating), equipment and process areas are classified in accordance with the NEC and API Standard RP 500.

The NEC is valued as the definitive tool for such classifications. Insurance companies and their inspectors generally insist that only electrical equipment, controls, and motors that have been so listed and approved by UL for such application can be installed in hazardous areas. If general-purpose electrical equipment is installed, approved methods must be used for protesting that equipment. Most state and municipal (as well as public service) enforcement authorities use the NEC as their inspection standard.

The initial step in specifying large motors is to apply these two codes to determine, first, whether the area is hazardous and, second, whether the electrical equipment should be specially designed for such an area.

The Pressurized Enclosure

If the area has hazardous vapors, some method must be found for rendering the electrical equipment explosion proof. Explosion-proof motor designs (i.e., providing totally enclosed water-cooled or air-cooled low-leakage motors for pressurizing with inert gas) can be very expensive, and in many cases are impractical.

One way of overcoming this problem of protection and cooling is to build a sheet metal enclosure around large general-purpose motors and

affected components and to supply a steady stream of relatively cool outside air under slight pressure (up to 1/2 in. water) for maintaining a
purged environment within the enclosure and around the motor and its
windings.

Such an enclosure must be large enough for people to get around the
motor to service it. If several motors are grouped within an enclosure,
or a building, the saving in equipment costs can far outweigh the initial
and operating costs for the pressurizing system.

Having decided to locate the motor in a pressurized enclosure, one
should obtain the following information from the motor manufacturer:

> Cooling-air requirements
> Air static pressure to be maintained within the enclosure
> Maximum atmospheric air temperature permitted within the enclosure
> Maximum particulate matter permitted in the air within the enclosure

With such information, plant layout can be started, including motor locations, air intake location, air intake dimensions, fan specifications, etc.
Figure 9.4 gives a typical layout that could be used for two separately enclosed motors.

Cooling Air

Cooling-air requirements will usually come to about 200 cfm per electrical
horsepower lost in the motor. Large motors are usually provided with
shaft-mounted fan blades built into the armature, so that the cooling air
must flow through and around the windings.

However, space limitations within the motor do not always provide
for ample air supply, so it may be necessary to include additional fan power for delivering air to the enclosure under a pressure sufficient to aid in
moving the air through the motor casing. This is a critical consideration.

When the cooling air is drawn from a dusty area, the dust must first
be removed by means of filters. These are preferably dry-type filters of
the throwaway class and are usually made of fiberglass, about 2 in. thick.
Especially dusty conditions should be reviewed with a reputable filter
manufacturer.

Appropriate dust removal reduces the accumulations in the motor
windings and thus remove the need for shutdowns for cleaning. The danger
of fire and short circuits within the motor windings is also reduced, while
the cooling effect of the air is enhanced. Within a hazardous area, a 50-ft
intake stack is satisfactory for reaching noncontaminated air, and employ-
ing such stacks is standard practice.

The Ductwork

Once the enclosure pressure has been set, and air-flow requirements
established, the ducts and stack can be sized.

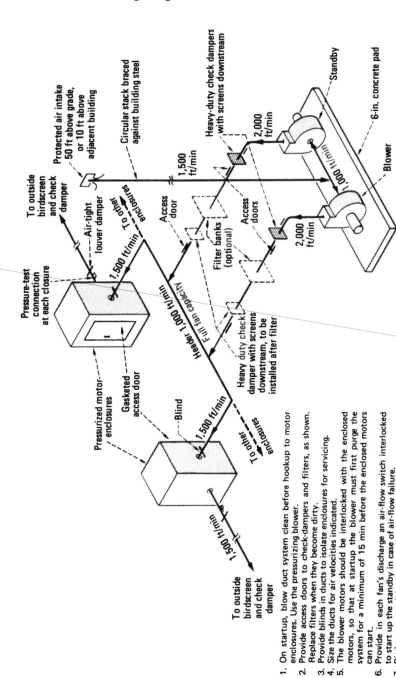

FIG. 9.4. Layout and design criteria to pressure-ventilate large general-purpose motors. (From Chemical Engineering, February 27, 1978.)

1. On startup, blow duct system clean before hookup to motor enclosures. Use the pressurizing blower.
2. Provide access doors to check-dampers and filters, as shown. Replace filters when they become dirty.
3. Provide blinds in ducts to isolate enclosures for servicing.
4. Size the ducts for air velocities indicated.
5. The blower motors should be interlocked with the enclosed motors, so that at startup the blower must first purge the system for a minimum of 15 min before the enclosed motors can start.
6. Provide in each fan's discharge an air-flow switch interlocked to start up the standby in case of air-flow failure.
7. Birdscreens are 1-in. square mesh, 10-gage galvanized steel wire.

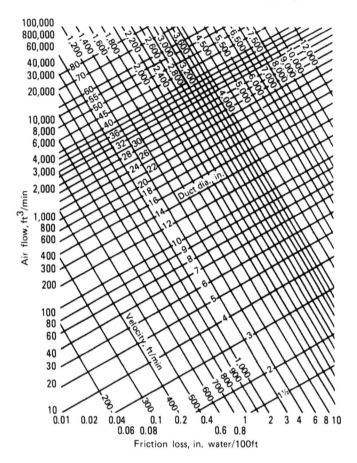

FIG. 9.5. Estimating friction loss for air flowing through straight ducts. (From Chemical Engineering, February 27, 1978.)

It is a simple matter to determine the friction loss of air flowing through straight ducts from published data and charts (Fig. 9.5). However, the determination of air-pressure loss through elbows, fittings, hoods, air intakes, louvers, screening, etc., involves both dynamic and friction loss and requires prior calculation of air velocity based on assumed duct dimensions.

Since each type of fitting causes a characteristic loss of velocity head for any given air velocity, calculated velocities can be converted to pressure losses for each fitting, provided the air density does not deviate significantly from normal (0.078 lb/ft^3, corresponding to 70°F dry air at 29.92 inHg barometric pressure). Pressure losses at different velocities may be found for different fittings by means of Fig. 9.6, without any corrections, as long as the ambient temperature of the air does not go above 100°F or the elevation is not more than 1500 ft above sea level.

Wherever possible, duct elbows should be made with a radius-to-width ratio (R/W) of 1.5. Whenever space limitations require smaller elbows, turnblades should be used. Divide the elbow into several parallel sections evenly spaced so that the R/W of each section is about 1.5, with the turnblades laid out to this ratio. With such arrangements, the pressure loss of the elbow will have the characteristic shown in Fig. 9.6.

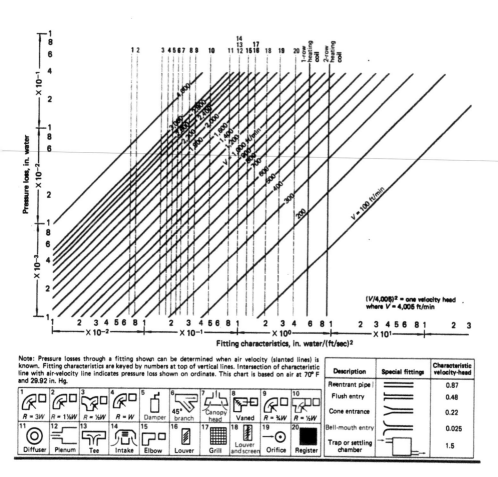

FIG. 9.6. Estimating pressure drop for air flowing through duct fittings. (From Chemical Engineering, February 27, 1978.)

Blowers

The air blowers should be centrifugal, with backward-curved blades producing nonoverloading characteristic curves. If located in a nonhazardous
area, they can be of standard construction, and their driven motors can be
general purpose. When located in hazardous areas, as at the bottom of an
intake stack, the fans should have nonsparking blades and wheels, static-
conducting belts, and explosion-proof totally enclosed fan-cooled motors.
A standby fan should always be provided. See Cheremisenoff, P. N., and
Young, R. A. (1974).

Backward-curved fan blades, while not common, provide several advantages. The motor will not burn out from overload because the steep
pressure-capacity curve prevents a runaway fan. An automatic shutoff is
tripped by free air delivery should a break in the duct system occur (i.e.,
if someone happens to open the enclosure access door). Also, such blades
have a high efficiency, low noise levels, lower (than forward-curved blades)
air velocities off the wheel, self-cleaning characteristics so that dust and
dirt do not accumulate, and less sensitivity to deviations between practice
and design values of system resistance.

Selecting such fans to operate within 55-65% of full-open capacity allows performance on the steep part of the pressure-volume curve. This
helps maintain constant flow through the system. For estimating purposes,
use a 50% fan efficiency to size the motor driver (Fig. 9.7).

Performance Requirements and Controls

Blowers should be provided with starters and controls to meet the following
criteria:

Either one of two blowers should function, with the other in standby.
    If the functioning blower fails to maintain flow and pressure, then
    the standby should start.
The starter for each blower should be provided with a local control
    switch and local lamps to indicate on, off, and malfunction.
Reverse flow through the standby blower should be automatically and
    positively prevented by a fan-discharge check damper.
Flow through the operating blower should automatically adjust to small
    changes in air-flow resistance due to the steep characteristic curve
    of the fan.
Each pressurized enclosure should be equipped with a differential-
    pressure gauge and transducer to actuate an alarm in the event that
    the system pressure drops.
Alarm contacts should be provided to show a tripped blower motor and
    a started standby.
Alarm contacts should be normally open and closed in the alarm
    condition.

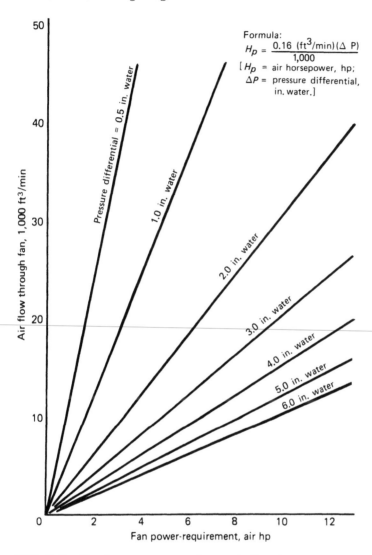

FIG. 9.7. Fan horsepower requirements for air-pressurized ducts and enclosures. (From <u>Chemical Engineering</u>, February 27, 1978.)

Materials of Construction

<u>Ductwork</u>   Ducts should be made of 14-gauge black iron for outdoor service,
or 16-gauge for indoor service. The air-intake stack should be 10-gauge
black iron. The automatic, gravity-action, backpressure check dampers

that are set in the discharge of each fan should be made of material at least
equivalent to that of the associated housings.

Balancing dampers should be of the opposed-blade type, with a hand
lever and locking device. The damper-blade shafts should be set in bronze
bearings so as to withstand air-flow velocities in excess of 2000 fpm.

Any blinds located at closure inlets should be of 12-gauge black iron,
while louvers and screens in the discharge ducts into the enclosure should
be standard 20-gauge sheet metal with galvanized bird screens.

Pressurized enclosures and pressurized fan-suction boxes should be
12-gauge black iron, flanged and cross braced for stiffness.

Dust construction   Outdoor ducts should be welded, with flanged sections
located at flanged outlets and at T connections. Indoor ducts should be
flanged on 8 ft centers. Ducts should be braced and should be equipped with
gasketed access doors at least 12 in. square, located at dampers and other
sections requiring access.

Blower motor   The blower motors should be designed for 460-V, 3-phase,
60-Hz electricity, with a standard NEMA service factor of 1.15 and should
be suitable for full-voltage starting and continuous duty at 122°F. Each
blower motor should be provided with a space heater to keep motor windings
dry at all times.

9.4. CONTROLLING AIR FLOW BETWEEN ROOMS

General

How does the designer establish pressure differentials to prevent air movement from contaminated areas to clean areas? Conventionally, the approach
has been to pump about 10% more supply air than exhaust per room. This
approach is qualitative at best but not quantitative, and a slightly more rig-
orous treatment is in order. See Heckert, F. (1968).

Rooms Under Positive Pressure

The pressure differential method will be used to determine supply and exhaust air volumes in rooms to control air flow between them. Air flow
should be in the direction of least contaminated to most contaminated area,
from which the final exhaust connection is made for vitiated air treatments.
See Heckert, F. (1968).

EXAMPLE 9.2. A room is 24 × 20 × 10 ft in height with an 80 ×
44 in. corridor door and an 80 × 30 in. door opening into an adjacent room. Find the supply air volume that provides a differential pressure of 0.1 in. w.g. between the given room and adjacent
spaces. The room is to be rendered contamination free from adjacent infiltration. Assume no leakage through building construction.

SOLUTION: First determine the corridor door leakage based on 1/16-in. crack around the full perimeter of door. See Fan Engineering, 6th ed., p. 343. Note that infiltration in a 20-mph wind (0.1 in. w.g.) is 227 ft^3/hr/ft of crack. Now

$$\frac{80 + 80 + 44 + 44}{12} \times \frac{1}{60} \ (227) \ = \ 78 \ cfm$$

Now determine leakage through the adjacent room door in the same manner.

$$\frac{80 + 80 + 30 + 30}{12} \times \frac{1}{60} \ (227) \ = \ 69 \ cfm$$

Total supply air = 78 + 69 = 147 cfm

This is equivalent to (24 × 20 × 10)/147 = 32-min air change, or about a 2-hr air change. It must be remembered that this is a differential volume requirement and that this calculated volume must be increased by the ventilation requirements of the pressurized space. Normally, a 10-hr air change will provide sufficient ventilation so that the total supply would become

$$\frac{24 \times 20 \times 10}{10/60} \ = \ 800 \ cfm$$

Thus, we see that there are other requirements that must be satisfied, and the differential volume must be maintained at 0.1 in. w.g. The use of counterbalanced dampers must be considered to maintain pressure and satisfy ventilation requirements.

Rooms Under Negative Pressure

Negative pressure is the condition that occurs when more air is removed from a room than is being supplied. This can result in a laboratory using exhaust hoods or in a room provided with an exhaust system. As we have seen, makeup air must be supplied to balance the system. Supply air volume then becomes the basis for establishing minimum acceptable air flow through a space under negative pressure.

By the pressure differential method, supply air is calculated as above, whereas exhaust air volume is the sum of the supply air plus total differential or leakage volume necessary to achieve the required negative pressure. Thus,

Exhaust volume = supply + differential volume

If building codes strictly prohibit the use of corridors as plenums, then pressurization cannot be accomplished unless an entrance vestibule or anteroom off the corridor is provided to reroute leakage air around the corridor.

Basic Rules for Pressurization

The following basic rules provide an orderly procedure for calculating
pressure differentials and gauge pressures:

> When air flows out of a space, the pressure within must be higher than
> that of the adjacent area, and the pressure differential should be
> considered positive. The algebraic sum of the pressure differential
> and gauge pressure of the adjacent area receiving the air is the
> gauge pressure of the space.
> When air moves into a space, the pressure within must be lower than
> that of the adjacent area, and the pressure differential should be
> considered negative. The algebraic sum of this pressure differential
> and the gauge pressure of the adjacent area from which air is re-
> ceived is the gauge pressure of the space.
> Areas connected to a pressurized space by doorways are at the same
> pressure if the air supply to each adjacent area is equal to the air
> exhausted from it. A sketch of the complex room arrangement and
> a tabulation of its design and calculated conditions is recommended.

The first step is to select corridor pressure as a datum pressure for adjoining spaces, to prevent any entry of air from outside the complex.
Some room pressures should be the same as that of the adjacent rooms to
prevent a loss of pressure when interconnecting doors are opened. Certain
other rooms may be considered part of the main corridor, and their volumes are added to the main corridor volume. Calculation of corridor supply and exhaust is the final step after the conditions in all adjacent rooms
are computed.

Supply and Exhaust Volumes for Main Corridor

Leakage or pressurizing air volumes that are calculated for all areas adjacent to the corridor can be listed in tabular form. Since the corridor is
to be maintained at a positive pressure, the required air changes per hour
dictate the exhaust volume.

 Leakage volume should be considered maximum when pressurizing
individual spaces and minimum when dealing with the actual quantity delivered on the low-pressure side of the same door. The total leakage air
volume actually flowing in and out of the corridor when the air system is
balanced and operating is between these maximum and minimum values.
Consequently, corridor air supply and exhaust ducts must be sized to handle maximum volumes. In addition, they must be provided with volume
control dampers to cover the range between the highest and lowest leakage
flow in the corridor. These limiting conditions may be set up in tabular
form.

 By inspection, the maximum air flow to be supplied to the corridor
may be determined, so too with the maximum exhaust flow. Use volume

dampers to regulate the air flow from zero to maximum, depending on
actual leakage encountered. These relationships may also be summarized
in tabular form. Balancing the dampers at each air inlet and outlet helps
control the attainment of design pressures by compensating for such var-
iables as air leakage, deviations from plans, and errors in design and
construction changes "as built."

Design of Pressurized Switch Gear Cubicle

On occasion, switch gear must be housed within a contaminated process
room and must be protected against dust or gases or vapors. To accommodate this requirement, a tight sheet metal enclosure with access panels
or doors is built around the switch gear sitting on supports. If the environment is dusty, pressurizing air may be taken directly from the room through
high-efficiency dry filters through a pressurizing blower (and standby blower) which discharges through ductwork directly into the enclosure and is
allowed to leak back out into the room. Air flow rate is determined in the
usual fashion by the crackage method. This is based on maintaining
0.1 in. w.g. air pressure within the enclosure at all times and using the
method outlined in Example 9.2. Pressurizing air would be a minimum
since switch gear gives off heat; cooling air must be circulated through the
enclosure and controlling pressure by check-dampers as described earlier
in this chapter. If the room is hazardous because of the presence of gases
or vapors, pressurizing and cooling air must be taken from a safe location,
either above the roof line or from a distance through a booster (and standby) blower and ductwork. Use Fan Engineering as a reference as in Example 9.2 or use the ASHRAE guide publications.

There are many applications of pressurizing technique in industry;
using the techniques discussed in this chapter will prove cost effective.

10

CLEARING THE AIR IN LABORATORIES FOR SAFETY AND HEALTH

10.1. INTRODUCTION

With the advent of the Occupational Safety and Health Act (OSHA), removal of toxic fumes and gases from the laboratory has become even more important. This chapter provides useful information on the selection and operation of hoods and exhaust systems that can make this facility safe and liveable.

The accepted method for containing and removing fumes, odors, and other contaminants emitted from laboratory work or chemical testing procedures is to restrict the operations to an enclosure. Ideally, the best procedure is not to emit, but the next best is to remove or exhaust directly and as close to the point of origin as possible to protect personnel and property. Fume exhaust systems, using properly designed hoods where room air is drawn across the hood face to capture and remove the contaminants, can be very effective. Before selecting such a system, however, the following factors must be analyzed and evaluated: capture velocities, fume hood design, makeup air source, air distribution, exhaust system, exhaust air treatment, and special systems. This chapter tells the story thoroughly and effectively.

10.2. CAPTURE VELOCITIES—A KEY CRITERIA

Capture Velocity

Air flow rates required for hood exhaust systems are based on a number of factors, the most important one being capture velocity. We have discussed this aspect of exhaust systems previously for local exhaust systems, and the capture velocities for those applications ranged in the very high figures. However, for laboratory hood exhaust applications, capture velocities will range from 50 to 200 fpm. The lower figure is used to control contaminants released at low speed into relatively quiet room air (15-25 fpm). The higher figure is for controlling contaminants released at high rates. Under special conditions, hood face velocities as low as 25 fpm have been used with induction-type hoods.

The matter of face velocity selection is a mixed bag. In the conceptual design of a laboratory facility, this is given much thought and argument, especially when air conditioning is to be included. It is worth remembering, and repeatedly so, that for every 1000 cfm of air exhausted through hoods, about 5 tons of refrigeration must be added to the system capacity for makeup air. At the present rate of $1500 per ton of refrigeration, the cost of exhausting 1000 cfm could range close to $7500. This certainly adds to hood burden and capital outlay.

Compromising Fume Hood Usage

Some designs emphatically forbid hood face velocities less than 100 fpm. Attempts have been made to relate face velocity to hood service by compromising fume hood usage with the added responsibility of supervision by laboratory personnel to ensure that fume hood usage is restricted to the type of contaminant for which face velocities were selected. To this end, a method of hood classification as a step toward economy of design and operation was offered by R. S. Brief (1963). He classified type "S" hoods for highly toxic contaminants [threshold limit values (TLVs) less than 0.1 ppm] requiring face velocities from 150 to 130 fpm. Type "A" hoods, for moderately toxic contaminants (TLVs of less than 100 ppm), can be sized for 100-80 fpm. Type "B" hoods (for nontoxic contaminants; TLVs of less than 100 ppm) are sized for 60-50 fpm. It should be emphasized that TLVs should be used with care and not as a sole criteria since they represent the airborne concentrations that most workers may be exposed to repeatedly during a normal 8-hr work day over a working lifetime.

Fume hood efficiency depends on the amount of air exhausted and on the hood design. To ensure flexibility of operation and maximum safety to personnel, a fume hood should be designed to exhaust air at rates ample for complete removal of all contaminants. This may be a logical step when only one or two hoods are involved in a single facility. However, with more than two, generous exhaust through all hoods can impose heavily initial and operating cost penalties on the air conditioning system. It is known from actual experience with laboratory design that it is difficult to select one hood design which will satisfy all situations. See Dalla Valle, J. M. (1936).

10.3. FUME HOOD DESIGN

Some Basic Points

It should always be remembered that the purpose of a hood exhaust system is to protect laboratory personnel from exposure. Thus, the heart of the system is the hood—and the design begins with the hood, which is, at best, a compromise between the ideal and the practical. Basically, a hood is a simple box. Without the necessary indraft used in a simple ventilated hood, the material inside the hood can become airborne and be emitted into the room by one or a combination of normal laboratory operations: thermal action and convection currents, mechanical agitation, or aspirating action by cross currents of the air outside the box. Material can escape only through the door or opening in the front.

In the simple ventilated hood, however, contaminants are kept inside by the action of the air flowing into the opening. To contain and keep the material from escaping, sufficient air must be exhausted to create and maintain a draft through the opening and into the hood.

Nearly all hood designs currently in use attempt to provide protection to personnel in three ways: via a mechanical shield, direction of air movement, and dilution of contaminants by mixing with large volumes of air inside the hood. The hood sash serves as the mechanical shield. It is in the raised position when an experiment is being set up. The sash is then lowered two-thirds or even closed off entirely during an unattended experiment. However, care should be exercised not to lower the sash to a level that can cause a high-velocity indraft that would overcool an experiment or snuff out a burner flame. Protection is provided by the direction of air flow across the back of the worker and into the hood proper, past the equipment within the hood, and into the exhaust system. Also, because large amounts of air are being moved through the hood, dilution of the contaminated air takes place readily, thereby further reducing the hazard of breathing hood air. There are seven basic hood designs currently in use (Figs. 10.1 through 10.7).

Seven basic hood designs

1. Conventional Hood   This is the simplest design, effective and low in initial cost. All exhaust air is taken from the room. However, high exhaust air rates place a heavy burden on air conditioning capital cost and operation.
2. Conventional Hood with Reduced Face Velocity   This is an attempt to compromise hood effectiveness to reduce air conditioning load

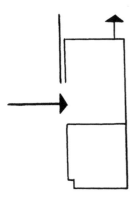

FIG. 10.1. Conventional hood. (From Research/Development, September 1972.)

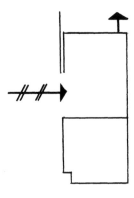

FIG. 10.2. Conventional hood with reduced face velocity. (From Research/Development, September 1972.)

chargeable to the hoods. Although low in relative cost, it does reduce air conditioning load, but its effectiveness in removing fumes generated within the hood is weakened.

3. Conventional Hood with Use Factor In this arrangement, a number of hoods may be needed at random intervals. As with other types of air conditioning loads, there is a usage factor or diversity factor that is apparent; yet it is difficult to define precisely. This factor depends upon judgment, experience, and logic. For example, a large number of hoods in a room does not necessarily mean that all will be operating at one time. On the other hand, it is the policy of some laboratories to keep all hoods operating 24 hr a day even though they are used intermittently. Much depends on the management of the facility, so it behooves the designer to explore the total operation with the ultimate user.

4. Internally Supplied Hood Required makeup air for this design is fed directly into the hood without affecting the over-all room air conditioning. This air need not be cooled in summer but merely

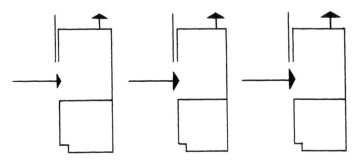

FIG. 10.3. Conventional hood with use factor. (From Research/Development, September 1972.)

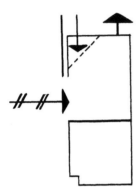

FIG. 10.4. Internally supplied hood. (From Research/Development, September 1972.)

tempered in winter. Although an additional air handling system is required, the saving on the air conditioning load can offset this. The cost of such a hood is medium to high. The hood must be carefully designed, and makeup air must be balanced or fume removal effectiveness may be poor.

5. Externally Supplied Hood   Because of the additional ductwork required, this system is more expensive. There is also a low cost effect on air conditioning. Since air is exhausted across the hood face, fume removal effectiveness is good.

6. Perforated Ceiling Supply Hood   This design allows ample opportunity for the conditioned air to mix with room air. It often becomes necessary to sensibly cool (but not dehumidify) this auxiliary supply. Because air is exhausted across the hood face, fume removal effectiveness is good.

7. Horizontal Sliding Sash Hood   Compared with the conventional hood with its vertical sliding door, the horizontal sliding sach unit represents much less area to be exhausted. Total exhaust is thereby

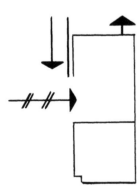

FIG. 10.5. Externally supplied hood. (From Research/Development, September 1972.)

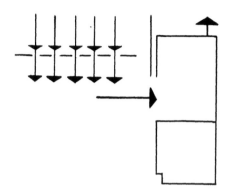

FIG. 10.6. Perforated ceiling supply hood. (From Research/Development, September 1972.)

reduced. The cost of the hood is low, and since less air is exhausted, air conditioning costs are low. Air conditioning and fume removal effectiveness are good.

To keep hood face disturbances to a minimum, high-velocity streams from the air conditioning system should not be permitted to disturb the even, smooth flow of air across the hood face.

10.4. MAKEUP AIR SOURCE

Need for Balance

Makeup air to balance the air that is being exhausted is the most essential design feature of any hood exhaust system. When a fume hood is operating poorly, close analysis will often reveal an inadequate supply of makeup air. There is no air for the hood to "breathe," and an improperly sized makeup system will starve the hood and consequently restrict its intended operation.

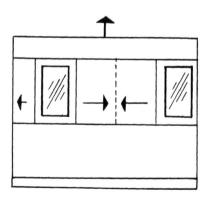

FIG. 10.7. Horizontal sliding sash hood. (From Research/Development, September 1972.)

Some designs depend on air drawn from adjoining corridors and office spaces. Introduction of makeup air by indirect means is an economical approach. However, such a system can lead to balancing problems and cross-contamination among laboratory spaces. Positive introduction of air from corridors and office spaces by transfer fans can improve this. Experience has shown that the most reliable, flexible, and easiest to maintain system is that in which an adequate supply of outside conditioned makeup air is provided to the laboratory to balance the air being exhausted. It is good practice to supply a little less makeup air than that being exhausted. A slight negative pressure will thus be maintained, drawing air through door louvers from corridors or offices.

Air Exhausted from Hoods is Never Recirculated

Air exhausted from a hood is never recirculated so that hood burden goes up. Operating costs can be reduced by supplying makeup air from an auxiliary source instead of from the cooling system. The air handled is filtered and tempered in winter only. Of the seven basic hood designs mentioned, only the internally supplied, externally supplied, and perforated ceiling supplied hoods make use of the auxiliary system. Such a system can be either a central unit or unitary type with an outside air inlet for each laboratory. Correct selection of the type of makeup air system can be made only by an engineering analysis and flow sheet of the hood exhaust system.

One of the most important characteristics of an exhaust system is that at some point the system must end and discharge to the atmosphere. Unfortunately, while the exhaust system has ended at this point, the problems associated with the system may have just begun. If too much discharged air is recirculated through the supply system, not too much good has been accomplished. If the exhaust air is not properly located with respect to the intakes of their supply systems, potentially disastrous results can be attained. Higher exhaust velocities, taller stacks, better weather caps, and better separation of discharge and intake openings will not solve this type of a problem—although one or more of these can contribute to the cure. The real remedy must start back at the source of contamination itself.

Because the pattern of natural air flow around buildings is not predictable, contamination by the location of vent effluents and air intakes is difficult to avoid in practice. J. Halitsky (1963) and J. H. Clarke (1967) have advanced theoretical knowledge and rule-of-thumb guidance that can aid greatly in the solution of such problems.

10.5. HOW TO HANDLE AIR DISTRIBUTION

Air movement within each room of a laboratory complex must be such that a definite flow pattern is maintained throughout the building, along with flow

from noncontaminated to potentially contaminated areas. To bring about
this differential flow pattern, the natural barriers between the various
classes of rooms will assist. The pattern will also be helped by supplying
clean outside air to the noncontaminated and semicontaminated areas and
by exhausting air only from moderate and extreme areas. In general,
supply fans should take suction from the upper portions of the building.
Also, the exhaust fans should discharge to the outdoors through stacks
whose heights vary depending on adjacent structures. To help, the building
should be maintained at a slight positive pressure with respect to the outdoors. Laboratory rooms should be kept at a negative pressure with respect to the surrounding rooms. It is suggested that the reader refer back
to Chapter 9 for maintaining differential pressures between rooms.

Only an adequate supply of makeup air to satisfy exhaust needs will
keep the building in balance aerodynamically. This certainly implies that
there must be an excess of supply over exhaust needs. In actual installations, experience shows that when two fans are exhausting from the same
space with no provisions for makeup air, the stronger fan will take com-
mand and outside air will enter the room through the weaker fan system.
When there are multiple exhaust hoods and no makeup air, with one hood
off, outside air can downdraft through the idle fan. When a fan must exhaust from a room without makeup air, fan capacity will be reduced from
design and will result in less control at the hood.

10.6. EXHAUST SYSTEM

Roof Fan

Since the exhaust system is under negative pressure, any air leakage will
be drawn into the system, thus confining contamination. The best location
for an exhaust fan serving hoods is on the roof, then all exhaust ductwork
will be on the suction side of the fan and will be indoors. But this is not
always possible. If the fan location must be indoors, say just above the
hood, then careful attention must be paid to duct tightness on the discharge
side. When flammable material is handled, mounting the fan on the roof
is a distinct advantage because an explosion-proof fan motor may not be
required. However, the fan wheel should be nonferrous and the inside
casing should be protected (by use of an epoxy coating, for example) against
corrosive attack.

Exhaust Duct Materials—Which to Use?

In many buildings ductwork is often concealed in ceilings or inside walls,
making duct inspection and replacement a major problem. Where this
condition exists it is reasonable to use ductwork with long life expectancy.
For chemicals used in laboratories, galvanized iron and black iron ductwork are highly susceptible to corrosion. Stainless steel, Transite,

polyvinylchloride (PVC) coated steel, or fiberglass-reinforced plastic (FRP) ductwork, although costly, will not require early replacement. Actually, selection of materials will depend on the nature and concentration of contaminants or chemical reagents, space conditions, cost, and accessibility. Whatever materials are selected, duct joints must be leak-proof, and the ductwork should have ample supports. For the best service life, all longitudinal duct seams should be along the top panel. An extensive duct system should have inspection and cleaning facilities. Ducts that could develop condensation loading should pitch downward toward a pocket in the bottom of the duct run and be provided with a trapped drain.

Type 316 passive stainless steel may be used for bacteriological, radiological, perchloric acid, and other general chemical purposes. This steel is easy to work but is not suitable for chemical hoods handling concentrated HCl and H_2SO_4.

Exhaust Air Treatment

Gases that are bubbled through reaction mixtures and then discharged to the hood are generally, by their very nature, reactive enough to be eliminated by some kind of scrubber. For acidic materials, a simple caustic scrubber is all that is necessary to ensure essentially complete control. For basic materials, an acid scrubber may be used. For materials that do not react rapidly with either caustic or acidic solutions, a column filled with activated charcoal will usually provide the desired control.

For perchloric acid, which is highly soluble in water, hoods have been developed with packed sections built into the hood superstructure. To prevent the buildup of perchlorates, which are explosive on contact, water wash rings are provided in the ductwork downstream of the scrubber. Fume hoods handling highly radioactive materials should have high efficiency particulate air (HEPA) filters upstream and downstream of the hood. For highly hazardous bacteriological experiments, safety can be achieved only by incineration (at about 650°F) of the exhaust stream.

10.7. SPECIAL SYSTEMS PROVIDE DIVERSITY

Lowered Sash Operation

A hood exhaust fan maintains a proper capture velocity when the sash is wide open, but the exhaust hood's vertically sliding sashes are sometimes lowered to within a few inches of the work surface when the hood is in operation. Use of a two-speed fan can reduce any waste of conditioned air and also achieve a more constant face velocity over the range of sash positions. When the sash is pushed up the fan operates at high speed. A microswitch mounted in the hood is tripped by the sash when it is lowered below a predetermined position. The volume of air pulled by the fan at low speed is adequate to maintain the desired face velocity for the small cross-sectional area. The proper placement of the switch setting can be 50-60% of the vertical face opening (fan velocity would drop to low speed when the sash is lowered to 50-60% of the full opening). This applies to all exhaust hoods despite differences in hood dimensions and other variations in exhaust systems. It has been found to apply also to hoods with minimum face velocities of 80, 100, and 125 fpm. The volume of conditioned air that is normally lost is reduced by about 33% when the sash is below the set point.

In a conventional hood with a single-speed fan, the excessively high face velocities experienced at low sash settings and the cooling effect on the backs of laboratory personnel using the hood have an adverse effect. Further, when an individual stands in front of an operating hood his body presents an obstruction to the flow of air into the hood. Thus, a low-pressure area develops in the space between him and the hood. Under certain conditions, this can cause fumes to be aspirated from the hood and out into the room. The reduction in face velocity using the two-speed fan reduces the probability of such a hazardous condition developing.

Fan speeds on type S hoods should be such that air velocities will never exceed 250 fpm at any point across the hood face. Another way to control this is to provide bypass dampers in the exhaust duct just downstream of the hood.

Bypass Hoods

Bypass hoods provide a constant rate of room exhaust and uniform face velocities at any door position. They stabilize the room exhaust and the room air supply. The bypass may be an integral part of the hood itself (Fig. 10.8). As the hood door begins to close, the damper starts to open.

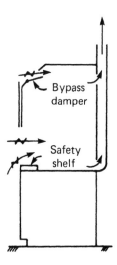

FIG. 10.8. Bypass hood can have its interior purged continuously even when sash is closed. (From Research/Development, September 1972.)

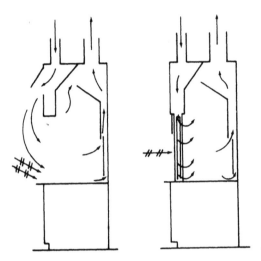

FIG. 10.9.   Low room air consumption is a feature of supply-air-type hoods.   Unit at top has auxiliary air introduced outside and in front of sash, while unit at bottom has air fed directly into interior.   (From Research/ Development, September 1972.)

Another important advantage is that the hood interior is continuously being purged of fumes even while the door is closed tight.

Supply Air Hoods

Two types of supply air hoods are commercially available (Fig. 10.9). One has auxiliary air introduced outside and in front of the sash, normally from the overhead position.   The auxiliary air is drawn into the sash open- ing as a part of the room air.   The cost of this hood compared with a con- ventional unit is high.   The relative cost of air conditioning is low because the amount of room air exhausted is reduced.   Air conditioning effective- ness, fume removal effectiveness, and convenience to personnel are good. However, acceptability to local authorities should be investigated.

In the second type of supply air hood, auxiliary air is fed directly into the hood from the inside.   Relative cost is high, air conditioning cost is low, and effectiveness is good; but fume removal effectiveness is poor.   Be- cause effective face velocities can drop below the safe value needed to pre- vent the leakage of fumes, its use is discouraged by many health authorities.

Induction Venturi

For many applications, the conventional method of passing gases through
the fan casing can be potentially hazardous. As indicated earlier, for example, perchloric acid fumes can cause a buildup of explosive crystals on
the duct walls and fan. Induction venturi systems with a water-wash capability can prevent this. The systems are provided with spray rings or
nozzles and are washed down internally at regular intervals. Drainage is
provided to a trough attached to the back of the hood table (Fig. 10.10).
See Kravath, F. F. (1940).

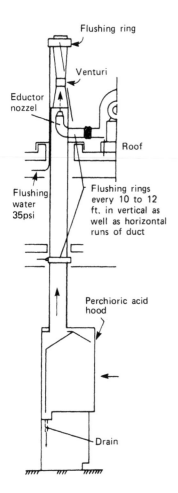

FIG. 10.10. Induction venturi system
with water-wash capability permits
safe handling of perchloric acid fumes.
Spray ring prevents buildup of explosive
crystals. (From Research/Develop-
ment, September 1972.)

The induction venturi system operates in the following manner. A high-velocity air jet inside the specially designed venturi induces a flow of gas into the venturi inlet. This induced flow exhausts the hood without letting any gas pass through the fan. The venturi is made usually of 316L stainless steel; the blower is made of mild steel. When used to exhaust 1200 cfm against 1/2 in. w.g., such a system requires a 500 cfm primary flow to clean air and 3/4 hp fan motor.

Other perchloric acid systems use PVC fans but wash the gas upstream of the fan. Each hood should be provided with its own exhaust system; no combinations should be manifolded. Organic compounds must be avoided in the construction of the system as well as for testing inside the hood.

Multihood Single-Fan System

Should each hood have its own fan, or should several hoods be serviced by a common fan? The latter system may suffice if the facility handles similar and compatible chemical reagents. In a chemical research facility, where the nature of reagents to be used cannot be predicted in advance, the safest procedure is to use separate and individual exhaust fans and ducts.

General Treatment

Exhaust stacks should be vertical, straight, and discharge up; no weather caps should be used. To prevent excessive indraft velocities on conventional hoods when open-face velocities exceed 125 fpm, R. S. Brief (1963) suggests that an atmospheric damper be installed downstream of the hood just before the exhauster. At high face velocities laboratory equipment placed within the hood should be set so that the points of release of the contaminant are at least 6 in. in back of the hood face. This can be ensured by placing a 1/4-in.-thick 6-in.-wide edging on the bench top near the hood entrance face. R. S. Brief (1963) found that concentrated heat loads within the hood proper, exceeding 1000 Watts/ft of hood width create thermal vectors that require higher face velocities for control. Any obstruction of hood face by large objects is discouraged; blockage causes control problems in the hood.

Getting Peak Performance

Here are eight suggestions to follow when selecting and installing a laboratory fume exhaust system. These guidelines, when combined with the various criteria discussed in this chapter, will help you determine the most efficient and economical design for your specific application.

1. Choose a hood dry-bulb operating temperature and relative humidity in the upper range of the comfort zone. Since relative humidity is critical to operating costs, place major emphasis on this aspect.

2. Select a hood face velocity sufficiently high to control the fume hazard, using the recommendations outlined by R. S. Brief (1963). Review hood operation carefully since not all hoods require the same face velocities.
3. In cooperation with laboratory management, determine the minimum number of hoods that require continuous operation. If a hood (or hoods) can operate intermittently, determine if its exhaust flow can be disregarded insofar as its effect on air conditioning load is concerned.
4. Avoid using hoods to store material or merely to provide local exhaust.
5. Determine the acceptability of using face screens, shields, or horizontal sliding panels.
6. Locate hoods away from doorways and frequently traveled aisles.
7. Determine if management is willing to accept a "slip" in room conditions if more air must be exhausted than was originally planned.
8. Consider the use of a perforated-ceiling spot-cooling arrangement with conditioned air supplied through the ceiling-mounted diffusers.

Laboratory Safety Guidelines

Safety rules should be followed at all times. A shortcut may save you a few minutes, but it could cost you your life. And so here are a few guidelines that may make your laboratory safer.

1. Hoods   Equipment in use should be completely enclosed in a hood with adequate room allowed for experimental procedures. When the apparatus is too large to be housed in a hood and there is no possibility of toxic or flammable materials being released, anchored shields of safety or wired glass should surround the equipment. Hoods are not designed to be used as storage areas; remove unused equipment and chemicals and store them in their proper places.

2. Emergency Equipment and Procedures   Well-equipped chemical laboratories have eyewash fountains, deluge safety showers, fire blankets, fire extinguishers, and emergency exits. This equipment should be tested periodically. In addition, being familiar with the locations and uses of the equipment may save needed time during an emergency.

3. Personal Protection   Rubber aprons, asbestos gloves, safety glasses, full face shields, and approved respirators must be available to protect personnel from spills, burns, spattering chemicals, flying fragments, and irritating fumes. In addition, the laminated safety glass doors on chemical fume hoods protect personnel from mishaps in the hood.

4. Health Monitoring   When biological agents or carcinogens are used in the laboratory, special medical control programs are necessary to monitor the workers' health. If radioactive materials or radiation-producing equipment such as an X-ray defraction unit are used, dosimeters or film badges should be worn to monitor exposures.

5. Labeling Chemicals must be prominently and accurately labeled. When a small quantity of material is removed from a large storage container, immediately label the smaller container. Containers for hazardous chemicals should have precautions such as "poison" or "flammable" indicated directly below the label. After having completed working with a particular material, return the container to storage or dispose of the material. Nothing should be left in open containers. Equipment should be labeled Underwriter's Laboratory (UL) or Canadian Standards Association (CSA) listed and meet all federal and local codes.

6. Eating, Drinking, and Smoking Food, beverages, cigarettes, pipes, and cigars should not be permitted in the chemical laboratory under any circumstances. Chemical glassware should never be used to hold food. Always wash hands well before eating, drinking, or smoking.

7. Pipetting Never pipette toxic, corrosive, or radioactive chemicals by mouth; always use a rubber bulb or syringe.

8. Glassware Cracked or chipped glassware should be discarded to prevent cuts or scratches which can cause further complications if chemicals contact the injury. Always place a towel or cloth over glass tubing being cut or broken, and fire polish sharp ends. When inserting a rod or piece of glass tubing through a perforated stopper, wrap a towel around your hand for protection.

9. Waste Disposal Disposal of hazardous waste materials requires special handling:

Place all broken glass in specially marked metal containers, never in waste baskets or containers used for paper or rags.
Flush dilute acids and alkalies down the drain with large quantities of water.
Never pour flammable liquids not miscible with water, compounds that give off toxic vapors, or corrosive materials down the drain. Special disposal containers are needed for each of these wastes.

10. Storage An efficiently placed storage room is essential for everyone's safety. Chemical storage rooms should be equipped with fire doors, safety lights, fire extinguishers, as well as good ventilation and sprinkler systems. Remember to carefully group liquid reagents to prevent hazardous combinations which may produce fumes, fire, or explosion. Remember to segregate incompatible materials. Remember to keep volatile liquids away from ignition sources such as heat, flames, or electric sparks. Remember to store all solvents in safety cans. Remember to store and frequently vent drummed chemicals according to the supplier's instructions. Remember to secure compressed gas cylinders. Remember to replace valve caps when not in use. Smaller laboratories that don't have separate storage rooms should have noncombustible storage cabinets. Large quantities of flammable solvents should be placed outside in ventilated, noncombustible buildings.

11. Housekeeping Good housekeeping is essential for safe laboratory operation. All passages, exits, safety showers, fire extinguishers, electrical controls, and stairways must be kept clear of equipment and obstructions. Remove unused equipment or chemicals from work spaces. Clean up spilled chemicals immediately to prevent dangerous chemical combinations, burns, or spills and falls.

10.8. MAINTENANCE AND TESTING

Maintenance

Since the hood performance may be affected by the cleanliness of the exhaust system and the direction of rotation of the exhaust fan, it is important to provide a maintenance schedule of inspections and performance testing through the year to make certain that the fume hoods are operating safely and efficiently.

If filters are used to remove dust and other particulates from the exhaust air, they must be periodically inspected and replaced if necessary. Corrosion of ductwork and damper mechanisms should be watched and debris should be removed from inside the ducts, especially at startup time. Excessive corrosion of ducts may cause the leakage of air into the system or the failure of balancing dampers that will affect capture velocities well below their design figures. Remember to check fan rotation since this is the most often cause of poor exhaust performance. See Cutter, T. J. (1976) and Tuve, G. L., et al. (1939).

Performance Testing

Two performance tests should be conducted periodically on all hoods: One for fume leakage and the other for face velocity. The test for fume leakage consists of releasing odorous fumes such as ammonia or hydrogen sulfide within the hood. If fumes are detected outside the hood, especially around the face opening, the capture velocity at the sash opening may be inadequate, or there may be an interfering air disturbance. Cleaning the exhaust system, adjusting the air flow damper, or increasing the fan speed may improve the performance if low face velocity seems to be the problem. If, on the other hand, the leakage seems to be caused by interference from an auxiliary air supply stream or other air velocity near the sash, the nature of the interference may be investigated as follows. Placing liquid titanium tetrachloride on masking tape around the periphery of the sash opening and on lengths of string strung in a grid pattern across the entire sash opening. Observations can then be made of the path of visible fumes to determine where there is spillage into the room. Smoke bombs have also been used to determine the flow patterns at sash openings and to identify interference.

A hot wire anenometer is usually used to measure actual face velocity. This is done as a traverse over the entire sash opening, including especially all edges and corners. The overall average face velocity is obtained by averaging the velocity readings at prescribed positions of the traverse.

These testing procedures are difficult to standardize and are dependent on subjective observations. Thus, they are considered to be unadaptable and inadequate. The American Society of Heating, Refrigeration, and Air Conditioning Engineers (ASHRAE) has set up a research project for developing fume hood performance criteria and new test procedures for such laboratory equipment.

10.9. SAFETY FEATURES

Interconnection of Hoods

If two or more hoods independently serve a single room or an interconnecting suite of rooms, all of the hoods in these rooms should be electrically interconnected so that the operation of one will require the operation of all. If this is not done, there is a strong possibility that fumes will be drawn from a hood that is not in operation to makeup air demands of those not in operation.

Alarm for Hood Malfunction

All hoods should be equipped with safety devices such as a sail switch to warn personnel that the air volume exhausted from the hood has dropped to a point where it will not provide sufficient capture velocity for safe operation.

Fire Dampers

Most building codes require fire dampers in all ducts that pass through fire walls or floors. However, it is important not to install them in fume exhaust systems. Should a fire occur in a hood, or if heat from a fire near such a damper should cause the damper to close, the fume backup into the facility would prove disastrous.

Exhaust from Laboratories

A laboratory should exhaust 100% of the air fed to it. If the materials that are being handled or tested in the laboratory are hazardous enough to need a hood, the presence of these materials in itself should dictate 100% exhaust. An accidental spill or accidental release of materials at a bench or hood can result in recirculation throughout the entire building. Accidental recirculation is a serious hazard and should be guarded against.

10.10. MATERIALS OF CONSTRUCTION

General

Although basic fume hood design has changed very little, many advances
have been made in the materials from which hoods are constructed. Here
are some of the basic materials and their distinctive features.

Materials

Wood

> Generally poor chemical resistance.
> Inexpensive to fabricate and modify in the field.
> Can present a fire hazard in applications involving heat and flame.
> Poor light reflectivity causes a dark interior.

Sheet Metal (cold rolled steel or aluminum)

> Requires secondary treatment for chemical resistance.
> Demands extreme care to avoid damaging the coating since corrosion
> can occur in damaged areas.
> "Oil-canning" due to light gauge metal causes noise in operation.
> Relatively inexpensive.
> Usually heavy and cumbersome to install.

Fiberglass

> Excellent chemical resistance.
> Lightweight for ease of installation or relocation.
> Easily modified in the field with readily available tools.
> Sound-dampening because of physical construction.
> Some inexpensive grades can cause fire hazards and are not chemically
> resistant.
> Available with good light reflective properties for a light and bright
> work space.
> Shapes are limited to tooled mold configurations, but can be molded
> with covered interiors.

Cement/Asbestos (Transite)

> Excellent chemical resistance.
> Has inherent sound dampening quality.
> Excellent fire resistance.
> Heavy and difficult to install.
> Extremely brittle, requiring care in handling to avoid breakage.
> Poor light reflectivity.
> Stains badly when exposed to many acids, etc.
> Easily modified in the field with only minor tooling difficulties.
> Inexpensive.

Stainless Steel

   Better general chemical resistance than cold rolled steel.
   Not well suited to many acid applications.
   Generally provided in type 316 for specific applications to which it is
      well suited, such as perchloric acid.
   Heavy.
   Expensive.
   Difficult to modify in the field.
   Excellent fire resistance.

Polyvinyl Chloride

   Excellent chemical resistance except for some solvents.
   Good fire-retardant properties.
   Particularly well suited to acid digestion applications using such acids
      as sulfuric or hydrofluoric acid.
   Easily modified in the field.
   Generally not available in molded configurations.
   Expensive.
   Distorts when exposed to intense direct heat.

Stone

   Excellent chemical resistance.
   Excellent fire resistance.
   Difficult and extremely heavy to install.
   Extremely difficult to modify in the field.
   Expensive.

Basic Performance Criteria

The following may be used as a general guide for the selection of hood blower systems that will provide optimum average face velocities for various
exhaust materials. This compares with our earlier discussion on the same
subject. Tables listing the TLVs of various chemical compounds are
readily available from the American Conference of Governmental Industrial
Hygienists (ACGIH).

Condition	Hood face velocity
Very low toxic level materials; noxious odors; nuisance dusts, and fumes	80 fpm
General lab use; corrosive materials; moderate toxicity level materials (TLV of 10-1000 ppm); tracer quantities of radioisotopes	100 fpm

Condition	Hood face velocity
Higher toxic level materials (TLV less than 10 ppm)	125-150 fpm
Pathogenic microorganisms; high alpha or beta emitters; very high toxicity level materials (TLV less than 0.01 ppm)	An enclosed glove box should be used

Special Purpose Fume Hoods

Perchloric acid fume hoods   Due to the potential explosion hazard of perchloric acid in contact with organic materials, this type of hood must be used for perchloric acid digestion. It must be constructed of relatively inert materials such as type 316 stainless steel, Alberene stone, or ceramic-coated material. Wash-down features are desirable since the hood and duct system must be thoroughly rinsed after each use to prevent the accumulation of explosive residue. Air flow monitoring systems are recommended to assure 150 fpm open face velocity operation. An additional monitoring system for the wash-down facilities are also recommended.

Radiological fume hoods   Hoods used for radioactive applications should have integral bottoms and covered interiors to facilitate decontamination. These units should also be strong enough to support lead shielding bricks in case they are required. They should be constructed to facilitate the use of HEPA filters.

Canopy fume hoods   Canopy hoods are a type of local exhauster which normally has limited application in a laboratory. Their main disadvantage is the large amount of air required to provide an effective capture velocity. Since the contaminant is drawn past the operator's breathing zone, toxic materials can be quite dangerous. A canopy hood can, however, provide a local exhaust for heat or steam.

Integral motor-blower   Many hoods are available with motors and blowers built directly into the hood superstructure. From the standpoint of convenience, the hood is relatively portable and can be installed easily. A built-in motor-blower should not be used for highly toxic applications since it causes a positive pressure in the exhaust duct system, and any leaks in the duct could spill the effluent into the lab area. There may be more noise associated with this type of hood since the motor-blower is closer to the operator.

Glossary of Terms Related to Fume Hood Selection

Baffle: an air director mounted off the hood's inner surface which causes air to move in specific patterns.

Blower: an air-moving device utilizing a rotating impeller within a housing to exhaust air.

Capture velocity: air velocity at the hood opening necessary to overcome opposing air currents and cause contaminants to flow into the hood.

Duct: a pipe system used to convey and constrain a moving air stream.

Ejector: an air-moving system which consists of a high-pressure air source passing through a Venturi nozzle, creating a suction at the nozzle entry.

Face velocity: the speed of air measured in feet per minute (fpm) across the fume hood sash opening perpendicular to the sash.

HEPA filter: a high-efficiency particulate air filter rated 99.97% effective on particles 0.3 μm in size or larger.

Inches of water: a unit of pressure equal to the pressure exerted by a column of water one inch high at standard temperature, and abbreviated w.g.

Manometer: an instrument for measuring pressure. It is essentially a U-tube filled with a liquid, normally water and mercury.

Negative pressure: pressure within a system below that of atmospheric pressure, causing an inward flow of air.

Plenum: an air compartment maintained under pressure which serves as a reservoir for a distribution duct.

Positive pressure: pressure within a system above that of atmospheric pressure, causing an outward flow of air.

Scrubber: a device used to wash effluent air streams to remove contaminants.

Static pressure: the pressure exerted in all directions when air moves through a duct stream creating a resistance to air flow; measured in inches of water.

TLV (threshold limit valve): the amount of airborne toxic materials that represents the maximum concentration to which an average person may be exposed for 8 hr a day with no adverse effects [usually expressed in parts per million (ppm)]. Formerly this expression was known as MAC, or the maximum allowable concentration.

Transport velocity: the minimum air velocity required to move particulates in the air stream.

11

MOISTURE CONTROL IN PROCESS BUILDINGS

11.1. INTRODUCTION

Evaporating water in a building raises the dewpoint and, during cold weather, results in condensation on the inside surfaces of walls and roofs. This
problem may be solved by providing ventilation air, by adding insulation
to the cold walls and roofs, or by doing both. However, merely adding insulation will not solve the overall problem since, if moisture is still generated in the building, it can penetrate the insulation material and condense
within the layers of insulation, causing structural corrosion and rot of
wooden members.

Ventilation, whether by mechanical means or natural, is required in
buildings for a number of reasons in addition to controlling moisture buildup. The need may be to prevent carbon dioxide buildup, to eliminate or
dilute odors, to dilute toxic or volatile gases, or in many cases, to maintain reasonable temperature levels for human comfort during warm weather.

Recently, there has been an emphasis on improving building insulation
as a way of saving energy, and money. Plant engineers have increased
wall and roof insulation, installed storm sash, and put up weather stripping
and window and door caulking. But such treatment can be too good. When
a building is made too airtight, chances are that moisture can build up un-
noticed within walls and roof spaces, causing structural members to rust
and rot and even, in some cases, to collapse.

In this chapter moisture control will be discussed, and problems will
be analytically solved. Also, recommendations will be made to alleviate
the problem.

11.2. GENERAL

Surface Condensation

It is frequently necessary to check by calculation the maximum relative
humidity that may be maintained within a building during severe winter
weather without causing condensation on interior surfaces. A second part
of the problem which is seldom considered is the possibility of moisture
penetrating the walls and ceiling and causing damage to the structure itself.
Paradoxically, treatment to prevent condensation on the inner surface
(usually by the application of insulation) may actually increase the possibility of trouble from condensation within the walls. Surface condensation is due to insufficient thermal resistance, whereas interior condensation is due to too much thermal resistance without provision for preventing
water vapor penetration.

Causes of Condensation

Condensation is formed on the inside surfaces of buildings when the thermal
resistance (reciprocal of transmittance) of the structure is so low that the

inside surface is chilled to a point below the dew point temperature of the room. The condensation point for perfectly smooth surfaces is undoubtedly lower than for decorative plasters with high peaks and low valleys because of the pocketing of air in the valleys.

Condensation is formed within walls, roof, etc., when the thermal resistance is high enough to keep the inside surface temperature above the room dew point but the wall structure is porous and thus pervious to water vapor. The difference in vapor pressure between interior and exterior building surfaces will force a penetration of water vapor into the interior structure. If the interior temperature is below the dew point of this moisture-laden air, condensation will occur within the material. If the interior temperature (within the wall structure) is below freezing, serious damage may result.

Correcting the Condition

Condensation on inside surfaces is objectionable because it will cause staining of the surfaces, dripping on machinery and furnishings, and damage to materials in process of manufacture. Before condensation occurs, with relative humidities 80% and above, there is danger of propagation of mold spores, particularly in industrial work involving food products. The condition may be corrected by one of the following methods:

1. Control the room dew point to keep it lower than the inner surface temperature of the surface on which condensation must be avoided.
2. Increase the thermal resistance of the walls or roof by increasing the thickness or insulation value. The thermal resistance of glass may be increased by installing two or three panes with air space(s) between. In extreme cases, electric or other heat, under control, may be applied between the glass of double-glazed windows.
3. Surface resistance can be decreased by increasing the velocity of air passing over the surface. This method is commonly used by store merchants to prevent frost or condensation on show windows and is normally done by placing electric fans in windows or by directing air supply streams at the window.

Condensation Within Walls

Condensation within walls, though not always visible, may cause even greater damage: wood may rot, iron may rust, or brick work may chip or crack, especially if the moisture freezes. This is an indication that the life of the building may be seriously shortened.

The only way known to correct for condensation within walls is to make the inner surface of the structure impervious to water vapor. Insulation, which is not resistant to water vapor, will aggravate the condition because the moisture will condense between the insulation and the other building materials. This is particularly true in frame construction where the insulation is placed between the studding.

In connections with ceilings installed for acoustical effectiveness (and, to a lesser extent, for ordinary plaster furring), it is customary to leave a dead air space of 1/2 in. or more between the acoustic material and the ceiling proper. Due to the porosity and insulating value of air, and the hygroscopicity of some acoustic materials, the dew point in the dead air space is practically the same as in the room, while the dry bulb may be much lower than room temperature. And so we see that the relative humidity in the furred space is much higher than in the room, and there is a danger in extreme cases of condensation or the growth of mold. When perforated ceilings are used for air distribution, saturated or near saturated air is supplied to the furred space.

The following vapor resistant materials are recommended:

1. Sheathing paper impregnated, and the glossy surface coated, with 35-50 lb of asphalt per 500 ft^2 roll.
2. Laminated sheathing paper made of two or three sheets of kraft paper cemented together with asphalt.
3. Double-faced reflective insulation mounted on paper.
4. A thick layer of asphalt paint.
5. Two coats of aluminum paint which offer some resistance to moisture penetration; ordinary paints are not effective.

Any one of the above vapor barriers must be located on the side of higher vapor pressure in order that it prevents entrance of the water vapor. The higher vapor pressure side is the warmer side of the room.

11.3. DESIGN FOR PREVENTION OF AIR-MOISTURE CONDENSATION

Application of Graph

As we have seen, evaporating water in a building raises the dew point, and during cold weather results in condensation on the inside surfaces of walls and roofs. Estimating the amount of outside air needed to prevent this requires a knowledge of the inside surface temperatures and of the increase in dew point caused by the moisture release. Where high release rates of steam prevail (e.g., steam vats or open tanks), the outside air must be tempered in winter.

Given the overall heat-transfer coefficient U and the dry bulb temperatures indicated in Fig. 11.1, this graph may be used as shown in these examples:

EXAMPLE 11.1. Estimating the Inside Wall Surface Temperature ($T_{w,i}$) What is the $T_{w,i}$ value of a 6-in.-thick solid-concrete wall if the inside room temperature (T_i) is 70°F and the outside air temperature (T_o) is -20°F, with a 15 mph wind velocity?

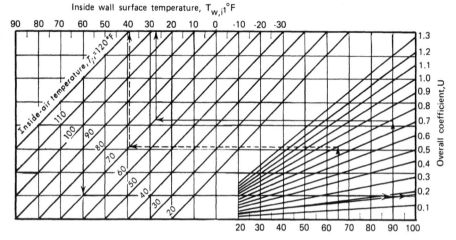

FIG. 11.1. Estimating inside wall surface temperature. (From Chemical Engineering, October 5, 1970.)

SOLUTION: We first calculate the overall heat resistance R, bearing in mind that the temperature drop through a wall is directly proportional to R, and that $U = 1/R$. If the inside surface coefficient for air at 15 mph standard velocity $= 6.0$, and the conductivity of the wall material $= 12.0$ Btuh/ft^2/°F/in. thickness), then the summation of resistances R is computed as follows:

$$R = \frac{1}{1.65} + \frac{1}{6.0} + \frac{1}{12.0} = 1.27$$

From which

$$(U) = \frac{1}{R} = \frac{1}{1.27} = 0.79 \text{ Btuh/ft}^2/°F$$

Once U is determined, Fig. 11.1 can be used to find $T_{w,i}$ under various conditions. For this example, a vertical line is drawn from 90°F $(T_i - T_o)$ scale to $U = 0.79$. From this point, a line is extended until it meets the 70°F T_i line, from which another line is drawn upward to the $T_{w,i}$ scale to read 27°F. The accuracy of the graph can be determined as follows:

$$\frac{T_i - T_{w,i}}{T_i - T_o} = \frac{1}{1.65} \times 1.27 = 0.477$$

$$T_i - T_{w,i} = 0.477[70 - (-20)] = 43$$

Therefore, $T_{w,i} = 70 - 43 = 27°F$.

EXAMPLE 11.2. Estimating the Insulation Thickness   For the
same wall, what insulation thickness (conductivity 0.30) would be
required to raise the temperature of the inside surface from 27
to 60°F?

SOLUTION: Since $T_i - T_{w,i} = 10$ and $T_i - T_o = 80$, the heat resistance from the inside wall surface to the outside air must be
80/10, or eight times that from the inside air to the inside wall
surface, or 8(1/1.65) = 4.85. Therefore, the resistance of the
added material is

$$4.85 - \frac{6}{12} + \frac{1}{6} = 4.19$$

and the thickness of the insulation is 4.19 X 0.30 = 1.25 in. The
new U = 1/(1.27 + 4.19) = 0.183.

This new value of U can be found in Fig. 11.1 by drawing a
line downward from 60°F on the $T_{w,i}$ scale to the T_i value of
70°F, and then projecting a horizontal line on the $T_i - T_o$ scale.
From here, draw a slanted line to the U scale to read 0.18.

EXAMPLE 11.3. Estimating the Dew Point of Mixed Air and
Water Vapor   The use of Fig. 11.2 is demonstrated by this other
example. If 42 lb/hr of water vapor are liberated into a space
being maintained at 65°F, and 290,000 cfh of saturated outside air
at 20°F is mixed with the vapor, what is the resulting dew point?

SOLUTION: To solve, enter Fig. 11.2 horizontally from the left
at 42 lb/hr water vapor; also enter the graph vertically at
290,000 cfh and establish the point of intersection of the two lines.
Now draw a line through this point from the vertex of the graph.
The point B at which this radial line passes through the incoming
air temperature line of 20°F is the dew point, which as shown on
the graph is 32°F. The accuracy of the graph (Fig. 11.2) may be
determined mathematically. Essentially, a room at 65°F is being fed 290,000 cfh of saturated air, plus 42 lb/hr of water vapor.
The moisture content of the 20°F saturated air is 14.9 grains/lb
(from a psychrometric chart); its density may be taken as
0.075 lb/cf. Thus, the weight of the air involved is 290,000 X
0.075 = 21,700 lb/hr.

Since water evaporation is 42 X 7000 = 294,000 grains/hr,
after the mixing is completed 294,000/21,700 = 13.5 grains
water/lb air have been added. The final moisture after mixing is

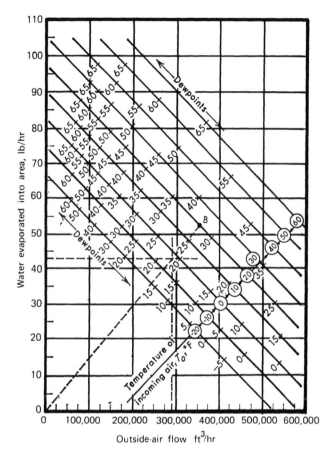

FIG. 11.2. Estimating dew point of mixed air and water vapor. (From Chemical Engineering, October 5, 1970.)

therefore 14.9 + 13.5 = 28.4 grains/lb. From the psychrometric chart, the equivalent dew point is 33°F, which compares favorably with 32°F determined from Fig. 11.2.

Adding Makeup Air

Spaces may require makeup air for satisfying exhaust needs, which is another facet of building condensation. Vapor generated may be high, and the outside air must be tempered to avoid fogging. Most spaces will be supplied with heating anyway.

EXAMPLE 11.4. In a tank room of a processing plant, the water
evaporation rate is 2820 lb/hr. The tank contents are at 200°F.
The outdoor temperature is 0°F; the indoor conditions are 90°F
and 50% relative humidity. Building transmission losses (heat
leak) are 960,000 Btuh, including internal sensible heat gain.
Determine the temperature of makeup air entering the room and
the amount of exhaust air required to balance conditions.

SOLUTION:

$$\text{Grains per minute} = 2820 \times \frac{7000}{60} = 3.29 \times 10^5$$

Room conditions give a dew point of 68.7. From the psychrometric
chart read 105.5 grains moisture per lb of bone dry air. The
outside air condition of 0°F gives a moisture content of 5.5 grains/
lb. The difference is the carrying capacity of the air, or 105.5 -
5.5 = 100 grains/lb of dry air.

The volume of air needed for moisture load pickup, assuming
ideal mixing, is $3.29 \times 10^5/100 = 3290$ lb per min. This is the
equivalent of 3290×14.2 ft^3/lb at room conditions, or 46,700 cfm.
Since the building heat leak amounts to 960,000 Btuh, the temperature difference becomes 960,000/46,700 × 1.08), which is about
20°F. With tempering, air should enter the room at 90 + 20 =
110°F. It is also recommended that the space be maintained at a
slight positive pressure, say 0.1 in. w.g. (inches of water).
Reasonable results can be achieved by exhausting 75% of the makeup air. Thus, the amount of exhaust air needed to balance conditions is $46,700 \times 0.75 = 35,000$ cfm.

Cost of Heating Makeup Air

The following equations may be used to predict makeup air heating costs on
an hourly or yearly basis. Since makeup-air-unit efficiency is included,
the resulting figures will be low if the air is permitted to enter by infiltration only—a most unlikely situation in real practice.

$$\text{Hourly cost} = \frac{0.001 \times \text{cfm} \times \text{Btuh per 1000 cfm}}{\text{gross heating value of fuel} \times \text{efficiency}} \times \text{fuel cost}$$

$$\text{Yearly cost} = \frac{0.154 \times \text{cfm} \times \text{operating time, hr per week} \times \text{degree days}}{\text{gross heating value of fuel} \times \text{efficiency}} \times \text{fuel cost}$$

EXAMPLE. 11.5 What is the hourly cost of tempering 20,000
cfm of makeup air to 70°F in St. Louis, Missouri, with oil at
$1.00 a gallon? The average temperature is 35°F.

SOLUTION:

$$\text{Hourly cost} = \frac{0.001 \times 20,000 \times 38,000}{106,500} \times 1.00 = \$7.13$$

EXAMPLE 11.6. What is the annual cost for the same city? The number of annual degree days is 6023 and the operating time can be assumed at 40 hr/week.

SOLUTION:

$$\text{Yearly cost} = \frac{0.154 \times 20,000 \times 40 \times 6023}{106,500} \times 1.00 = \$6950$$

The solution using the annual presentation is more representative of true cost because both the length and severity of the winter season are taken into account. Degree days may be obtained from the American Society of Heating, Refrigeration, and Air Conditioning Engineers (ASHRAE) Handbook & Product Directory— Systems, Chapter 43.

Moisture from Combustion

When direct-fired makeup air heaters are used for the combustion of either natural gas or commercial propane gas, it is helpful to know that the products of combustion released directly into the space carry along moisture from combustion. Natural gas will yield 0.1 lb water vapor for every 1000 Btu fired; commercial propane will yield 0.078 lb/1000 Btu fired. With these figures, it is a simple procedure to determine the resulting dew point from data generated and inserted in Fig. 11.2.

11.4. MOISTURE INFILTRATION THROUGH BUILDING CONSTRUCTION

Moisture Load

The infiltration that will be dealt with here is the transfer of moisture through the building construction itself from the side of high-moisture to that of low-moisture concentration in the air adjacent to it. This is independent of the commonly accepted infiltration of air into the space, bringing with it both sensible and latent heat.

The moisture infiltration under consideration is that which takes place through building construction exposed to air on both sides. Cases where there is water or water-soaked soil on one side of the wall and air on the other will not be discussed since such a condition must be corrected to prevent free moisture from penetrating the wall structure. We refer to cases where water soaks through the wall and not to condensation on cold walls due to high humidities inside the space.

Information Available

It has been generally assumed that the infiltration is in direct proportion to
the difference in vapor pressure in the air on the two sides of the wall, the
flow of moisture being from the side of high vapor pressure to that of low
vapor pressure. Recent studies have shown that vapor differences are not
the only driving force. There is a second force, a capillary effect, which
may have considerable influence in the case of some materials. Despite
the meagerness of data and methods for accurate calculation, it is now
agreed that moisture infiltration is an almost universal phenomenon and
that there is no way in which it can be positively prevented, should it be
desired to do so, except to adopt a wall construction, or lining, which is
definitely gas tight (such as sheet metal with soldered joints) and which is
impervious to absorption of moisture.

Calculation of Moisture Infiltration

It is possible to estimate moisture infiltration by methods described below.
These will serve in fixing the approximate total moisture load. These determinations should not be considered exact, and where the moisture infiltration is an appreciable part of the total moisture load, estimates should
be liberal to avoid difficulties later. See Carrier (1965) and Carroll, B. T.
(1976).

Table 11.1 lists a number of moisture infiltration coefficients for a
number of building materials. These may be used for estimating purposes.
The coefficients tabulated are for "grains moisture per square foot of surface per hour per pound per square inch of vapor pressure difference."
The total transmission is taken to be proportional to the vapor pressure
difference the same as the heat transfer is proportional to the difference
in temperature for sensible heat transmission. The vapor pressures in the
air adjacent to the two sides of the wall are those corresponding to the air
dew points as found from the psychrometric chart.

The overall transmission value of a composite wall, or for materials
of different thicknesses from those tabulated, is determined exactly as with
sensible heat transfer and as illustrated in the example below.

EXAMPLE 11.7. A wall is made up of (1) plaster base and plaster,
(2) air space, (3) 3/4 in. wood sheating, (4) building paper, and
(5) painted siding. Outside air conditions are 95°F dry bulb and
75°F wet bulb and inside air conditions 80°F dry bulb and 50% relative humidity (RH). What is the overall coefficient of vapor
transmission U_V for the wall and total vapor transmission per
square foot of wall?

SOLUTION: The individual coefficients are as follows:

Plaster base and plaster   30.0
Air space; has no effect   0.0

TABLE 11.1. Vapor Transmission Coefficients

Material	Coefficient
3/4 in. plaster board and plaster	30.0
3/4 in. fir sheating	6.0
Waterproof paper (ordinary building paper)	100.0
Pine lap siding	10.0
Paint film	7.0
3/4 in. Celotex	25.5
4 in. brick masonry	2.2
Bright-foil-surfaced reflective insulation, double faced	0.17-0.26
Roll roofing	0.27-0.35
Duplex or laminated waterproof Kraft paper (30-30-30)	2.80-5.3
Plaster on wood lath	2.3
Plaster with three coats lead and oil	7.7
Plaster with two coats aluminum paint	2.4
Plaster on fiberboard or gypsum lath	4.2
1/2 in. five-ply fir wood	5.7-6.8
Insulating lath and sheating, board type	53-70
Insulating sheating, surface-coated 3/16 in. compressed fiber board	10.4
1 in. insulating cork blocks	12.6
4 in. mineral wood	60

Note: Coefficient is given in grains per square foot per hour per pound per square in. water vapor pressure difference.

Wood sheathing	6.0
Building paper	100.0
Siding	10.0
Paint film	7.0

The overall coefficient is

$$U_v = \frac{1}{1/30 + 1/6 + 1/100 + 1/10 + 1/7} = 2.19$$

The vapor pressure inside and outside are determined as follows:

    95°F dry bulb and 75°F wet bulb = 0.67 in.Hg
    80°F dry bulb and 50% RH = 0.52 in.Hg
    Difference = 0.67 - 0.52 = 0.15 in.Hg
    Difference in pounds per square inch = 0.15 X 0.492
        = 0.0735

The total transmission per square foot per hour is

$$2.19 \ X \ 0.0735 \ = \ 0.161 \ grains/ft^2/hr$$

Note: For a more complete treatment of vapor transmission
through building materials see the Carrier "Handbook of Air Conditioning System Design" (1965).

11.5. STOPPING CONDENSATION UNDERGROUND

General

In unconditioned spaces below grade, moist outside air can lead to condensation on room and equipment surfaces. Here is a method for quickly determining the atmospheric relative humidities that contribute to condensation
in unventilated and unconditioned spaces where a close control of humidity
is not required. Spaces that fit into this category are sewage lift stations,
underground cable rooms, pipe tunnels, and similar structures that operators, service personnel, or inspectors occasionally visit. Underground
spaces occupied by people over relatively long periods of time are not
candidates for this method, because environmental conditions in them differ markedly.

Cause of Dampness

Excessive dampness in unconditioned underground spaces is caused by the
condensation of water vapor in the air entering a space by infiltration
through structural openings and cracks. When the relative humidity of outside air is high, moist air coming in contact with cold walls, structural
steel, uninsulated cold-water piping, electrical controls, switch gear, and
idle motor windings in underground spaces will condense on these surfaces
and result in corrosion and possible short circuiting.

Where Method Applies

At a level of 6 ft below ground, a constant temperature of approximately
50°F prevails, regardless of atmospheric temperature. At lower levels,
ground temperature increases as depth increases; in such underground

TABLE 11.2. Relating Key Temperatures (°F)

Outside air	-30	-20	-10	0	+10	+20
Ground	+40	+45	+50	+55	+60	+65

Source: Power, February 1975.

spaces, forced ventilation and dehumidification measures must be used, and the method proposed here is not valid.

From the 6-ft level upward, however, ground temperatures for estimating purposes vary in accordance with the outside design temperatures in Table 11.2. Use of Fig. 11.3, together with local weather bureau data and ground temperatures, provides a useful tool for estimating condensation

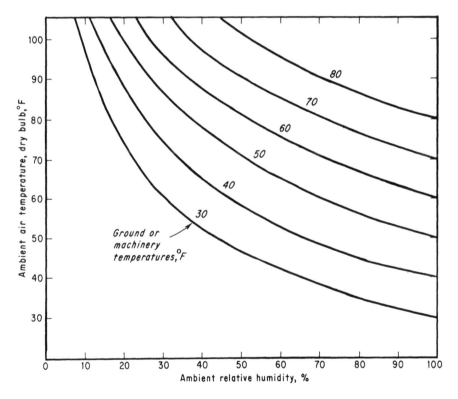

FIGURE 11.3. Estimating condensation below ground. (From Power, February 1975.)

rates in spaces 6 ft or less below ground. If air-temperature and relative-humidity coordinates in Fig. 11.3 intersect <u>above</u> the ground temperature curve, condensation will take place, and some means of dehumidification is recommended.

Preventing Condensation

Knowing that condensation will take place is only a small part of the problem—just the beginning step. We must also be able to estimate the amount of water vapor that must be removed from the space atmosphere to <u>prevent</u> condensation. When forced ventilation is not used, the dehumidification load may be calculated on the basis of one air change per hour. This rate is adequate, based on the assumption that no humidification load is added to the space other than outside infiltration air.

To find the dehumidification load, first estimate the gross space volume (wall-to-wall and floor-to-ceiling), then apply the following formula:

$$C = \frac{(v)(n)(m_1 - m_2)}{7000} \tag{11.1}$$

where C = pounds of condensate per hour, v = gross space volume (cf), n = number of air changes per hour, and $m_1 - m_2$ = moisture content of the air (grains/cf) before and after dehumidification. The value of grains of moisture may be obtained from Table 11.3 (7000 grains = 1 lb). Interpolation may be applied if necessary.

Providing Dry Air

Three approaches to providing dry air are suggested for the underground spaces in question:

    Small package units recirculating room air
    Small package units with once-through outside air connections
    Larger units, with duct connections from the outside and distribution
        systems

The last two methods pressurize the space slightly, but relief is obtained through an open vent to the outdoors. These methods are preferred.

Packaged dehumidifiers are available with hermetically sealed R-12 or R-22 refrigeration-type compressors, expansion coils, fan, and condenser coil all in one unit. The moisture removal capability of the machines varies with the temperature and relative humidity within the space to be dehumidified.

Units are usually sized on the basis of capacity for moisture removal; from 10 to 25 pints daily are common for the portable or smaller sizes. Control of humidity is adjustable; equipment is provided with low atmospheric-temperature cutouts. Condensate drip, which is collected, may be piped to a sump, and from there pumped up to ground level.

Larger and more elaborate units for use in multispace complexes with distribution ductwork range from 500 to 12,000 cfm (dry air). Where low space temperatures cannot be tolerated, reheat coils must be added.

When applying Fig. 11.3 to machinery-storage problems, ground temperature is equivalent to machinery surface temperature. Or, for graph use generally, any solid surface that might experience condensation replaces ground temperature in the calculations. Let's run through some examples.

EXAMPLE 11.8. Critical Relative Humidity In an underground space, dry bulb temperature is 70°F. If the ground temperature is 50°F, what is the critical relative humidity?

SOLUTION: Enter Fig. 11.3 at the left along the 70°F line and proceed horizontally to the point where it intersects the 50°F ground temperature line. Read vertically down to 50% relative humidity. This is the critical or equilibrium point above which air within a space must be dehumidified. Thus, if the space were at 70°F dry bulb and 60% relative humidity, it would need dehumidification.

EXAMPLE 11.9. Dehumidification An underground space 15 ft wide, 20 ft long, and 10 ft high has a surface temperature of 55°F. Outside air conditions are 70°F dry bulb temperature and 60% relative humidity. Will condensation take place? If so, what will the dehumidification load if one air change per hour is assumed?

SOLUTION: First, let's check for condensation. From Fig. 11.3, 70°F dry bulb temperature and 60% relative humidity intersect at a ground temperature of 55°F. Therefore, condensation will take place. To prevent it, space air must be dehumidified to a low dry bulb temperature of 50°F and a relative humidity of 30%. From Table 11.3 it can be seen that the moisture content is 4.788 and 1.223 grains/ft^3 before and after dehumidification, respectively. The dehumidifier load is (15 × 20 × 10)(4.788 − 1.223)/(7000) = 1.528 lb/hr. Since the weight of one pint of water is approximately 1 lb, the total requirement for dehumidifier capacity is 1.528 × 24 = 37 pints daily.

EXAMPLE 11.10. Maximum Relative Humidity Goods are to be moved from storage in a 42°F dry-bulb-temperature room to another room for more convenient handling. The latter space is to be maintained at 60°F. What relative humidity must be produced coincidentally to avoid corrosion and spoilage?

TABLE 11.3. Moisture Content of Air at Various Temperatures and Humidities (grains/ft^3)

Temperature[a] (°F)	Relative humidity (%)									
	10	20	30	40	50	60	70	80	90	100
-20	0.017	0.033	0.050	0.066	0.083	0.100	0.116	0.133	0.149	0.166
-15	0.022	0.044	0.065	0.087	0.109	0.131	0.153	0.174	0.196	0.218
-10	0.028	0.057	0.086	0.114	0.142	0.171	0.200	0.228	0.256	0.285
-5	0.037	0.074	0.111	0.148	0.185	0.222	0.259	0.296	0.333	0.370
0	0.048	0.096	0.144	0.192	0.240	0.289	0.337	0.385	0.433	0.481
5	0.061	0.122	0.183	0.244	0.305	0.366	0.427	0.488	0.549	0.610
10	0.078	0.155	0.233	0.310	0.388	0.466	0.543	0.621	0.698	0.776
15	0.099	0.197	0.296	0.394	0.493	0.592	0.690	0.789	0.887	0.986
20	0.124	0.247	0.370	0.494	0.618	0.741	0.864	0.988	1.112	1.235
25	0.155	0.310	0.465	0.620	0.776	0.931	1.086	1.241	1.396	1.551
30	0.194	0.387	0.580	0.774	0.968	1.161	1.354	1.548	1.742	1.935
35	0.237	0.473	0.710	0.946	1.183	1.420	1.656	1.893	2.129	2.366
40	0.285	0.570	0.855	1.140	1.424	1.709	1.994	2.279	2.564	2.849

45	0.341	0.683	1.024	1.366	1.707	2.048	2.390	2.731	3.073	3.414
50	0.408	0.815	1.223	1.630	2.038	2.446	2.853	3.261	3.668	4.076
55	0.485	0.970	1.455	1.940	2.424	2.909	3.394	3.879	4.364	4.849
60	0.554	1.149	1.724	2.298	2.872	3.447	4.022	4.596	5.170	5.745
65	0.678	1.356	2.035	2.713	3.391	4.069	4.747	5.426	6.104	6.782
70	0.798	1.596	2.394	3.192	3.990	4.788	5.586	6.384	7.182	7.980
75	0.936	1.871	2.807	3.742	4.678	5.614	6.549	7.485	8.420	9.356
80	1.093	2.187	3.280	4.374	5.467	6.560	7.654	8.747	9.841	10.934
85	1.274	2.547	3.821	5.094	6.368	7.642	8.915	10.189	11.462	12.736
90	1.479	2.958	4.437	5.916	7.395	8.874	10.353	11.832	13.311	14.490
95	1.712	3.425	5.137	6.850	8.562	10.274	11.987	13.699	15.412	17.124
100	1.977	3.953	5.930	7.906	9.883	11.860	13.836	15.813	17.789	19.766
105	2.275	4.550	6.825	9.100	11.375	13.650	15.925	18.200	20.475	22.750
110	2.611	5.222	7.834	10.445	13.056	15.667	18.278	20.890	23.501	26.112

[a]Dry-bulb temperature.

Source: Power, February 1975.

SOLUTION: Assume that the temperature of the goods is at ground temperature, or 42°F. From Fig. 11.3, at 60°F a maximum relative humidity of 50% is required.

11.6. REMOVING MOISTURE FROM BUILDINGS

Exhaust Ventilation

Ventilation, whether by mechanical or natural means, is required in buildings for several reasons. The need may be to prevent CO_2 buildup, to eliminate odors, to dilute toxic or volatile gases, or more commonly to maintain reasonable temperature levels for human comfort during warm weather.

In parts of the country where winters are prolonged and outside temperatures reach 0°F or lower, condensation or moisture accumulation within walls and roof spaces has become a subject of considerable concern to plant engineers, home owners, and builders themselves.

Why is there so much more interest in this condition now than there used to be just a few years ago? The answer is relatively simple. During the last few years, there has been a marked tendency to improve buildings with the idea of decreasing operating costs and expenses. Prominent among these improvements is the increasing use of storm sash, insulation, weather stripping, caulking around windows and doors, and other means of decreasing heat losses and wind infiltration.

Effect of Higher Humidities

Because of the tighter construction, the normal humidity or vapor pressure is higher than in buildings less tightly constructed. In older buildings with higher infiltration rates, vapor pressure does not have a chance to build up. As a health and comfort measure, the normal humidity is usually deliberately augmented, by evaporating water in humidifiers. In industrial buildings open tanks and vats used in the processing of products cause a buildup of water vapor within the building.

Because of the present trend to higher indoor humidities and, therefore, high water-vapor pressure within doors, there is a constant outleakage of water vapor. The amount depends on the tightness of windows and doors, the permeability of the wall and roof construction materials, and upon other factors. If doors and windows are loose, water vapor will pass out readily, and if they are tight, the leakage will be minimized. However, attempts to protect a building against high humidities have proved to be, for the most part, imperfect. Vapor barriers, vents in siding, or methods of ventilating the outer layers of the building walls all have disadvantages.

Exhaust Ventilation Effective

Ventilation from the interior by means of exhaust fans has proved effective
in preventing moisture buildup in the types of buildings we have been dis-
cussing. Further, this ventilation wastes less heat than one might imagine.
The rate of exhaust needed to dispel the water vapor generated within a
building depends on the relative humidity within the structure.

The lower this humidity, the more air needs to be exhausted to remove
the moisture generated. As the relative humidity is increased, less air
needs to be exhausted to dispel the same amount of water vapor, and less
heat is thereby removed from the building. So the designer can plan for
optimum comfort and health by maintaining 40-50% relative humidity, and
at the same time reduce ventilating costs.

This, in turn, has an effect on the building materials and construction.
To live with the higher humidities, the structure must be built or remodeled
so that it can withstand them. The cost of providing that protection must be
weighed against the reduction in ventilation heat losses and the increased
level of comfort.

Venting Individual Processes

In addition to the use of general ventilation, the designer should consider
venting individual processes and providing makeup air that is tempered and
controlled. Mild weather conditions should also be considered, since increased exhaust may be necessary due to higher specific humidity outdoors. For best results under these conditions, local exhaust systems take
preference over dilution ventilation methods, which require that larger
volumes of air are exhausted.

Figure 11.4 gives the amount of air, in cubic feet required to remove
1 lb of water vapor as a function of room temperature and room relative
humidity when the outdoor specific humidity is negligible. With some time
and effort, a designer can prepare a similar family of curves for his particular locale and weather conditions, thus improving the precision of the
estimate of exhaust requirements. In the case of exhaust ventilation for
moisture control and removal, an increase in outside temperature conditions would demand a higher ventilation rate.

The following examples show how Fig. 11.4 may be used in ventilation
design.

EXAMPLE 11.11. A building has a gross volume of 30,000 ft^3
and an outside air infiltration rate of two air changes per hour.
At 70°F dry bulb temperature indoors and 0°F outdoors, a mois-
ture-liberating process maintains a 30% relative humidity indoors.
As a conservation measure, the building is sealed to minimize

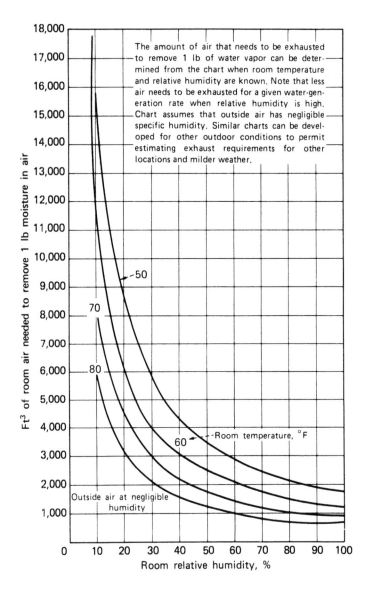

FIG. 11.4. Volume of air needed to remove 1 lb of water vapor. (From *Chemical Engineering*, May 19, 1980.)

infiltration and is adequately protected to permit maintaining 45% relative humidity. What will be the exhaust rate necessary to remove the water vapor liberated by the process?

SOLUTION: From Fig. 11.4, it is seen that the exhaust of 3000 ft^3 of air removed 1 lb of water vapor at the original room conditions. The water removal rate is then

$$\frac{30,000 \times 2}{3000} = 20 \text{ lb/hr}$$

After the building is protected and maintained at the higher relative humidity, the new ventilation rate required to remove 1 lb of water vapor is seen from the graph to be 1900 ft^3. Then, to remove 20 lb/hr of water vapor, the exhaust rate can be calculated to be

$$1900 \times 20 = 38,000 \text{ cfh}$$

The new rate reduces the outside air changes from the original two per hour to

$$\frac{38,000}{30,000} = 1.27 \text{ air changes per hour}$$

For the unprotected building, the ventilation heat losses are

$$30,000 \times \frac{2}{60} \times 1.08 \times (70 - 0) = 76,000 \text{ Btuh}$$

For the protected building they are

$$30,000 \times \frac{1.27}{60} \times 1.08 \times (70 - 0) = 48,000 \text{ Btuh}$$

EXAMPLE 11.12: A processing room is adequately ventilated by a 3000-cfm exhaust-makeup air system while maintaining 60°F and 25% relative humidity at 0°F outdoors. A new process liberating an additional 100 lb/hr of water vapor is under consideration. Without changing building construction, what modifications are required to maintain 70°F and 50% relative humidity with the new process added?

SOLUTION: With the existing conditions, the water removal rate is

$$\frac{3000 \times 60}{60} = 37.5 \text{ lb/hr}$$

This is also the vapor generation rate. Then, for the new system, the water vapor removal rate would be

$$37.5 + 100 = 137.5 \text{ lb/hr}$$

For the new room conditions, Fig. 11.4 shows that 1700 ft^3 of air must be exhausted to remove 1 lb of vapor. Thus, the ventilation rate becomes

$$\frac{1700 \times 137.5}{60} = 3900 \text{ cfm}$$

This represents a 30% increase over the old system. Study the fan ratings and contact the fan manufacturer to see whether an increase in fan speed and horsepower would safely handle the new load. If not, then a new fan, drive, and motor may be necessary.

12

THINK QUIET—DESIGN FOR NOISE CONTROL IN INDUSTRY

12.1. INTRODUCTION

Noise: the ignored contaminant! What we accept as normal everyday levels of noise in our homes, workplaces, and recreation areas may be permanently damaging our hearing.

Noise is the single most omnipresent noxious contaminant in the environment. Despite its effect on virtually every American, little attention has been paid to the dangers of noise, and relatively small amounts of money have been spent to control it compared with other threats to our environment like water and air pollution.

To the scientist, noise is an unwanted disturbance occurring within an audible frequency band that interferes with communication. To the acoustician it is an erratic, intermittent, or statistically random oscillation. To the man in his workplace, excessive noise causes ringing in the ears, hearing impairment, irritability, and inability to communicate with others.

To the plant engineer, noise poses a challenge to their engineer's precision, their creativity, their curiosity, and their skill in solving problems. Thus, this chapter's intent is to provide plant engineers with noise criteria, their evaluation and use, and guidelines for engineered in-plant control. P. N. Cheremisenoff and N. P. Cheremisenoff (1973) provide an excellent noise glossary.

12.2. NOISE CRITERIA

Their Evaluation and Use

A noise problem must be evaluated to establish the noise level for a particular site that will be acceptable to those who will be living with it. The

acceptable noise level is known as the "noise criterion" for that location.
It is also important to appreciate the fact that it can vary widely for different locations and situations.

In developing noise criteria, certain conditions must be considered:

The kind of activity that the worker is engaged in near the noise
   source
The amount of noise absorption from natural barriers in the noise path
Sound absorption characteristics of elements of the occupied space
   such as the walls, ceiling, and floor
The presence of background noise that could mask the noise under study
Relative distance from acoustic center to the worker in his normal
   work location

Criteria are only statistical in nature. One noise level that may be considered a damage risk to one person may not apply to another. Reactions
from people are not time invariant, that is to say, not consistent or uniform.
People react to noise in different ways. A dripping faucet may not be considered annoying during the daytime, but heaven help the dripping faucet at
night when it can easily be considered quite disturbing. The public may
react to the noise of aircraft overhead quite differently after a series of
plane crashes. The noise from a room air conditioner can be quite acceptable since it provides a degree of comfort.

Range of Human Hearing

The frequency range of human hearing stretches from about 20 Hz (cycles
per second) to 10,000 Hz. Although there could be exceptions, this range
has come to be accepted for most practical purposes. For most engineering applications, this audio range is subdivided into eight frequency bands
called "octave bands" which cover the range of frequencies somewhat as
the octaves on a piano cover the range of pitch. The octave bands used
have the identifying center frequencies and ranges listed in Table 12.1.

When noise levels are plotted on a graph, they are most often divided
into these eight octave bands. In this way it is possible to observe the
variation of a noise level with change in frequency. This variation is important in any noise problem analysis because human beings display a different sensitivity and response to low-frequency sounds as compared with
high-frequency sounds, and engineering solutions for low-frequency noise
problems differ from those for high-frequency noise problems. Refer to
Fig. 12.1.

Sound Basics

The frequency range of audible sounds for healthy young ears is usually
considered to extend from 20 to 20,000 Hz, although there is evidence to
indicate that hearing extends beyond these limits. But for all practical
purposes the top limit is 10,000 Hz. The simplest type of sound, called a

pure tone, is described as having a single frequency. Sounds, as encountered in nature, rarely consist of a single frequency. Indeed, music,
speech, and noise are each composed of many frequencies. Those com-
prising speech are principally between 250 and 3500 Hz. This range is considered most important to humans since hearing losses for speech sounds
would handicap the individual in most daily activities.

The magnitude of the pressure variations constituting a sound provide
a measure of its strength or intensity. Actually, the pressure variations
producing audible sound are quite small. Normal atmospheric pressure is
approximately 1×10^6 dyne/cm^2, i.e., 14.7 psia. The faintest sounds
that can be detected by the human ear are produced by pressure variations
of approximately 0.0002 dyn/cm^2. The pressure involved in producing
the background noise levels we encounter in offices and factories or similar
places is on the order of 1 dyn/cm^2, or about one-millionth of the barometric pressure. The unit microbar is equal to 1 dyn/cm^2 and the terms
are used interchangeably.

The Decibel Scale

The decibel scale is a simplification for the use of large numbers expressed
as pressures. The nature of the scale is logarithmic and the formula for
computing sound pressure level in decibels (dB) is

$$dB = 20 \log_{10} \times \frac{P_1}{P_0} \qquad (12.1)$$

TABLE 12.1. The Frequency Range of Human
Hearing

Band no.	Center frequency (Hz)	Frequency range (Hz)
1	63	37.5-75.0
2	125	75.0-150
3	250	150-300
4	500	300-600
5	1000	600-1200
6	2000	1200-2400
7	4000	2400-4800
8	8000	4800-9600

Source: Consulting Engineer, December 1973.

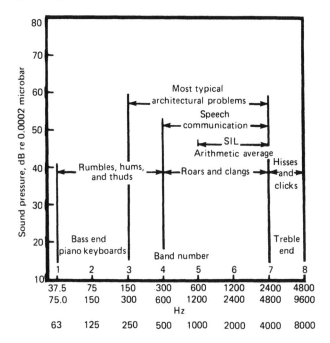

FIG. 12.1. Octave band versus intensity chart with superimposition of useful parameters in understanding noise. (From Consulting Engineer, December 1973.)

where P_1 is the pressure of the sound being measured and P_0 is a reference pressure. In industrial hygiene work, 0.0002 dyn/cm^2 is usually the reference pressure. This value corresponds to the weakest sound pressure that the human ear can detect under the most ideal listening conditions. Sound pressure level measurements must always state the reference value being used. Unless otherwise stipulated, all sound pressure level measurements hereinafter are given as re 0.0002 microbar. The sound pressures and decibel equivalents for some common sounds are given in Table 12.2.

Single Number Rating System

The use of an octave band analysis of a sound is rather complicated, so many attempts have been made to express the frequency content (quality) and sound pressure level (intensity) of sounds using a single number system. The most common method used is the A-B-C weighting network of sound level meters. Sound level meters with these weighting circuit networks attempt to simulate the human ear's response to sound at different pressure intensities. At a relatively low pressure level, the human ear is considerably more sensitive to high frequency than to low frequency. This difference,

TABLE 12.2. The Sound Pressures and Decibel Equivalents for Some Common Sounds

Sound pressure (microbars)	Sound pressure level (dB re 0.0002 microbar)	Example
0.0002	0	Threshold of hearing
0.00063	10	
0.002	20	
0.0063	30	
0.02	40	
0.063	50	Residence
0.2	60	Conventional speech
0.63	70	
1.0	74	
2.0	80	
6.3	90	Subway
20	100	Looms in textile mill
63	110	Woodworking
200	120	Hydraulic press
2000	140	Jet plane

Source: Consulting Engineer, December 1973.

however, becomes less noticeable at higher sound levels where the ear approaches more nearly equal sensitivity for low-frequency as well as high-frequency sounds. Thus it is important to realize that sounds of equal sound pressure level may not be equally loud. At sound pressure levels near 100 dB (re 0.0002 microbar), frequencies between 20 and 1000 Hz sound equally loud. At lower sound pressure levels the lower frequency-sounds do not seem as loud as the 1000 Hz tone. For example, a pure tone of 70 Hz having a sound pressure level of 50 dB does not sound any louder than a 1000 Hz pure tone having a sound pressure level of only 10 dB. At sound pressure levels below 40 dB, frequencies below 80 Hz are inaudible. Curves called loudness level curves have been developed showing the sound pressure levels and frequencies required to produce similar loudness levels.

A-scale Weighting Network

The A-scale weighting network is the most popular in use today and is the basis for regulations established by the new Federal Occupational Safety and Health Act (OSHA). The A-scale weighting network is designed to simulate the human ear's response for low pressure sounds of about 40 dB. Such levels are characteristic of quiet offices and residential areas. The A weighting is also used in many sound rating codes and noise ordinances and, as we have already said, by OSHA.

The B-scale weighting network is designed to simulate the ear's response for medium pressure sounds of about 55 dB. It is sometimes also known as the 70 dB weighting network, and it approximates ear response at a level of 70 dB. This covers the range from business offices to fairly quiet factory operations. The C-scale weighting tends to provide nearly equal response in all frequencies and is used to approximate the ear's response above 85 dB. Such levels are typical of a noisy factory.

A-B-C scales ratings have been used because of their simplicity of statement. They may have value in some sound comparison situations, but such data are of little value in making an engineering evaluation of an equipment or space noise problem because no indication of the frequency content or character of the noise is apparent. For example, two different types of pumps could have the same A-scale rating, but one could have most of its energy in the low-frequency bands (rumbles, hums, and thuds), while the other could have its energy concentrated in the high-frequency bands (roars, clangs, hisses, and clicks). A single-number rating will give no indication of this, and its use could lead to erroneous and costly misjudgments. Once single-number ratings have been established and have values that are in violation of sound rating codes or OSHA regulations, then an octave band analysis should be made of the offending machine or area.

Figure 12.2 illustrates data obtained from an octave band analysis of two different wide-band noises having the same total sound pressure level of 98 dB. The energy contained in one sound appears to be uniformly distributed across the eight octave bands. The other (dotted line) noise, however, shows its acoustical energy to be concentrated largely within one or two bands. This analysis would be helpful in making judgments about their loudness. As we have already noted, the ear does not respond equally to different frequencies. Hence, noises having the same total sound pressure level may not be equally loud because of differences in frequency content or in the manner in which the various frequency components contribute to the total sound pressure level. Knowledge about the spectrum of a noise is also important in evaluating its potential harmfulness.

Single-number ratings have limited applications for the following reasons:

Pieces of equipment may yield similar overall sound levels, yet their distribution of sound energy with frequency may be greatly different.

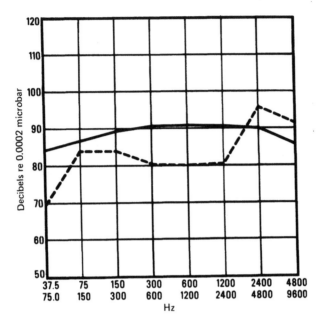

FIG. 12.2. Spectral differences between two sounds having the same over-all sound pressure level of 98 db. (From Consulting Engineer, December 1973.)

The human ear hears high frequencies more easily and calls them loud-er than low frequencies even at equal intensity (db).

There is a great difference in the case of propagation of low frequencies through walls and ducts (walls) as compared with high frequencies.

The levels of masking environmental or background noises differ widely at various frequencies.

Noise Criteria by the Tangent Contour Method

Noise may be compared and criteria developed involving the use of a set of contours known to acousticians as NC curves (noise criteria curves). Fig-ure 12.3 shows these contours by octave band. Table 12.3 lists NC con-tours with representative areas of activity.

The noise criteria are two-fold because the sound spectrum has to be such that the high-frequency sounds do not interfere with normal speech communication and the low-frequency sounds do not produce excessive loud-ness. The NC curves accomplishing this purpose match the sensitivity of the human ear. From these NC values a design level may be selected that

TABLE 12.3. NC Contours with Representative Areas of Activity

NC number range	Activity
NC-20 to NC-25	Sleeping, resting, relaxing: homes, apartments, hotels, hospitals
NC-20 to NC-25	Suburban and rural
NC-25 to NC-30	Urban, executive offices
NC-15 to NC-20	Excellent listening conditions required: concert halls, recording studios
NC-20 to NC-25	Very good listening conditions required: Auditoriums, theaters
NC-25 to NC-30	Large meeting and conference rooms
NC-30 to NC-35	Good listening conditions required: private offices, school classrooms, conference rooms, radio and television in the home
NC-35 to NC-40	Fair listening conditions required: large offices, small engineering and drafting rooms, restaurants, retail shops and stores
NC-40 to NC-45	Moderately fair listening conditions acceptable: business machine areas, large engineering and drafting rooms, lobbies, cafeterias, laboratory work areas, satisfactory telephone use
NC-45 to NC-55	Not recommended for any office. Acceptable working conditions with minimum speech interference: light to heavy machine spaces, industrial areas, and commercial areas such as garages, kitchens, laundries
NC-45 to NC-70	Light manufacturing
NC-55 to NC-75	Heavy manufacturing
NC-values above 70	Determined from octave band analyses described in the text.

Source: Consulting Engineer, December 1973.

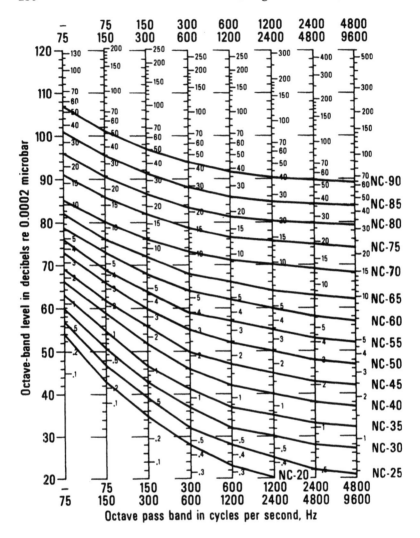

FIG. 12.3. Noise criterion "NC" curves. Note that the contours above
NC-70 have been extrapolated by the author to explore their use for process-
ing and high levels of noise in heavy manufacturing areas. (From Consulting
Engineer, December 1973.)

provides proper balance between the miscellaneous ambient sound sources
in a space and the sound effect of the piece of equipment under consideration.

Normally, the ambient sound pressure levels are assumed to be below
the respective occupancy noise criteria so that they do not influence the

design sound pressure level. However, the NC objective should be no more
than 15 dB above the expected occupied ambient sound level without the added equipment in operation. On the other hand, the reverse is unattainable
because it is below the level of external or extruding sounds.

At the outset, we pointed out the importance of recognizing that acceptable noise levels may vary widely for different areas and situations. If the
ambient sound levels are high, the selection of sound noise criteria can approach these higher levels. If the space sound level is extremely low, the
design noise criteria should be established at the low levels.

Effect of Equal Decibel Levels

Two sounds, not of the same frequency but both having equal decibel levels,
result in a combined sound level 3 dB higher than either one. However, it
can be shown that if two sounds have a 10 dB difference, the combined sound
level is less than 1 dB higher than the higher of the two. What then becomes
apparent is that the greater the dB spread between sound levels, the lower
the dB increase in the combined level. The curve in Fig. 12.4 shows this
relationship well.

Predicting NC Values of Equipment Sounds

NC values of equipment sounds may be predicted from octave band analyses
by the tangent contour method. In this method the octave band analysis is
plotted on a family of NC curves as shown in Fig. 12.5. The noise is then
rated simply by the highest NC band penetration. This value is the NC number for that noise spectrum. Space noise level criteria as well as equipment noise criteria may be similarly established. All that is needed is the
family of NC curves and an octave ban analysis.

EXAMPLE 12.1. The octave band analysis for a gas compressor
room is as follows:

Octave band (Hz)	Sound pressure level (dB re 0.002 microbar)
31.5–75	90
75–150	89
150–300	80
300–600	82
600–1200	85
1200–2400	80

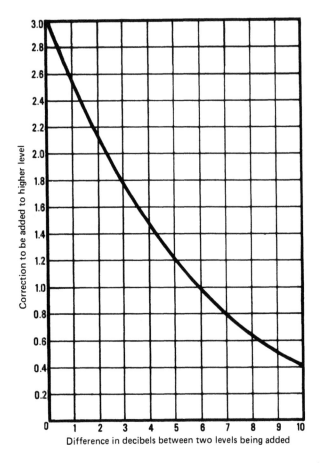

FIG. 12.4. The greater the dB spread between sound levels, the lower the dB increase in the combined level. (From Consulting Engineer, December 1973.)

Octave band (Hz)	Sound pressure level (dB re 0.002 microbar)
2400–4800	78
4800–9600	74

Determine the NC criterion for the compressor room.

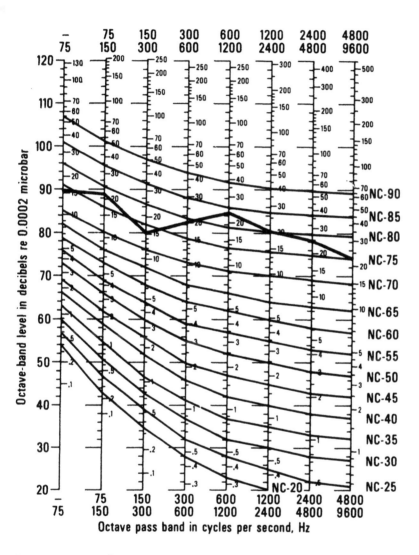

FIG. 12.5. Predicting NC values of equipment sounds from octave band analyses via the tangent contour method. (From Consulting Engineer, December 1973.)

SOLUTION: Plot the given noise spectrum as shown in Fig. 12.5. The point of highest penetration is NC 85. This is the NC criterion.

Sound Control Criteria for Industrial Buildings

As we pointed out initially, different sound pressure levels are acceptable for different rooms or processing areas. Table 12.4 lists the range of design noise criteria level decibels (re 0.0002 microbar) for a number of such spaces. These have been determined from the literature and have been used in actual practice with acceptable results. From these values a design level may be selected that will provide a proper balance between the miscellaneous ambient sound effect of mechanical or processing equipment. Normally, the sound pressure levels are assumed to be below the respective occupancy noise criteria so that they do not influence the design sound pressure level. The main purpose of the low- to high-level range is to provide acceptable flexibility. See Bruce, R. D., et al. (1976).

For extremely noisy processing or manufacturing areas, use speech interference levels (SIL). SILs may be calculated from the octave band analysis. First determine the sound pressure level (SPL) in dB from three octave bands: 5, 6, and 7. Then average these arithmetically, adding the three dB values and dividing by 3. SILs greater than 75 should be carefully evaluated.

EXAMPLE 12.2. H. B. Karplus and G. L. Bonvallet (1953) gave the octave band analysis for a fabric-coating process at low temperature at a 3-ft distance as follows:

Band	dB (re 0.0002 microbar)
1	72
2	71
3	68
4	74
5	76
6	69
7	69
8	67

Calculate the SIL.

SOLUTION: The average of bands 5, 6, and 7 is

$$\frac{76 + 69 + 69}{3} = 71$$

TABLE 12.4. The Range of Design Noise Criteria Level Decibels (re 0.0002 microbar) for Different Rooms or Processing Areas

| | Noise criteria | |
Space	Low	High
General office areas	35	50
Executive offices	30	40
Conference rooms	25	35
Secretarial offices	25	35
Accounting rooms	35	50
Large engineering and drafting offices	35	50
Assembly or meeting rooms	30	35
Cafeterias	40	50
Laboratories	35	45
Guard houses	35	45
First aid rooms	30	40
Control rooms	35	45
Foremen's rooms and offices: manufacturing	40	50
Corridors and hallways	35	45
Kitchens	40	50
Locker rooms	35	45
Computer rooms	40	60
Private offices	30	45
Board rooms	20	30
Office machinery rooms	40	60
Stenographic rooms	35	50
Laundries	40	60
Supervisor room	30	45
Lobbies	35	45
Mechanical equipment rooms	55	65
Switchgear rooms	50	60

TABLE 12.4. (Continued)

Space	Noise criteria	
	Low	High
Tank rooms (metallurgical)	50	70
Blower and compressor rooms	60	70
Tool maintenance	45	70
General storage	50	65
Light machinery assembly	55	70
Machine shops	45	65
Plating shops	60	70
Foundries and heavy manufacturing	55	75
Rock crushing and grinding	60	75
Punch press shops	60	75
Chipping and grinding areas	60	75
Shot blast rooms	65	75
Electric furnace rooms	60	75
Pulverizing ball mill rooms	65	75
Riveting operations	65	75
Heat treatment rooms	60	75
Boiler rooms	65	75
Die rooms	65	75
Inspection rooms	55	65
Shipping rooms	50	65
Burning-off area cutting torches	60	70
Lunch room: crusher building	50	60
Jaw crusher building: one crusher	65	75
Lunch area: ball mill floor	50	60
Wash room: ball mill floor	55	65
Diesel engine room	60	70
Electric power station	60	70

TABLE 12.4. (Continued)

Space	Noise criteria	
	Low	High
High speed blowers: inside	65	75
Crusher building ambient	60	75

Source: Consulting Engineer, December 1973.

This is the SIL and may be considered, for all intents and purposes, to be the NC.

A rule-of-thumb criterion for rating rooms and spaces with regard to
speech interference is given in Table 12.5. These are maximum permissible values of SILs for men with average voice strengths. The actual SILs
should be less than the values given in the table to have reliable conversa-
tion at the distances and voice levels shown.

No matter which criterion is used, the point to remember is that the
ability to communicate depends upon the intensity (dB) and frequency (Hz) of
the message as compared with the intensity and frequency of the background

TABLE 12.5. A Rule-of-Thumb Criterion for Rating Rooms and Spaces
with Regard to Speech Interference

Distance (ft)	Normal	Raised	Very loud	Shouting
1/2	71	77	83	89
1	65	71	77	83
2	59	65	71	77
3	55	61	67	73
4	53	59	65	71
5	51	57	63	69
6	49	55	61	67
12	43	49	55	61
24	37	43	49	55

Source: Consulting Engineer, December 1973.

noise. Below 65 dB, SIL interference is minor; at SILs above 75 dB, speech communication in industry becomes difficult.

The purpose of these criteria can be shown by the following example.

EXAMPLE 12.3. Assume we are to put a small conference room in a factory space. By measurements we determine that noise within the space is 65 dB and that the SIL for the conference room is 30 dB. The structure then must be designed to attenuate the noise from the factory space by about 35 dB to have a conference room that will be satisfactory as far as background noise level is concerned.

These criteria in combination with room effect, taking into account room size and area, sound absorption characteristics of the room, space configuration, distance of worker to sound source, and source location, specifications. See Tetorka, S. G. (1976) and Constance, J. D. (1973) for a procedure that explains acceptable methods for prediction of sound power requirements for mechanical equipment.

12.3. ENGINEERED NOISE CONTROL

General

Noise control for a manufacturing plant, chemical plant, oil refinery, or simply a building in the design stages should be given consideration and evaluation by the design team on a continuing basis. Success in this area will depend on their ability to accurately evaluate the acoustical environment and obtain guidance from noise control legislation, factory codes, zoning ordinances, and other effecting legislation such as OSHA.

Not all engineers can be acoustical experts, but if they are involved in a design that requires some knowledge of the noise-producing characteristics of the equipment to be installed, they should have more than a passing acquaintance with what to look for as the design progresses. We will focus on the more important sources of noise and what steps should be taken for their attenuation and control by first reviewing basic methods of control.

Basic Methods of Control: Quieting the Source

The greatest benefits in noise control are derived from quieting the source. Surveys have shown that more than 50% of power generating and other industrial machines produce at least 90-100 dBA of noise, and 50% of all plant working areas have noise levels of between 85 and 95 dBA. The ideal approach is noise reduction through new machinery design. This will prove to be the most economical in the long run since, even though there may be some choice, the design engineer may be forced to confine location of equipment because of the nature of the operation. On the other hand, such equipment as valves and piping can be designed to control noise propagation by devices and pipewall lagging applied to the outer surface of the equipment. Gear noises, loose bearings, noisy conveyors, escaping steam, and compressed-air sources can be quieted through engineering knowhow at the drawing board stage.

Equipment Placement

Where there are choices, avoid locating conference rooms and other rooms that require similar noise levels (see Tables 12.3 and 12.4) next to turbine and pump rooms. If this cannot be avoided, consider additional attenuation devices or heavier construction, or a combination of the two. Where air intake and discharge louvers are within earshot of occupied spaces, they should be sized for velocities of under 1000 fpm, and the connections should be acoustically lined a 4-10-ft distance back into the approach duct to each outlet.

Avoid placing bag filters and exhaust fan combinations within areas with low noise NC levels (see Tables 12.3 and 12.4). When a cooling tower cannot be placed at the highest point of a building, or when an adjacent structure is higher, specify a centrifugal fan-type tower or sound baffles. Coordinate the mechanical layout with the structural design to avoid flanking noise paths. Study the possibility of isolating equipment by moving or locating the operation or process in an area where a minimum number of workers would be exposed or by isolating the source in a room. The designer may elect to construct a wall or other acoustical barrier between the source and the exposed workers.

Substitution of Materials

Substitution of materials, equipment, or operations can be an effective means of controlling any type of noise hazard. However, in noise control there are limited applications. But there are certain areas where substitution may show considerable promise. Typical examples include substitution of squeeze-type equipment or welding for conventional riveting and chemical cleaning of metals for high-speed polishing wheels in the plant shop.

Study how to increase the distance between the noise source and the worker, or if that is not possible, provide soundproof booths to cut down exposure time. Reducing the noise exposure by increasing the distance follows the inverse square law: thus, by doubling the distance from the noise source, the sound intensity is reduced to one-fourth of the original intensity. In the outdoors and in a highly absorptive environment with no reflects or buildup, sound can be reduced by about 6 dBA for each doubling of the distance from the source.

Most factory structures are built of essentially hard, reflective materials. The noise within such buildings tends to reverberate, reflect, and build up, thus providing only limited attenuation with distance. Noise levels in such instances can often be reduced effectively by the addition of sound absorptive elements readily available from manufacturers of acoustical materials.

Sound-absorbing Elements

After all treatments of both the source and path of the sound have been completed, sound levels can frequently be reduced another 5 or 10 dBA by adding sound elements. Such a reduction is possible only where most of the sound reaches the area after at least one reflection. Sound-absorbing elements are available as suspended ceilings, wall coverings, and suspended unit absorbers. Porous surfaces are typically good sound absorbers. Wall and ceiling materials for this purpose are made from mineral or glass fiber blankets, molded or felted boards (panels and tiles), foamed open-celled plastics, sprayed-on fibers, and porous plasters.

Apparent buildup can be theoretically reduced as much as 10 dBA by lining all surfaces. However, in practice it is most unlikely that this will be achieved. Also, the reverberant noise level in a room theoretically decreases by about 3 dBA for each doubling of the total absorptive surfaces. Remember, too, that even a very hard surface will have some absorptive characteristics. In most cases it is not feasible to treat more than 50% of the room surface. The noise reduction gained beyond this amount is slight.

Isolation of the Worker

Isolation as a method of noise control is similarly applicable to the exposed worker. In situations where the number of workers is small and the nature of the operation is favorable, isolation of workers in a separate room is effective. A partial enclosure or sound barrier with both absorptive and sound transmission loss qualities, correctly placed, can provide noise reductions on the order of 8-12 dBA. A complete enclosure cab provides a greater degree of reduction ranging from 30 to over 60 dBA, depending on design.

Quiet rooms are different from enclosures in that a quiet room may be defined as a room where the undesired sound is outside the room and a desired quiet environment is maintained inside the room. This is the opposite from enclosures, in which case the undesired sound is inside the structure and a quiet environment outside the enclosure is the goal.

Selecting Equipment

Equipment should be selected such that it will operate at top efficiency. Induced draft and forced draft fans should be selected such that they will operate at peak efficiency on the brake horsepower curve for least noise operation. Fan discharge velocities should be chosen according to the discharge static pressure required. Check for "masking" noise levels which may serve to correct interroom transmission of unwanted noise. For air conditioning systems, select induction and fan-coil units and check with the manufacturer for their acoustical ratings. Take into account "room effect" when selecting unducted equipment. See Constance, J. D. (1973).

Gas Path Noise

If a noise source is a part of the gas path (the turbine inlet and exhaust), total enclosure is clearly impossible. Any acoustical treatment must pass the exhaust and inlet gases freely but block acoustical radiation.

In installations where some of the exhaust heat is recovered in a regenerator or a heat-recovery boiler, some, or all, of the exhaust silencing may be provided in the heat-recovery equipment, while the remainder is provided by a silencer which dissipates acoustic energy. Inlet silencers of simple-cycle machines are always dissipative. Figure 12.6 shows the loss achieved by typical heat-recovery equipment. The regenerator was of the split-fin design and about 8 ft in length. The heat-recovery steam generator was of the type which is capable of supplementary firing. The heat-recovery steam generator attenuation data are only up to 1000 Hz because the loss was greater than could be reliably measured at higher frequencies. While the attenuations shown are not nearly so large as can be attained with specially designed silencers, they are not negligible. The regenerator, for example, is roughly equivalent to a conventional silencer which is about 5 ft long.

Dissipative Silencers

Dissipative silencers achieve their attenuation through the use of sound-absorbing material such as fiberglass or mineral wool. In its conventional form, the silencer consists of parallel baffles of fibrous material, with passages in between for the gases as shown in Fig. 12.7. The materials are

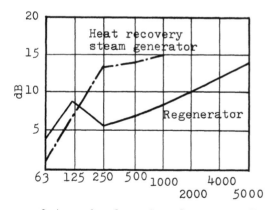

FIG. 12.6. Sound attenuation of heat recovery equipment.

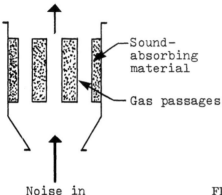

Noise in   FIG. 12.7. Parallel baffle silencer.

suitably chosen to withstand and endure the temperatures and gas velocities which are to be expected. By proper choice of the thickness of the baffles, the width of the gas passages, and the acoustical material, the attenuation can be adjusted as required. For example, exhaust service might call for relatively thick batts of mineral wool to accommodate the low frequencies and high temperatures typical of the exhaust, while an inlet silencer might use thinner baffles of fiberglass, these being better suited to the low temperatures and high frequencies associated with the compressor or the gas turbine.

Another device is a switchback silencer, so-called because it uses a folded-path principle (Fig. 12.8). Instead of constricting the flow between batts of fibrous material, the switchback may be thought of as a series of acoustically-lined chambers. While the silencer has interior features which allow the exhaust gases to flow freely, the noise "sees: the device as a series of discontinuities which block sound propagation.

Isolating Equipment, Pipes, and Ducts

In the equipment room or generator room layout, allow space for inertia blocks and springs. This will vary depending on location (bed rock, penthouse steel, etc.). Review piping flexibility and provide spring hangers. Insulate service piping passing through partitions for an air-tight seal against the transmission of high frequencies via interroom paths. Large, heavy, motor-driven equipment such as forced and induced-draft fans, pumps, and compressors are prime examples of equipment that vibrates severely during operation. By placing such machine on mounts, the shock can be contained. The vibrations produced are blocked from traveling beyond the machine itself so that the vibration will not be transmitted to the floor, structural members, or rigid sections of electrical distribution systems.

The simplest ways to control the transmission of vibration and shock is with isolation pads or felt, cork, elastomers, steel, aluminum, or combinations of these materials. Pads can simply be placed under the legs of the base of the machine. Elastomers are ideal vibration isolators that curtail detrimental vibrations which otherwise would transmit to floors, foundations, and adjacent machines. These pads protect the equipment from impact and vibration forces transmitted through the floor and foundation by other machines and from vibrations caused by the machine or equipment itself. Isolators also provide a slight leveling action because of their resilience and keep the structure free of nonuniform stresses that might be produced by a vibration from external forces. Most pads resist petroleum products, cleaning compounds, and the deteriorating effects of sun, light, or air.

Inertia Blocks

Inertia blocks are widely used when there is a possibility that shock and vibration forces will be transmitted through the foundation. These blocks are concrete sections which are set in floors or foundations and are isolated from the surrounding floor by vinyl bonded pads. These pads are inserted before the concrete is poured to act as an impervious barrier. Motors and equipment can be mounted on massive inertia pads that are spring-mounted above the floor slabs. The construction of these pads varies: one of several possibilities consists of a reinforced concrete deck with an outer steel frame incorporating the spring housings.

Vibration control can also be accomplished by using steel springs in combination with sound-absorbing materials. Because of their effectiveness, springs are widely used in machine foundation design. The advantages to springs are

1. Smoother and quieter machine operation.
2. Reduced machine maintanance.
3. Reduction or elimination of the effects of vibration on the structure.
4. A decrease in the size and mass of the foundation under the equipment.

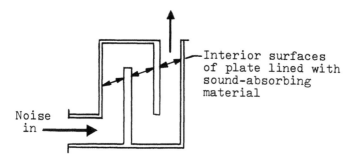

Noise in →

Interior surfaces of plate lined with sound-absorbing material

FIG. 12.8. Switchback silencer.

5. More accurate design because their properties are known and readily predictable.
6. Springs can be considered permanent for the life of the machine because their properties are not affected by time.
7. Leveling adjustment is possible in spring units.
8. Versatilty of installation.

Designing Ductwork for Optimum Fow

Duct and pipe flow velocities should be reviewed since sound power level increases 15 dB for each doubling of velocity. Make smooth transitions and shape takeoffs from high pressure risers for smooth flow.

Some of the most common vibration sources are compressors and pumps. Simple vibration isolation of these items from the floor is generally of limited benefit. This is due to the high amplitude of vibrations which are transmitted along the connecting pipeline to many other areas of the plant. In addition, mounting brackets for the piping will frequently act to short circuit the equipment isolators, making them almost totally ineffective. Consequently, it is usually necessary to support the piping on, or hung by, vibration isolators. Of further benefit is the prevention of coupling to the piping in the first place. For this purpose, flexible pipe couplings are available and should be used.

Flexible couplings act as vibration breaks in the piping system and ease the problem of pump-to-pipe alignment when the pump must be isolated from its support structure. In addition, these couplings can help compensate for changes in the piping system due to thermal expansion and contraction.

Noise Control and Maintenance

Vibration is detrimental because it can cause machines to deteriorate faster, produce higher maintenance costs, and lead to production rejects. Excessive vibration may be due to faulty installation or improper maintenance. Equipment should be periodically checked. Any gradual increase in vibration shoud be examined during routine maintenance. Sudden increases in vibration call for action to remedy or correct the condition. Increased vibration in machinery can be caused by the following:

1. Rotation imbalance which requires rebalancing
2. Misalignment of couplings or bearings
3. Eccentric journals
4. Defective or damaged gears
5. Bent shafts
6. Mechanical looseness
7. Faulty belt drives
8. Rubbing parts and resonant conditions

TABLE 12.6. Possible Noise Control Procedures for Typical Industrial
Equipment

Equipment	Noisy components	Possible control procedures
Forced draft furnaces	Burner casings	Lagging
	Forced draft fan intake	Location change/muffler
	Burner ducting	Bury ducting/lagging
Natural draft furnaces	Combination oil/gas burners	Plenum with intake muffler
	Primary air inspirating burners	Primary air muffler/plenum with intake muffler
Steam-generating boilers	Forced draft fan intake	Location change/muffler
	Boiler resonance	Design of boiler internals to avoid resonance
Compressors	Intake and discharge piping	Enclosure
	Casing	Lagging
	Recycle valve	Lagging quiet valve/muffler
Electric motors	Rotor, magnetic noise	Enclosure
	Windage noise	Muffler
Gas turbine	Casing	Enclosure
	Intake and exhaust	Muffler
Gear boxes	Gear mesh noise	Enclosure
Air-cooled heat exchangers	Propeller noise	Reduce rpm, increase blade pitch

Sudden increases in vibration may be traced to malfunctions of equipment due to lack of lubrication, overload, or misalignment. In pumps,
cavitation may erode an impeller. In fans and blowers, dirt may adhere to
the fan or impeller blades and break off unevenly, causing imbalance. Look
for any change in operating speeds. Examination of the foundation may un-
cover settling that can cause misalignment. Table 12.6 lists a number of
possible noise procedures for typical industrial equipment.

Holes and Openings

Any hole or opening, however small, is an acoustical "leak." This includes
the openings around ducts, pipes, or conduits, where they pass through

walls or slabs, door undercuts, or relief grilles. Such openings can completely vitiate a well-designed wall or structural system.

Openings around pipes, conduits and ducts, where these services pierce walls or floors, should be packed with glass fiber or a similarly resilient blanket material; or the pipe may be wrapped with a sleeve of foamed elastomers such as some of the available low-temperature insulation materials. The visible joint should be sealed with nonhardening plastic caulking cement. Large openings, which would require grouting, should be minimized.

Construction Elements

The partitions, floors, and ceilings of a building provide resistance to the transmission of airborne and structure-borne noise. Their efficiency as sound barriers is dependent on several factors:

1. Mass: the heavier the construction, the greater its resistance to sound transmission.
2. Isolation: separation of opposite surfaces of a construction will improve sound isolation. Surfaces may be separately supported with no structural connections between them or may be resiliently mounted to common supports.
3. Damping: addition of sound attenuation wool within the construction effectively dissipates sound energy by converting it to heat.
4. Leaks: cracks, penetrations, or any openings, however small, readily conduct airborne sound.
5. Flanking paths: sound is transmitted along the path of least resistance, which is usually through the structure and around sound barrier walls and floor-ceilings.

Effective Structural Sound Control

Wall and ceiling construction should provide approximately the same degree of sound control through each assembly. Where a dry wall partition is used for sound isolation, the construction should extend from slab to slab. Sound can travel through a suspended ceiling, although acoustically protected, up and over a partition attached to the suspended ceiling and into other areas (Fig. 12.9).

Optimum sound isolation requires that the integrity of dry wall partitions and ceilings never be violated by cutting holes for vents or grilles or by recessing cabinets, light fixtures, etc. Instead, they should be surface mounted. Door and borrowed light openings are not recommended in party walls. The septum layer in the triple solid drywall partition should always remain whole.

Where holes are necessary, avoid placing them back to back and immediately next to each other. Electrical boxes should be staggered, preferably at least one stud space. A nonhardening resilient caulking material

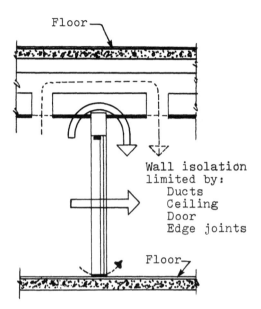

FIG. 12.9. Flanking noise paths.

should be used to seal all cutouts, such as around electrical and telephone outlets, plumbing escutcheons, and wall cabinets. The backs and sides of electrical boxes should also be caulked to prevent sound leaks.

Caulking should be used to seal all intersections with the adjoining structure, such as underfloor and ceiling runner tracks, around the perimeter where the assembly meets the floor, ceiling, partition, or exterior wall, and at vertical intersections occurring at columns and window mullions.

Avoid construction such as ducts, rigid conduits, or corridors, which act as speaking tubes to transmit sound from one area to another. Common supply and return ducts should have sound attenuation liners. Conduits should be sealed. Doors leading to a common hall should be gasketed around the perimeter and should not contain return air grilles.

To isolate structure-borne vibrations and sound, resilient ceiling systems and floor coverings are recommended. Vibrating or noisy equipment should have resilient mountings as heretofore discussed to minimize sound transfer to structural materials. Ducts, pipes, and conduits should be broken with resilient, nonrigid boots or flexible couplings where they leave vibrating equipment and should be isolated from the structure with resilient gasketing and caulking where they pass through walls, floors, or other building surfaces.

Noise Criteria Checklist

1. Discuss and set up power levels or noise criteria to be maintained in each category of space in the plant.
2. Interpret government (OSHA) regulations.
3. Develop and publish guidelines for noise control specifications for purchased equipment.
4. Review equipment specifications for compliance with established criteria, including major power plant equipment, vibration elimination devices, terminal devices, sound traps, mufflers and silencers, acoustical lining and covering, etc.
5. Spell out testing procedures for equipment not previously used.
6. Schedule the deflection required for each piece of equipment when operating on top of its vibration elimination device.
7. Review pipe and duct runs for flexibility and acoustical needs of covering or lining.
8. Schedule silencers and sound traps where required.
9. Obtain adequate data on the noise-producing properties of the equipment to be installed prior to design or estimate noise levels based on published data.
10. Reduce noise exposure by increasing the distance to the equipment; noise reduction follows the inverse square law. Thus, by doubling the distance between source and receiver, the sound intensity is reduced to one-fourth the original under "nonverb" conditions (open country). In open country, sound will be reduced by about 6 dB for each doubling of distance from the source.
11. Strive for a minimum of 10 dB of overall attenuation, a most significant recognizable change.

Architectural and Structural Checklist

1. Noisy areas should not abut areas requiring freedom from noisy intrusions. When spaces must abut one another, the smaller the common wall (length times height), the less sound energy will be transmitted, other things being equal.
2. Heavy wall construction reflects most sound energy back into the room. Lighter construction will permit more energy to pass into the receiving room.
3. The sound ratings of walls and partitions only reflect a direct airborne path; indirect paths can reduce the performance of barriers after installation in a finished building.
4. The transmissionl loss, which is the property of a sound barrier to block passage of sound from one space to another, varies from one frequency to another. In general, low-frequency or rumbling sounds readily pass through a material, i.e., heavy machinery and train noises, whereas high-frequency or hissing or whistling

noises tend to be blocked effectively even by lightweight partitions, i.e., speech, typewriter noises, etc.

5. Machinery room noises should be studied in the range of 20-300 Hz.

6. Noise from a typewriter, person talking, radio, TV, etc. should be studied in the range of 150-4000 Hz.

7. The effectiveness of a barrier depends on its mass, stiffness, discontinuity, and air tightness. The first three are most significant for low-frequency sounds, and the last for high-frequency sounds.

8. Transmission losses (TLs) afforded by mass are proportional to the ratio of masses, i.e., a two-fold increase in mass, either from 20 to 400 lb/ft, or from 50 to 100 lb/ft, produces the same improvement. Thus, it becomes uneconomical to increase the mass of a partition beyond a certain structural limit.

9. The use of two separate discontinuous partitions, completely isolated from each other by an air space, will provide considerable advantage because the two transmission loss values are approximately additive.

10. The best protection against the passage of high-frequency noises is air-tight construction.

11. Evaluate the effect of flanking transmission on the degree of transmission loss insulation requirements. Normal building practice, using masonry bearing walls and concrete floors, or their equivalent, with comparatively light construction for nonbearing partitions, places a limit of about 50 dB at medium frequencies on the maximum sound transmission loss obtainable by these traditional methods. When greater transmission losses (TLs) are required, discontinuous construction is called for.

12. Provide discontinuous construction to mitigate against the transmission of mechanical vibrations through the structure.

13. A perfectly discontinuous structure cannot be achieved in practice because ultimately all structures require support and the discontinuity fails at the points of support.

14. Choose and design points of support to provide a fair approximation to discontinuity within limits set by an analysis of conditions.

15. Use the air space concept to provide discontinuity (maximum deviation from homgeneity). Smaller but effective changes in discontinuity are provided by fibrous and granular materials of light density such as felts, asbestos, and cork, metal springs, and resilient materials like rubber and some corks. Lead sheets and lead plate may also be used under certain conditions.

16. Evaluate the effectiveness of air space as a coupling in light partitions and small air gaps.

17. The lighter a partition, the more effective is any particular coupling. The stiffer the coupling, the more effective it is as a coupling. The result in both cases is greater transmission of sound.

18. Attempts to improve transmission loss effectiveness between partitions by filling the cavity with sound-absorbing material (fiberglass, mineral wool, etc.) has the reverse of the desired results because, if the filling touches both partitions, it acts as an additional coupling. Light construction (up to 20 lb/ft^2) is particularly affected.
19. For partitions on the order of 20 lb/ft^2, air space should not be less than 2 1/2 in. Lighter partitions require a larger separation, thus a 21 oz double window needs a 6 in. minimum air space separation to attenuate low frequencies.
20. Wall ties should be twisted galvanized steel or copper wire of 9-12 gauge at maximum centers.

12.4. PROCESS PLANT NOISE

General

Once a process plant is on stream and is found to be noisy, any corrective steps are more costly and less effective than proper design of the original plant in the design office and on the drawing board. A more in-depth understanding, acceptance and the application of available technology, together with further development of technology are needed to ensure that the initial design results in a quiet plant. In this section designs for low-frequency noise control are discussed, the equipment, processes, and problems are common to a broad range of industrial plants.

Process Plant Furnaces

Considerable and intense noise emanates from process plant furnaces due to the high heat release rates inside the units. How does this noise source escape? Air register openings are the main source of escape. There are other aspects that can complicate the noise due to combustion, but they can be taken care of when steps are being taken to reduce combustion noise. In modern burners the flames are intensely turbulent and noisy. Broadband noise is generated and its frequency may be related to flame propagation speed divided by flame thickness. The sound pressure levels measured invariably have a broad peak in the octave bands centered at 125 through 500 Hz. These are the combustion roar frequencies. See Table 12.1.

Inherent in today's burners is combustion roar which must be confined to the firebox. Taking into account all aspects of noise control here, today there is but one way to control combustion noise and that is to prevent its escape from the firebox by external means. Acoustically treated air-intake plenums can be very effective in doing this job by using air intake baffles lined with acoustically treated liners. The alternative method is to acoustically line approaching air intake ductwork, but these can become quite cumbersome. The only practical way is to provide a circumventing and tortuous absorbent path for the entering air that will effectively attenuate the noise escaping through this path.

Fan-cooled Heat Exchangers

Fan noise is found almost everywhere in process plants as well as industrial plants. The fans of air-cooled heat exchangers are the greatest culprits. In general, all fan noise is produced by the turbulence created by the cutting of the air mass by the fan blades. The frequency range of greatest noise generation has been related to the blade speed divided by the effective blade thickness. Except for fans directly attached to motor shafts, external acoustically treated boxes are not practical. The most effective approach is to provide a streamline design to the fan blades themselves.

Fan noise may be related to the mechanical power that is dissipated in developing the turbulent wake. The fan-blade designer must first make sure that the flow separation is pushed back as far as possible toward the trailing edge by using a good aerodynamic blade profile. Such will reduce the thickness and intensity of the turbulent wake. In addition, the designer can vary the chord length and angle of attack to make the uniform loading of the air front possible. Seals at the shaft hub and tip can be used to prevent by-passing and vortexing around those upstream points. Blade loading must be carefully analyzed to reduce it by increasing the number and length of the blades. Octave band analyses versus sound pressure studies effectively define the improvements when soundproof enclosures are provided for all such equipment.

Motors

Air-cooled motors are provided with fans attached to the rotors and usually are major sources of noise. In large motors, electromechanical noise can become important. The use of higher temperature insulation and smaller fans can bring about a reduction in fan noise. As with fans heretofore discussed, the broadband noise calculation is the same (blade speed divided by effective blade thickness). These motors run at higher speeds, and so do the fans attached to them; the result is a higher frequency noise.

In motors of the fan-cooled variety with horsepower ratings of about 200, fan noise usually dominates and sound pressure levels usually differ little in the no-load and full-load conditions. In larger motors, in particular the weather-protected type with an enclosure, the inherent radial magnetic force fluctuations can produce a strange pulsating sound at low frequency. The broadband noise due to various enclosure vibration responses is also increased. The low frequency "wavering moo" usually manifests itself as a twice-slip-frequency modulation of the twice-line-frequency driving force. Such a noise is in most cases load dependent.

Fan noise can be attenuated by the use of acoustically lined fan covers and enclosures.

Control Valves

Control valves are the bane of piping systems. Control valves are responsible for nearly all the noise generally blamed on piping systems. Flow noise in pipes, vents, and piping fittings (elbows, reducers, etc.) is usually negligible by comparison. Once introduced into the piping system, valve noise can persist for long distances. The piping designer spends a considerable amount of time to design into the system smoothness of flow by the use of fitting selection. When valve noise dominates, smoothness in manifold design and piping systems is not very important.

It has been shown that control valve noise is related to the mechanical power developed within the valve itself. The broad band noise generated has a frequency related to the maximum velocity within the valve divided by the effective valve port width. Adequate schemes are available for predicting valve noise problems during design. The ordinary valve is always noisy in service when operating in a throttled condition, at any substantial flow rate. Standard designs do not provide configurations that will help solve the noise problem since all are variations on the simple orifice. Special valve designs must be used to achieve results here. These change the physical process of expansion and contraction that take place. For good noise control, valves with a special internal design or in-line silencers are available. A valve that approaches isenthalpic (constant enthalpy) performance by means of sharp turns is the most effective in controlling noise. It has been found that acoustic lagging is the least effective method for valve noise control since valve noise is still propagated downstream.

Rotating Machinery: Compressors

Rotating machinery working at high speeds is a major source of process plant noise. Centrifugal compressors generate intense broadband noise with a wide range of frequencies beginning at about 100 Hz through about 6000 Hz. Discrete frequencies in the 1000-4000 Hz range are generated inside the case at the fundamental, second, and even third harmonics of the blade-passing frequency. The discrete frequencies (or tones) may protrude above the broad band noise by about 15 dB.

Resonance between blade-passing excitation and gas response inside the associated piping causes increased noise. The design of the casing internals offers some distant hope of noise reduction. For example, reductions of 6 dB (10 dB would be more telling) have been made by the proper design and choice of stationary and rotating blade arrangement to effect wave cancellation and wave interference.

Today's large turbo machines reflect noise levels that exceed 90 dBA close to most of the machines. It may be seen that there can be situations

when machines that lack acoustical treatment that are going to be too noisy,
irrespective of what the "performance specification" may say and irrespective of what "guarantee" may have been wrangled from the supplier.

And so we can see that really effective silencing of these machines
and others like them is eventually going to involve the routine use of in-
line silencers in both the intake and discharge lines. Perhaps, even total
machine enclosure may be the way to go.

Systems of Piping

Many piping systems reflect natural response modes in the fluid flowing
and in the pipe itself. The disturbance energy introduced by control valves
and the connected machines all occur at about the same frequency. What
does this mean? It means that noise can build up within the fluid or escape
through the pipe walls, or both. This probably explains why a noise is occasionally found to be a real trouble maker.

Frequently, valve and machine noise persists for long distances in
piping systems. This is because the noise energy may be either in the
gas stream or in the pipewall itself. If it is mostly in the gas stream,
the noise suffers little attenuation. When the noise energy propagates primarily in the pipewall, it suffers considerable attenuation as it flows
across flanges, elbows, and rigid supports. If the energy is in the gas
itself, then the use of in-line silencers work well. As previously mentioned,
acoustical lagging is not effective unless large lengths of pipe are treated.
If the energy is concentrated in the pipewall, lagging is somewhat more
practical because the noise does not persist so far downstream. Vibration isolation would be more effective.

For high-speed compressors, generally, and also valves in gas
service, most of the noisy energy remains in the gas. Here in-line silencers are most effective. For pumps and control valves in liquid service,
most of the noise energy is transferred to the pipe. Here vibration isolation would be most effective.

Flares

Flares can be sources of community annoyance. Anyone passing a refinery
surely can't miss those torches high in the air. The intense combustion
noise and light are inherent, and steam injection used to reduce smoking
can aggravate the noise problem. Flare noise can be reduced to a degree
by the use of multiport steam nozzles. It was found that the quicker the
steam and gas were mixed, the sooner the noise was reduced. Nevertheless, the intense combustion noise and light remain.

Grade-level flares are used to help reduce the noise and light of elevated flare systems. These are more popular in Europe than here in the
United States, although their use is increasing domestically. The up-to-
date grade-level flare is lined with refractory and equipped with many

burners at its base. Although the grade-level flare's capacity is limited, it can be integrated into an elevated flare system that will take care of the normal majority of reliefs that are small and reserve the elevated flare system for emergencies. The grade-level flare is an expensive feature to be added to an elevated flare system.

Equipment Specifications

As we know, there are two kinds of equipment specifications. From the point of view of the owner, the person who will have to live with the unit, a performance specification that stipulates only the maximum noise level may not be exceeded seems simple, and is, accordingly, the most popular. However, pure performance specifications do not work out because the low bidder frequently lacks the capability for noise-controlled designs.

Noise control specifications based on performance can be little more than an "acoustic prayer and supplication" stating maximum noise levels, continuing with seemingly endless definitions and calculations procedures, spouting a few engineering platitudes regarding potential noise sources and possible solutions, and imploring the supplier's best efforts to achieve the stated noise levels. For those contractors or suppliers who know the answer, it becomes only necessary to state the noise control objectives. And for those who do not, there is no help. The laws of physics cannot be legislated, no one can be invested with knowledge he does not have by a decree.

That leaves the ultimate consumers in a state of quandry: How. can they tell the "good guys" from the "bad guys"? It should be required that each and every equipment supplier give evidence of performance for each system or item of equipment to be furnished. Noise test data should be submitted that was taken from a test on a unit of identical design and construction operating under normal conditions in an existing plant; or certified noise test data should be obtained at the supplier's factory.

Noise "guarantees" may be given by suppliers who do not really know if their offering will comply with the purchaser's requirements. They are playing it safe because of the loopholes in guarantee enforcement. Other suppliers may know what is required but, because they think that the competition is giving guarantees without providing any extra-cost items for sound control, will most likely do the same to maintain a competitive position and have a chance at the low bid. This is a simple fact of business.

Specifying Minimum Design Features

Here are two reasons why it is important to understand and specify minimum design features for noise control:

1. To provide a judging gauge which will help determine which suppliers are offering good designs and which are simply giving lip service "guarantees" in the hope of obtaining the contract with a low bid.
2. To provide a uniform bidding requirement and make it clear that certain extra-cost noise control features are expected in the supplier's offering if needed.

Guarantees should be sought and enforced if necessary. But guarantees are like accident insurance policies: the best ones are those which are never used. To avoid the need for enforcing guarantees, make sure the design is right in the first place. Simply writing performance specifications provides very little assurance that acceptable noise limits will be achieved. If a supplier knows a better way to achieve the goals and can prove it, everyone benefits. Thus, minimum design features go hand in hand with a design review. Such specifications are the key to successful process plant noise control.

12.5. POWER PLANT NOISE

Octave Band Analysis

The noise from a complete power plant comes from all of the separate components, including the turbine itself, the load equipment, and the auxiliaries. Table 12.7 shows the octave band analysis where ambient sound levels exceed the safe limits of a coal-burning electric power plant of about 700 MW capacity. The dBA readings are not equipment readings but are readings of areas within the plant where ambient sound levels exceed the 90 dBA minimum for exposure. Turbine plant noise and noise from the machine casing are generated by high-velocity turbulence flow and have a broad band, random nature with a "rushing" quality. Turbine inlet noise is pitched, with a frequency equal to the product of the number of first-stage compressor blades and the compressor speed.

If the load is an electric generator, you can expect broad band noise due to the electromagnetic forces usual in electrical machinery. Gas compressors typically introduce a periodic component in the line pressure that is heard as a whine, the intensity being dependent on construction features which vary with the manufacturer.

The pipeline itself can radiate compressor noise, as well as flow noise caused by bends, valves, orifices, and other discontinuous items in the piping system. Pipeline noise tends to be rich in high-frequency energy since the line is a relatively inefficient radiator of the lower frequencies. This comes about because the cross dimension of the pipe is small compared with the wavelength of sound in the frequency range.

TABLE 12.7. Noise Sources in a Coal-burning Power Plant

Power plant components	Sound levels (dBA exceeding 90 dBA)
Soot blower compressor	92–93
Ash sluice pumps	92–93
Sealed air fan	92–94
Sealed oil system	92–95
Air injector	92–95
Generator turbine	92–95
Bearing water cooler	92–95
Heater drain pumps	94–95
Fan steam condenser	94–95
Air conditioning pump	94–95
Ash hopper	93–96
Hot well	95–96
Station air compressors	92–97
Condenser	93–97
Turbine condenser	94–97
Crusher house hammermill	95–97
Turbine oil reservoir	95–98
Conveyor motors	93–99
Pulverizer mills	94–99
Electrostatic precipitator	97–99
Condensate regulator valve	98–99
Condensate pumps	95–101
Boiler hot spot fans	96–103
Inside caterpillar tractor	97–105
Boiler feed pumps	99–107
Pneumatic impact wrench	106–107
Forced draft fan	109–111
Coal car shaker	117–120

Silencing Procedures

As is often the case, the origins of the noise of a power plant are both
varied and complex, and many of the sources must be considered individually and quieted. This should be done in a rational manner by considering priorities of budgeting. The total radiation of acoustical energy is
divided up into the contributing forces. Then, logically, the difference
between the unsilenced output of the source and the output to be allowed
after silencing defines the amount of attenuation required to do the job.

If the sources to be quieted are not the gas path through the machine—
casing noise is an example—they may be quieted by some combination of
lagging, enclosures, and barrier walls. The attenuation increases as the
weight of the treatment increases, as sound-absorbing materials are
added to the side facing the noise sources, and as sound leaks are minimized. Noise from the load compressor may be controlled, if necessary,
by lagging around the compressor casing and by using a muffler, similar
to that used in automobiles, to smooth out pressure fluctuations before
they reach the pipeline.

Pipeline-generated noise may be minimized by avoiding such restrictions as valves and sharp bends. Burying the pipe silences it by preventing sound radiation. Above-ground piping runs may require lagging of
special coatings and pipe wrappings to reduce their noise. In many installations, the turbine itself, the load compressor, and a portion of the
piping are enclosed in a building. In that case, these sources may contribute relatively little noise in the neighboring community.

Noise control equipment tends to be more effective at high frequencies
than at low frequencies. As a consequence, the noise of an acoustically
treated plant will tend to have relatively little energy in the high-frequency
region where hearing is most acute.

Materials are available which can be used for various quiet room applications. Such materials can be used for enclosing either the noise
source or the receiver. If the operation of a piece of equipment can be
controlled from a distance, the operator can be placed in an enclosure with
viewing ports. On the other hand, the machine may be enclosed. But here
a word of caution: a tight enclosure around a piece of equipment can create heat problems, and ventilation must be provided as well as access
openings for worker entry, exit, servicing, and lubrication. Any opening
in the enclosure reduces its efficiency as a sound barrier. Openings must
be kept to a minimum.

Since many aspects of noise control in power plants apply to process
plant noise control, there is no need to repeat our discussion of noise generation sources and their treatment. The reader is referred to the other
pertinent parts of this chapter for details and guidance. See Constance,
J. D. (1980).

13

INDUSTRIAL HEAT AND ITS CONTROL

13.1. INTRODUCTION

This chapter will be devoted to some of the problems that a worker experiences when exposed to a hot environment and some of the physiological mechanisms that can be brought to bear in alleviating the condition of heat stress.

13.2. HEAT STRESS

Sources of Heat

For a worker in a hot environment two sources of heat are important:

1. Internally generated metabolic heat
2. Externally imposed heat from the environment

Metabolic heat results from the chemical processes taking place inside the
body cells, tissues, and organs. Under quiescent conditions with the body
at rest, the heat liberation is 300 Btuh. During hard physical work, the
body heat release rate can climb to 2400-3000 Btuh. As we can see, under
these conditions a large amount of heat must be removed from the body
to avoid an increase in body temperature. Heat from the working environment influences body heat release rate to maintain normal body temperature. The regulation of body temperature is an important physiological
function, and the simplicity with which it can be accomplished in determined and controlled by the worker's ambient environment—by air temperature, air movement, long-wave radiation, and solar radiation.

Body Heat Exchange

Body heat is exchanged with the environment through convection and con-
duction, radiation, and evaporation. If the ambient air is at a lower temperature than skin temperature, heat will leave the body. Obviously, if
the air is at a higher temperature, heat will be gained. The rate of heat
transfer is determined by the temperature difference. However, if there
is air movement, the transfer of heat is accelerated through convection.

Loss via Conduction/Convection

Sensible heat suffers by far the greatest loss of heat between the skin and
air. In this process, convection plays the biggest part. Complicated
mathematical explanations describe this well, but we are most concerned
with the end result. Respiration is an inward extension of the process between the skin and air, and there is an addition of latent heat to the surroundings through this mechanism.

Perspiration plays an important role in maintaining a healthy body
temperature. The body loses heat to the air through the evaporation of
moisture from the body skin surface. The rate of this evaporative heat
loss is directly dependent on the difference between the effective vapor
pressure of the moisture on the skin and that in the ambient air. But,
here again, air movement across the skin's surface has a telling cooling
effect through combined evaporation and convection.

Humidity

Humidity is expressed as absolute humidity and relative humidity. For a
quick explanation please refer back to Chapter 1. Dew point is another
measure of humidity and is closely related to vapor pressure and absolute
humidity. Various combinations of dry bulb temperature and relative
humidity with the same vapor pressure also have the same dew point. To
the heat loss by evaporation from the skin must be added that from the

respiratory tract into the inspired air which is expired naturally. See Carroll, B. T. (1976).

Heat Exchange by Radiation

Heat is gained or lost by the body through radiation between the body surface and all of its surroundings. This exchange increases as the fourth power of the absolute temperature (°F + 460 = °R). However, the intensity may be diminished below the theoretical maximum by the physical nature of the surface of exchange known as its emissivity.

Evaporative Heat Loss

It is not always possible to dissipate the required evaporation heat loss to the environment because of the limitations of the surrounding atmosphere upon the body's evaporative cooling system. Air velocity across the skin's surface and the vapor pressure of the air control the amount of heat that can be lost through evaporation.

Maximum evaporative cooling capacity is also limited by the worker's ability to produce sweat. The average man sweats at a rate of one liter of moisture per hour. To evaporate 1 liter of moisture requires 2400 Btu. Thus, maximum evaporative capacity is limited to 2400 Btuh even under the most favorable conditions.

Cooling Effect of Air in Motion

The feeling of warmth experienced by an individual is greatly influenced by air motion, for air movement over the skin lowers the body temperature. One's sense of warmth is less in moving air than in still air, though the dry bulb temperature remains the same. It is reckoned that heat loss from exposed parts of the body is approximately doubled by an increase in air motion from 15 to 65 fpm, and trebled by an increase from 15 to 150 fpm. Where high temperatures prevail, air motion can provide considerable relief from heat and can decidedly effect human capacity for work and the inclination to work.

It is generally found that at room temperatures between 70 and 75°F, a velocity of 100-200 fpm provides a comfortable cooling effect for workers seated and only mildly active. But when muscular work is performed in hot areas, velocities between 250 and 500 fpm are usually required to give relief from heat. Higher velocities are provided in some cases when workers are exposed to intense radiant heat for short periods.

The amount of air motion required for a cooling effect can be gauged to some extent from personal experience of outdoor air velocities. The feeling of freshness produced by a light breeze blowing through a window on a hot day is familiar to all. The velocity of what is officially called a

TABLE 13.1. Wind Scale

Description of wind	Average velocity (mph)	Velocity (fpm)
Calm	—	0–25
Light air	3	264
Light breeze	7	616
Gentle breeze	12	1056
Moderate breeze	18	1584
Fresh breeze	24	2112
Strong breeze	30	2640
Moderate gale	38	3344
Fresh gale	47	4136
Strong gale	56	4928
Whole gale	66	5808
Storm	76	6688
Hurricane	82 (or higher)	6688 (or higher)

light breeze is about 500 fpm. Table 13.1 shows wind velocities in feet per minute.

The cooling effect of air movement can be assessed in terms of the reduction in air (dry bulb) temperature which would give the same cooling effect in still air. The exact effect depends on humidity, temperature, clothing worn, etc., but the following table can be taken as representative. The conditions range from normal clothing at normal indoor humidity with temperatures around 70°F for the low air velocities to high temperature with dry air and workers stripped to the waist for the higher velocities.

Spot Cooling of Workers

Tests show that the output efficiency of workers decreases considerably when the environmental temperature increases above well-established limits and that worker peak efficiency is attained when environmental temperature is within prescribed limits. It has also been found that a worker's ability to compensate for atmospheric conditions varies with the work

intensity, from subjects at rest to a high degree of activity. As environmental temperature and humidity increase, productivity decreased.

The effect of temperature and humidity was also found to affect a
worker's accident frequency rate, which was lowest under comfortable
conditions and increased rapidly as the temperature increased.

It has been conclusively proven that it is economical to control heat
wherever practicable. Then what temperature do we use as a criterion?
What is the most suitable effective temperature? There are many operations in hot industries and others where "spot cooling" will cool workers
by blowing air over them as they work. However, the air stream must
not be so hot that it produces a heating effect instead of a cooling effect.
What air velocities give the best results? One important point must be
kept in mind: when the wet bulb temperature of the impinging air stream
is above that of the workers' bodies, this method of spot cooling will heat
them more and will increase their discomfort. Under these conditions,
the air must be cooled or dehumidified also.

Practically, air velocities of 50, 100, 200, 500, and 700 fpm may be
used with various degrees of comfort. See Table 13.2 for cooling effects.
A velocity of 200 fpm and an air stream temperature of 80°F is the most
practical. However, above the maximum velocity of 200 fpm, precautions
should be exercised in directing the air stream to avoid drafts.

Now the problem arises as to the location of fans or blowers with respect to worker location to realize what we have listed above. With the
size of blower available, how can it be placed to advantage to get 200 fpm
blowing over the worker? Assume no interference of the air stream.
Table 13.3 shows air flow characteristics of blowing over known distances
and gives terminal velocities as a percentage of opening velocity. Thus,

TABLE 13.2. Cooling Effect of Air Flow

Average velocity (fpm)	Cooling effect (°F)
20	0
50	1
100	3
250	6
500	10
1000	13
2000	16

TABLE 13.3. Discharge Pattern for Supply Outlets

Throw distance diameters	Percent of outlet velocity
1	100
1.5	90
3	80
4	70
5.25	60
7	50
9	40
12.5	30
18	20
36	10

with an outlet (fan, blower, or discharge grille) velocity of 2000 fpm, a residual velocity of 200 fpm will be felt 35 opening diameters away. The volume of air handled would depend on the area to be covered. If a duct outlet were used having other than a circular opening, we must first convert from square or rectangular to round. These conversions may be made using charts and graphs from the American Society of Heating, Refrigeration and Air Conditioning Engineers (ASHRAE) Book of Fundamentals for duct cross section conversions. Once obtaining the converted diameter, return to Fig. 13.1 to find the residual velocity at the desired terminal point.

There is another aspect that we must not overlook. The main air jet stream will entrain a certain amount of room air with it as it projects itself away from the discharge opening. The air leaving the discharge point may be at one temperature but will be affected by the main body of room air temperature. The total air movement may be determined by the use of Fig. 13.1 and the following example.

EXAMPLE 13.1. A flow of air is discharged from an outlet at the rate of 5000 cfm at a temperature of 80°F into a space having a temperature of 100°F. At a distance of 13 ft from a worker, what is the temperature of the total induced air flow?

SOLUTION: From Fig. 13.1 determine the air entrainment ratio to be 6.6. Then the total air movement is 5000 × 6.6 = 33,000 cfm. The final temperature of the "mix" is found to be

$$\frac{1}{6.6} \times 80 = 12.2, \text{ say } 12$$

$$\frac{5.6}{6.6} \times 100 = 85$$

Total induced temperature = 97°F for the "mix"

From Table 13.3 the velocity at 13 ft from the discharge is 30% of the discharge velocity, and if this is 2000 fpm, the velocity reaching the subject is 0.2 × 2000 = 400 fpm and the cooling effect is found to be about 7°F.

Shielding Techniques

When complaints are received that there is a heat problem, control measures in the form of shielding and/or ventilation should be instituted. Radiant heat is the most common source of heat that workers encounter in severe stress conditions. Radiant heat is not affected by air motion because it is a form of wave motion similar to that of light and sound. Pedestal or worker-cooler fans will not help at all. Radiant heat waves are emitted from hot surfaces, open flames, and flowing metal. This type of heat is common in those industries with very hot processes, such as foundries, glass-making plants, and chemical plants using carbide furnaces.

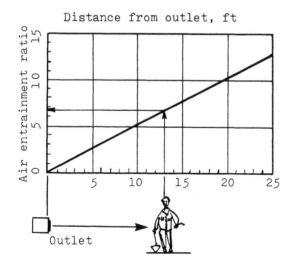

FIG. 13.1. Effect of free blow on air entrainment ratio.

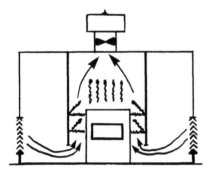

FIG. 13.2. Radiant shield extends down near floor and permits more air to flow past inner shield surface.

Since radiant heat waves travel in straight lines, they can be absorbed or reflected depending on the character of the material they strike; see Fig. 13.2 for application of principles of shielding techniques. Also see Lemke, R. C. (1961) and Polhemus, J. (1977). Because of this ability to be reflected, it allows for an inexpensive method of radiant heat control. Shiney metal surfaces reflect radiant heat well. Corrugated or flat sheet aluminum is easy to install. Aluminum screening has found wide use where the worker is required to observe conditions behind the reflective surface. Even dark metal screening has a retarding effect on radiant heat; for example, the screen across a fire place at home. Flexible reflective curtains are also available and have been used with good success as shields for the front of oven openings where rigid shields would block a continuous flow of materials.

A new shielding material is infrared reflecting glass. This can be used for radiant shielding where the worker must observe the operation. Radiant shielding with sheet aluminum is low in cost and will provide approximately a 50-60% reduction in the radiant heat load.

Worker Coolers

Worker coolers are limited in their effectiveness since they do not bring in cooler outside air. When workroom temperatures are below 90°F, they do help in cooling the worker by increasing the air velocity, which in turn helps body evaporation. However, when the workroom temperature exceeds 90°F, the use of a worker cooler will have the reverse effect since they will be blasting more warm air at the workers, heating them up. As previously pointed out, avoid using worker coolers in rooms requiring process exhaust ventilation because their high-velocity stream will upset the control of the exhaust stream.

Evaporative Cooling

Supplying outdoor air is effective as long as the outdoor air temperatures are low enough to provide inside relief. Evaporative cooling is a process of lowering the outdoor dry bulb temperature and can be applied effectively in many hot industries. The process is one in which air from the outdoors with a high dry bulb temperature is passed through an air washer provided with water sprays through which the air passes. As a result, the air is reduced in temperature to almost the temperature of the water. In a location with an average summer dry bulb temperature of 90°F and a wet bulb temperature of 75°F, the air can be reduced to 75-80°F, depending on the evaporative cooler design. This is a simple and inexpensive way to lower outdoor temperatures 10-15°F. Since the dry bulb temperature cannot be lowered below the existing wet bulb temperature, the wet bulb air temperature for a given locality limits the effectiveness of an evaporative cooling system. Therefore, give careful consideration to the wet bulb levels for the particular geographical location in question. See Marg, J. (1978).

In situations where evaporative cooling would not be practical for the general comfort cooling of large areas, it can still be effective when used in hot industries for spot cooling and cooling of larger process areas that are normally hot. To avoid the buildup of indoor humidity, evaporative cooling must be used with exhaust ventilation. Here are four simple precautions to observe when selecting evaporative cooling systems:

1. Use all outside air and do not recirculate during hot weather
2. Maintain adequate air motion around the workers who are to benefit. Although not scientifically backed, a minimum air velocity of 300-1000 fpm under severe heat conditions has proven successful. Automatic air dampers that can turn down 80% of velocity are essential to extend the system's usefulness during seasons other than summer when recirculation is permitted.
3. Provide a split system whereby evaporative cooling is used in conjunction with motorized roof exhaust ventilators and adequate fresh air openings. Thus, the heavy outdoor air volumes will hold down the overall temperature level in all areas of a hot operation and will sweep out the vitiated washed air.
4. Do not use evaporative cooling for offices and other areas free of hot operations except in recognized hot, dry climates of which the southwest is typical (e.g., Arizona).

Air Conditioning

Air conditioning finds its greatest acceptance in administration-type buildings where there is little or no process heat emitted. There are, however, an increasing number of manufacturing plants using air conditioning especially in the manufacture of precision parts and equipment in such places as clean rooms. Today, control rooms in oil refineries and chemical plants are air conditioned as a rule.

Excessive heat has physiological effects on the worker, and a comfortable working environment is recognized as a good investment for worker cooperation and welfare. The physical factors that relate to the makeup and severity of each individual heat problem must be understood so that effective measures can be provided for their abatement.

The Case for Industrial Air Conditioning

The case for industrial comfort air conditioning has been proved over and over again in hundreds of factories and plants. In production areas of a plant where there's a high internal heat gain from machinery, in the drafting room, engineering, planning, and research, there's bound to be a summer slump, a slow-down. Here are some yardsticks to help determine if air conditioning will pay in a factory or plant:

Is the plant located in an area of high summer heat and humidity?

Do production and quality go down during hot weather?

Is worker cooperation and teamwork important? Does hot weather affect smooth production lines?

Is absenteeism a problem during summer months? Is turnover high during the summer?

Are your products susceptible to damage from rust, dirt, or mildew?

Are there many sources of high internal heat gain, such as electric motors, ovens, heat treating furnaces, lights, solar gain, etc?

Are people involved in exacting labor, repetitive work, jobs where heat and fumes cause physical and emotional fatigue?

Does labor account for more than 25% of the manufacturing cost of your product?

How much does each department head feel air conditioning will save per hour per worker? Figure factors such as stopping work to wipe off sweat, extra trips to the water cooler, extra rest periods, and improved worker efficiency when heat stress is removed.

Ways to Reduce Cooling Costs

Here are 14 practical ways to reduce cooling costs:

Use the existing ductwork and air handling equipment, with minor modifications, to handle air conditioning.

Keep the plant closed up and run the cooling equipment at night to store cooling in walls, machinery, etc., and so reduce size of cooling equipment. Power rates are generally less at night.

For operations where air conditioning may not be practical, but heat is a problem, consider air conditioned "rest areas" where personnel can recuperate from heat exposure.

Check water consumption and use in your plant. Volume may be high enough that a water-cooled condenser can be used before going to the plant for process use, thus eliminating a tooling tower.

TABLE 13.4. Heat Control Methods

Method	Purpose	Application	Remarks
General ventilation (roof)	Removes convective process heat. Permits outside cooler air to replace the exhausted warm air.	When convective heat process adds to the overall problem. When outside makeup air is low enough (below 90°F) to provide inside cooling.	Makeup air should be directed to the lower 8-ft level where it can sweep across the work space. Buildings over 400 ft in width and areas with large machines hinder the cross-flow of air.
Local exhaust ventilation	To remove process heat, gases, vapors, and dust directly from the point of generation.	Process moisture increases the relative humidity, and gases and vapors contaminate the workspace.	Tempered makeup air equal in volume to exhausted air needed for winter operation.
Vapor absorption ventilation	Removes process moisture from large areas by absorbing moisture with makeup air of lower RH.	Process moisture increases space RH and cannot be exhausted with local ventilation.	Can be used in areas where dry makeup air is available. 100% makeup air is necessary. Tempered makeup air needed for winter operation. Introduce makeup air below 10-ft level.

TABLE 13.4. (Continued)

Method	Purpose	Application	Remarks
Evaporative cooling	Lowers temperature of dry hot outside air for distribution to hot plant areas.	A lower temperature cooling air is needed that can be obtained with outside air directly. Outside air temperature is above 90°F and will not give inside relief.	Evaporative cooling may be used for relief cooling in hot industries even in geographical areas where it would be impractical for general cooling due to high wet bulb temperature. Wet bulb air temperature governs the effectiveness of evaporative cooling. Evaporative cooling should be used with exhaust ventilation.
Air conditioning	Lowers the inside air temperature of the work space.	There is little process heat to add to the overall heat load.	Can also be used to control moisture in space air to prevent corrosion and condensation indoors on walls and roofs.
Reverse flow ventilation including spot cooling	Brings in cooler air at higher velocities.	Good air distribution to the lower regions of plant is needed. High-velocity supply air from outside is needed to improve body evaporation.	Duct outlets should be arranged to allow the workers to adjust air flow to accommodate themselves.

| Reflective shielding | Reflects radiant heat by placement of a shield between the source of radiation and the person or area to be protected. | High-velocity cooling air is needed for spot cooling at specific locations. Radiant heat adds to the body heat load generally when the mean radiant temperature is above 95°F. When radiant heat is converted to convective heat. | Sheet or corrugated aluminum is a good low-cost reflecting material. An added benefit is realized when convective heat within the area enclosed by the shield is removed by exhaust. |

Remember, it is not necessary to bring temperature and humidity down to levels found in offices. 80°F dry bulb temperature and 40% relative humidity (RH) is good enough in the plant area when it's 95°F dry bulb in the shade outside and the RH is 65% or higher. In general, it is as important to reduce the RH as it is the temperature, although both should be done. Reduced RH permits body-heat-removing functions to work at greater efficiency.

Install needed equipment in hottest "problem" spots now and add more later when the budget permits.

Consider lease arrangements for packaged air conditioning equipment.

Exhaust cooled, conditioned air out through hot spots, such as a foundry, paint spray rooms, etc., where air conditioning may not be practical.

Consider pinpointing air conditioning at isolated hot spots instead of cooling the entire plant in order to cool a few people. Package units are ideal for such applications.

Forget about 20-30 ft ceilings. Supply conditioned air at the 8-10 ft level. Compute your needs as if an all-glass ceiling existed 12 ft above the floor. If you use packaged units, avoid long duct runs. Deliver air right from the discharge plenum at the unit through grilles provided with the unit.

Supply air can be delivered at higher velocities than with commercial jobs since noise is not as much a factor with which to be contended.

Simply ventilate or partition off areas of extreme heat from the rest of the shop. Contain heat-producing areas so that you are only cooling the personnel.

Consider using radiation shields wherever possible.

Check the actual operating time and heat output of the machinery. You may be able to save by figuring a 50-hp motor that is running only 10% of the time as a 15 hp motor, thus cutting cooling costs. See Appendix A.5.

Summary of Heat Control Methods

Table 13.4 summarizes the various heat control methods available for use in industry.

EXAMPLE 13.2. The following information on the thermal environment has been reported: globe temperature* = 105°F; dry

---

*The globe thermometer is often used to measure the mean radiant temperature. A conventional globe thermometer consists of a 6 in. hollow copper sphere painted matte black on the outside and inside. For ordinary plant measurements, a common copper toilet float painted a flat black gives a sufficiently accurate reading. A thermometer is fixed in the center

bulb temperature = 84°F; wet bulb temperature = 70°F; air velocity is across the body. What is the effective temperature corrected for radiation?

SOLUTION: Determine the absolute humidity by using dry and wet bulb temperatures of the air obtained from a psychrometric chart. Absolute humidity = 84 grains per lb dry air.

Determine the pseudo-wet bulb temperature using the absolute humidity and globe temperature obtained from a psychrometric chart. Pseudo-wet bulb temperature = 75.8°F. Determine the effective temperature corrected for radiation by using the pseudo-wet bulb temperature as a wet bulb temperature and the globe temperature as a dry bulb temperature on the effective temperature chart in Fig. 3-5 in Industrial Ventilation, 8th ed. (1964). Finally, the temperature corrected for radiation is 84°F.

---

of the sphere with the stem protruding to the outside through a sealed opening. The temperature of the air inside the globe at equilibrium is the result of a balance between the heat gained or lost by convection. In terms of heat transfer relationships

$$MRT^4 = (T_g^4 + 0.103 \times 10^9 \times V)(t_g - t_a) \tag{13.1}$$

where

MRT = mean radiant temperature, °F

T_g = globe temperature, °R

V = air velocity at the globe, fpm

t_g = glove temperature, °F

t_a = ambient air temperature, °F

It will be noted from the above equation that the air temperature and air velocity around the globe must be determined. It is the determination of this velocity which presents the greatest problem in the use of the globe thermometer. A period of 15 to 25 min usually is required for the globe to reach equilibrium.

Measurement of low air velocity is always difficult. In addition to being low, the air velocity in an open room is quite random in direction, and a nondirectional instrument should be used for its measurement. Thermal anemometers of the heated thermocouple, hot wire, or heated thermometer types are best suited for such measurements. They will prove useful data if they are maintained in calibration and if the user understands their operation and limitations.

APPENDIX A

A.1. SOLVE GAS-PURGING PROBLEMS GRAPHICALLY

Here are instructions for making a chart that will help you to determine the amount of purge gas to use in various situations. Acetylene is used as an example.

When handling explosive gases, either in pilot plants or large-scale plants, the purging of process vessels, tanks, and piping is usual before start-up or after shutdown. The gas most often used for purging is nitrogen because of its inert characteristics and low cost.

Later on, we will show how a purging chart can be constructed that will "map" the entire purging procedure.

Inert gases such as nitrogen not only depress or narrow the explosive range of a combustible gas or vapor, but also prevent the formation of explosive mixtures when these inert gases are mixed in suitable proportions either with air, with the combustible gas, or with an explosive mixture of both.

Object of Purging with Inert Gas

By displacing (or mixing) the air in a piece of equipment to be placed in gas service, with a suitable amount of inert gas (in our case nitrogen), combustible gas may subsequently be introduced into the equipment without the formation of an explosive mixture. Similarly, by displacing or mixing the combustible in a container with a suitable quantity of nitrogen, air may later be introduced without forming an explosive mixture. During the purging procedure, the contents must constantly be sampled and the samples analyzed, using standard accepted methods of chemical analysis.

Gas Flammability Limits in Air

A flammable mixture of gases, such as acetylene and air, may be diluted with one of the constituents (acetylene or air) until the mixture is no longer flammable. The dilution limit of flammability is the borderline composition—a slight change in one direction supports burning, whereas in the other direction, combustion cannot be maintained. See Coward, H. F., and Jones, G. W. (1938).

281

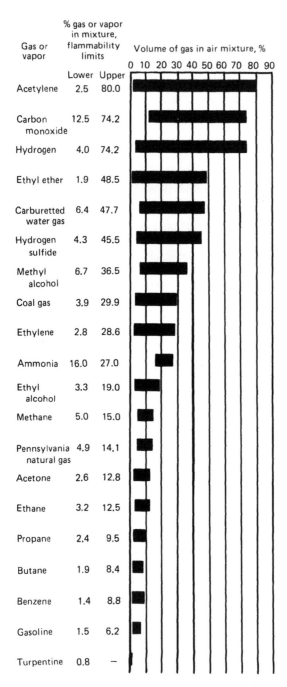

Gas or vapor	% gas or vapor in mixture, flammability limits		Volume of gas in air mixture, %
	Lower	Upper	
Acetylene	2.5	80.0	
Carbon monoxide	12.5	74.2	
Hydrogen	4.0	74.2	
Ethyl ether	1.9	48.5	
Carburetted water gas	6.4	47.7	
Hydrogen sulfide	4.3	45.5	
Methyl alcohol	6.7	36.5	
Coal gas	3.9	29.9	
Ethylene	2.8	28.6	
Ammonia	16.0	27.0	
Ethyl alcohol	3.3	19.0	
Methane	5.0	15.0	
Pennsylvania natural gas	4.9	14.1	
Acetone	2.6	12.8	
Ethane	3.2	12.5	
Propane	2.4	9.5	
Butane	1.9	8.4	
Benzene	1.4	8.8	
Gasoline	1.5	6.2	
Turpentine	0.8	—	

FIG. A.1. Upper and lower explosive limits of various combustible materials when mixed with air. (From Chemical Engineering, December 29, 1980.)

There are two well-defined limits within which self-propagation of flame will take place after ignition. These are the "upper" and "lower" limits that are defined in terms of the percentage volume of gas present in the mixture of gas and air. The combined chart and table (Fig. A.1) lists these limits for some of the common gases and vapors at atmospheric pressure and ambient temperature.

Within these limits, the gas-air mixture liberates enough energy to continue propagation of flame from one layer to the next. Mixtures above the upper limit may burn on contact with external air, since the air can form a new mixture. Certain conditions effect a shift in the limits, either increasing or decreasing the spread between them. These include ignition source, intensity of ignition, direction of flame propagation, size and shape of containing vessel, temperature, pressure and humidity in the containing vessel, oxygen content, and turbulence.

Some of the explosibility data reported in the literature are not applicable in purging problems. From the standpoint of safety, it is desirable not only that the widest explosive limits of the given combustible gas be selected, but that an ample safety factor also be provided. For acetylene-air mixtures at atmospheric pressure and temperature, the accepted values for the lower explosive limit (LEL) and upper explosive limit (UEL) are 2.5 and 80.0% acetylene in air, respectively. These are the widest limits shown on the bar chart for all gases listed (at normal pressure and temperature; (see Fig. A.1).

In every case involving combustible gas handling or processing, one must be constantly aware of the inherent dangers to life and property. In the case of acetylene, it is an acknowledged fact that it is an unstable gas at any pressure, and whether or not a decomposition would take place depends on the intensity of the initial source of ignition. Higher pressures have the effect of lowering the initial energy necessary to start a decomposition. See Tomkins, S. S. (1934).

Acetylene: A Few Fundamental Facts

Given a sufficiently high initial pressure, the possibility of a propagation acetylene decomposition depends very much on the kind and strength of ignition. With decreasing ignition energies, the initial pressures of the acetylene-air mixtures must be correspondingly increased in order to bring the total gas volume to decomposition conditions.

The size and shape of the process vessel, as well as its material of construction, have a profound influence on the ignition limits of combustible gas mixtures. The same holds for acetylene decomposition. It is all a matter of heat balance in the combustion process. The position of the ignition source is also of importance. In the case of a vertical cylindrical vessel, the widest explosive range is obtained when the ignition takes place at the base of the container.

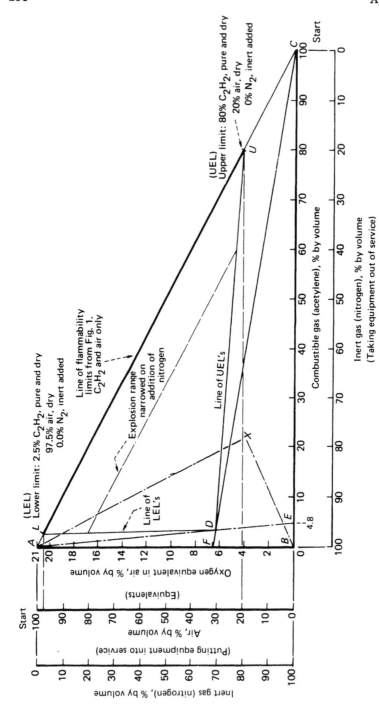

FIG. A.2. Acetylene-air-nitrogen purging chart (atmospheric temperature and pressure). (From *Chemical Engineering*, December 29, 1980.)

Water vapor, with its attendant high humidity, acts as a dilutor and an inert gas. This is a typical effect for all combustible gas-air mixtures.

As far as the effect on explosion limits, the ratio of vessel surface to sectional area is important from the point of view of heat balance or cooling. Long, slender vessels, having high ratios of surface-to-sectional-area narrow the limits of explosibility. (It is all a matter of heat removal rate). Also, since increased temperatures induce turbulence due to convection currents being set up, the limits are widened.

Tests on each of the above variations can tell the effects on widening or narrowing the explosibility range. However, once established, the LEL and UEL that have been determined experimentally can be used to develop a purging chart that will be discussed later on.

Effect of Inert Gas

The effect of inert gas on the explosibility of combustible gases in air may be shown graphically in Fig. A.2, represented by acetylene-air mixtures. This is simple to develop once the limits for any configuration and condition are experimentally determined.

As nitrogen is added to mixtures of gas and air within the explosive range, a series of new mixtures are formed. Each of these mixtures has a different UEL and LEL from the preceding mixture, and the explosive range is narrowed. As the oxygen and combustible gas contents of these mixtures are reduced by the addition of nitrogen, the line of lower limits and line of upper limits converge and meet at a point, in this case D. Here the explosive range has been reduced to zero. No mixture of this combustible gas, air, and nitrogen that contains less oxygen than the lowest point on the line LDU (point D) is explosive in itself, but all mixtures within the area bound by LDU are within the limits of explosibility and therefore will be explosive.

Again, in Fig. A.2 line ADE is drawn tangent to the curve LDU at D. Any mixture represented by point X to the right of line DE and below the line of upper explosive limits, DU, is not explosive in itself. However, on dilution of that mixture with air, a new series of mixtures will be formed having the composition falling along line XA, which passes through the explosive area. Similarly, any mixture represented by a point to the left of lines LD and DE will not form explosive mixtures when they are further diluted with air.

Note tha line LD is not vertical but swings to the right as it drops.

Application of the Chart

When placing gas equipment into service, say at startup (that is, purging from air to inert gas), the object is to reduce the oxygen content of the air in the equipment to such a point that acetylene (or another gas) may be subsequently introduced without forming an explosive mixture. From Fig. A.2 it may be observed that the safe condition will be reached when the oxygen

content of the atmosphere within the container has been reduced by the introduction of nitrogen to below approximately 6.6% by volume, denoted by point
F, where FC drawn tangent to LDU at D intersects the vertical axis, AB.
Any mixture of this combustilbe gas, nitrogen, and air having an oxygen
content represented by a point below this line, FC, may be diluted with the
combustible gas without forming an explosive mixture.

On Shutdown

Similarly, when withdrawing equipment (and piping) containing acetylene gas
from service or when purging from a combustible to an inert gas, the object
is to reduce the combustible gas content of the atmosphere in the equipment
(and piping) to such a point that the air may subsequently be introduced without the possibility of forming an explosive mixture. It may be seen from
Fig. A.2 that a safe condition will be reached when the combustible gas content of the atmosphere within the equipment or piping has been reduced to
below 4.8% by volume; this is denoted by point E.
     There may be occasions when mixtures of acetylene, nitrogen, and air
are to be diluted with a further quantity of inert gas so as to render them
nonexplosive or incapable of forming explosive mixtures on later additions
of air. The object here is to add sufficient nitrogen to convert the existing
composition of the mixture to some composition corresponding to a point on
the chart that lies to the left of LD and DE. Assuming that the mixture is
again denoted by point X, then, on addition and dilution of the mixture with
nitrogen, successive mixtures will be formed along XB. The point where
XB crosses DE denotes the safe end-point composition. Then, on the further addition of air (intentional or accidental), the line of mixtures will fall
to the left of LDE.
     In practical operations, it is desirable to decrease the proportions of
oxygen and combustible gas below the determined values, to provide a factor of safety. To prevent explosion in industrial processing, it is necessary
to keep the air-gas, air-vapor, or mixture of gas, air, and nitrogen below
the LEL within the processing vessel or piping most likely to be affected.
An established safe practice is to keep the mixture well blended with air or
inert gas so that the composition, as calculated or determined, never
reaches more than 25% of the LEL, or any other low limit as determined
from the chart at temperatures below 250°F. Equipment should be placed
into service or taken out of service when the system has been depressurized
to atmospheric pressure.
     During start-up or shutdown of systems, mixture contents should be
sampled downstream of the point of injection of nitrogen for proper mixing
of gases before sampling. Obviously, taking samples from stratified
streams would produce erroneous results. Samples should be taken from
piping systems downstream of elbows and valves (open) for greatest mixing.
Even though these may not be required for the normal design of the piping

system, mixing elbows and valves should be designed into the system at the drawing board stage.

The Nitrogen Supply

The use of inert gases derived from the combustion of hydrocarbons should be avoided. An upset condition in the operation of the inert-gas generator's combustion process could permit unburned hydrocarbons to enter the system being purged, and could thus render the purging procedure unsafe and unpredictable. These are important considerations.

Pureness and dryness of the purging medium are of paramount importance and can best be achieved from a bottled-gas arrangement or by use of a cascade liquefied nitrogen system.

Nitrogen for purging may be supplied from such cascade systems, or directly from "bottle" trailers under pressure, normally 2000 psig. When drawn from large cascade systems or reservoirs, the nitrogen is piped into a "running tank." This tank is then pressurized and its contents are expanded through pressure regulators, as desired for purging. When pressurized trailers are used, the high-pressure gas is also regulated down to the desired pressure for purging. See Glitwitzky, W. (1940).

Purging-chart Designations and Use

Point D	No mixture of acetylene, air, and nitrogen that contains less than 6.4% oxygen is explosive.
LDU	All mixtures within area of triangle LDU are explosive.
Point X	Any mixture such as that denoted by point X is not explosive.
Line XA	On dilution of the mixture denoted by point X with air, new mixtures along XA are formed.
LDE	Any point to the left of LDE will not form explosive mixtures on dilution with air.
FDC	Any mixture of acetylene, nitrogen, and air represented by a point below FDC may be diluted with acetylene without forming an explosive mixture when placing equipment into service.
Point F	Safe point reached after air has been displaced with nitrogen and you are ready to add acetylene (6.6% oxygen). This is the situation when placing equipment into service.
Point E	Safe point reached after acetylene has been displaced with nitrogen and you are ready to add air (4.8% acetylene). This is the situation when taking equipment out of service.

Steps in Setting Up a Purging Chart

---

1. Draw right triangle, ABC, whose size can accommodate the required ordinate and abscissa scales.
2. Fill in both ordinate and abscissa scales for the combustible of concern.
3. From Fig. A.1, superimpose the explosive range of the combustible gas of concern on line AC, using the abscissa scale values.
4. Using the experimentally determined value equivalent of point E, strike that value on line BC.
5. Draw line AE.
6. Draw lines LD and UD.
7. Draw line FDC.
8. Establish any point X below line FDC.
9. Draw lines AX and BX as shown.
10. Complete the chart by adding the notes and other embellishments.

Draw the chart carefully so that the various points can be determined with accuracy. And remember to use a safety factor in applying the chart figures, i.e., 25% of the chart values (points E and F) when taking equipment out of service and when putting equipment into service, respectively.

A.2. CONTROL OF EXPLOSIVE OR TOXIC AIR-GAS MIXTURES

Explosive and toxic gas-air mixtures can be made safe by diluting the mixtures with sufficient air. Here is how to determine dilution-air amounts with the help of easy-to-use formulas and charts.

Why risk explosion in handling solvents or dangerous gases in industrial processing, when mixing the gases or vapors with sufficient air can make the mixture explosionproof? For example, a flammable mixture such as methane and air may be diluted with one of the constituents until the mixture is no longer flammable. The dilution limit of flammability is the borderline composition. A slight change in one direction supports burning; in the other direction, combustion cannot be maintained. By means of the accompanying charts and formulas, the air quantities needed to make gas-air mixtures explosionproof and nontoxic can readily be found.

Explosive and Health Hazard Limits

There are two well-defined limits within which self-propagation of flame will take place after ignition; they are the upper explosive limit and the lower explosive limit. The limits are defined in terms of percentage volume of combustible gas present in the mixture of gas and air.

If the temperature of a flammable, volatile liquid is gradually increased, the air above the liquid becomes progressively richer in vapor. At a certain concentration, the air-vapor mixture can just be ignited with an open flame or spark of sufficient thermal intensity and will propagate flame. This is the LEL for the vapor.

As the concentration of vapor in air increases, it becomes easier to ignite the mixture, and the combustion becomes progressively more violent until a maximum concentration of vapor is reached. A further increase in concentration will result in a gradual decrease in the violence of explosion, until a point is finally reached where the mixture will no longer propagate flame but will still burn at the point of ignition. This is the UEL.

Within these limits, the combustible air mixture liberates enough energy to continue propagation of flame from one layer to another adjacent one. Mixtures above the UEL may burn on contact with external air because these are formed in the zone where gases mix.

Certain conditions effect a shift in the limits, either increasing or decreasing the spread between them. These include ignition source, direction of flame propagation (up or down), container (room) dimensions, humidity, oxygen content, pressure, temperature, and turbulence.

The data that are shown in Table A.1 are representative of typical gases and vapors and provide materials' characteristics pertinent to this discussion. For more extensive listings, consult Industrial Ventilation, A Manual of Recommended Practice (1970), Sax, N. I. (1968), National Safety Council (1964), Hemeon, W. C. L. (1964), National Board of Fire Underwriters*, U.S. Department of Health, Education, and Welfare (1967). Note that in this table the LEL and UEL values given are at atmospheric temperature and pressure. Maximum allowable concentrations (MAC), presently known as Threshold Limit Values (TLV), are based on an 8-hr exposure per worker.

The LELs are assumed constant for temperatures up to 250°F. Above this, LELs should be decreased by a factor of 0.7 because explosibility increases with higher temperatures. Since here we are concerned with standard pressures, no further correction is required.

MAC values appearing in the table are those termed threshold limit values in the recent literature. These values pertain to airborne concentrations and represent conditions to which, it is believed, nearly all workers may be repeatedly exposed, day after day, without adverse affect.

However, because of wide variations in individual susceptibility, exposure of an occasional individual to such concentrations—or even lower ones—may not prevent discomfort, aggravation of a preexisting condition, or occupational illness. MACs or TLVs should be used as guides in the control of health hazards and should not be regarded as fine lines between safe and dangerous concentrations because there are exceptions.

---

*Pamphlet 86, Standard for Class A Ovens and Furnaces.

TABLE A. 1. Explosive Limits and Maximum Concentrations for Vapors of Hazardous Chemicals in Air

Substance	Molecular weight	Vapor LEL (%)	Vapor UEL (%)	Vapor TLV (ppm)
Acetone	58.05	2.55	12.80	200
Ammonia	17.0	15.50	27.0	50
Benzene	78.05	1.40	7.10	25 (skin)[a]
Carbon bisulfide	76.13	1.25	50.00	20 (skin)[a]
Cellosolve	90.12	2.6	15.7	25 (skin)[a]
Ethyl alcohol	46.07	3.28	18.95	1000
Ethylene	28.05	3.0	34.0	—
Gasoline	86	1.3	6.0	—
Hydrogen	2.0	4.1	74.2	—
Hydrogen sulfide	34.08	4.3	45.5	10
Methyl alcohol	32.04	6.72	36.5	200
Methyl chloride	50.49	8.25	18.70	100
Methyl ethyl ketone	72.1	1.81	9.5	200
Naphtha (petroleum)	—	1.4	5.9	—
Toluene	92.13	1.27	6.75	200
Turpentine (turpene)	136.23	0.8	—	100

[a]Refers to potential contribution to overall exposure by cutaneous route—including mucous membranes and eyes—either airborne or, more particularly, by direct contact with the substance itself. Cutaneous absorption should be prevented.

Calculation Procedures

To prevent an explosion in industrial processing, it is necessary to keep the air-vapor (or air-gas) mixture below the LEL within the area or processing vessel most likely to be affected. An established safe practice is to keep the mixture well blended with air so that the calculated concentration never reaches more than 25% of the LEL in temperatures below 250°F.

To calculate the fresh-air requirement and the allowable concentration, Avogadro's law and the pound-mole concept are applied. According to these, one pound-mole of any gas or vapor occupies the same volume as one pound-mole of any other gas or vapor, providing no chemical reaction occurs in the mixture. We know this molal volume to be 379 ft^3 at 60°F and atmospheric pressure (14.7 psia). Process gases or vapors should never be considered harmless or nonflammable. Wherever they are handled, their characteristics should be checked with insurance carriers, governmental agencies, or manufacturers to make certain that correct and up-to-date values are applied in air requirement calculations. The National Board of Fire Underwriter's Standard for Class A Ovens and Furnaces lists and describes a number of safeguards and interlocks that must be always considered with air dilution when applied to processing vessels.

The range within which there is danger of explosion is sharply defined for every air-vapor mixture through the lower and upper explosion limits "as published". However, through the addition of vapor (or gas) of another dangerous substance, the published lower and upper limits are shifted. According to Le Chatelier, the more important limit—the LEL—can be determined approximately, but acceptably, as follows:

$$\text{LEL (mixture)} = \frac{100}{P_1/C_1 + P_2/C_2 + P_3/C_3 + \cdots + P_n/C_n} \quad (A.1)$$

where C_1, C_2, C_3, and C_n stand for the LEL of each individual explosive vapor expressed as percent by volume in air, and P_1, P_2, P_3, and P_n are percentages of individual vapor in the mixture when

$$P_1 + P_2 + P_3 + \cdots + P_n = 100 \quad (A.2)$$

Thus, the LEL of the mixture C_m (i.e., LEL_{C_m}) of three vapors in the percentage ratio of 30, 40, 30—with individual LELs of 1, 2, 3—is

$$\text{LEL}_{C_m} = \frac{100}{30/1 + 40/2 + 30/3} = 1.666 \quad (A.3)$$

This calculation applies soley to mixtures of explosive gases or vapors and not to mixtures of nonexplosive gases (or vapors). Here, a word of caution is necessary. Since calculated LEL_{C_m} values frequently show a marked discrepancy from observed values, when in doubt regard the mixture as consisting only of air and of the component with the lowest individual LEL; than calculate the air quantity on this safe basis.

Correction Factors

For enclosed processing vessels, such as drying ovens, this formula may be used:

$$A_d = \frac{379}{M} \times \frac{1}{B} \times \frac{100}{0.25\text{LEL}} \quad (A.4)$$

where A_d = amount of dilution air (cu ft^3), M = molecular weight of the substances, LEL = lower explosive limit, 0.25 = safety factor, and B = correction factor that takes into account that the LEL of a vapor-air mixture
decreases at elevated temperatures.

For mixture temperatures up to 250°F, B = 1; above 250°F, B = 0.7.
The multiplier 0.25, which is an industry-wide accepted figure, should never
be exceeded. There are exceptional cases when the factor of safety (1/0.25 =
4.0), which is acceptable for continuous-process ovens, becomes 10 for
batch ovens with peak drying rates. For improperly ventilated ovens or
similar enclosures, factors greater than 10 may be necessary. Experience
plays an important role in the selection of this factor.

Under certain high-temperature operations, a temperature and volume
correction-factor must be applied to Eq. A.4. An altitude correction factor may also be necessary. For operating temperatures up to 100° F and an
elevation of 1000 ft above sea level, such corrections are not required. Reference 1* is an excellent source of information on this aspect.

Figure A.3 facilitiates the calculation of the amount of dilution air needed for air-vapor mixtures. It has been developed from Eq. A.4 for temper-
tures below 250,F.

> EXAMPLE: Gasoline vapor is to be used in an enclosed process
> vessel. What is the volume of fresh air needed, for every pound
> of vapor handled, to dilute to 25% of LEL? Assume a temperature
> below 250°F and standard atmospheric pressure. The molecular
> weight of gasoline is 120, and its LEL is 1.3.
>
> SOLUTION: First, the specific volume factor(SVF) is calculated:
>
> $$\frac{379}{120} = 3.15 \text{ ft}^3/\text{lb.}$$
>
> Then
>
> $$25\% \text{ of LEL} = 0.25 \times 1.3 = 0.325.$$
>
> Now enter Fig. A.3 at the bottom at the SVF value of 3.15, and
> move upward to meet the 0.325 sloping line (interpolating as req-
> quired). The answer, 970 ft^3 of dilution air, is read on the left
> column. If the temperature were above 250°F, the corrected vol-
> ume would be 970/0.7 = 1386 ft^3.

Dilution Because of Health Hazard

When workers are exposed to toxic or hazardous vapors, dilution ventilation
rates should be much greater than those discussed above. In such cases,
dilution rates for health-hazard control are always applied. Note in the
table that if a space or work room is adequately ventilated for health pur-

---

*"Industrial Ventilation," manual of recommended practice, ACGIH, 11 ed.
(1970).

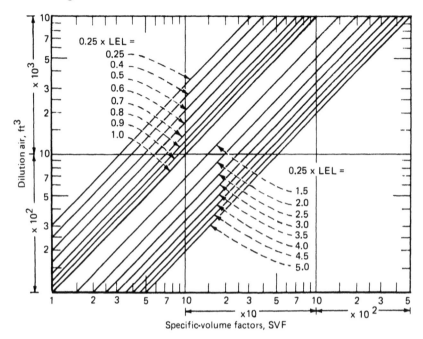

FIG. A.3. Air required to dilute combustible mixture to 25% of LEL value at temperatures under 250°F. (From Chemical Engineering, December 29, 1980.)

poses, explosion hazard does not exist. For instance, 10 ppm of hydrogen sulfide is equivalent to 0.001%, whereas 25% of the gas LEL is 1.075% by volume.

The MACs shown in the table are based on an 8-hr exposure per worker. Therefore, the "toxicity" ventilation rate is based on the same daily exposure.

Dilution-air requirements in cfm to render an open room or large vessel safe for worker occupancy may be calculated from

$$A_d = \frac{1540ST}{M \times MAC \times K} \tag{A.5}$$

where S = gas or vapor expelled over an 8-hr period (lb), M = molecular weight of vapor or gas, MAC (TLV) = maximum allowable concentration (ppm), T = room temperature (°R), and K = air-mixing factor for nonideal conditions, which varies between 3 and 10. See also Chapter 5 also for the use of these factors.

If the space temperature is assumed to be 100°F, there is no temperature correction, and Eq. (A.5) becomes

$$A_d = \frac{862,400S}{M \times MAC \times K} \tag{A.6}$$

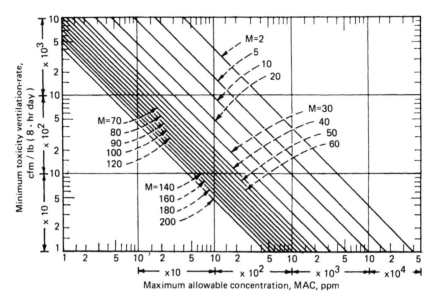

FIG. A.4. Minimum air ventilation rate needed to render harmless toxic gas-air or vapor-air mixtures. Graph based on S = 1, T = 560°R. (From Chemical Engineering, April 19, 1971.)

For every pound of gas or vapor expelled over an 8-hr period, when S = 1, Eq. (A.6) becomes

$$A_d = \frac{862,400}{M \times MAC \times K} \tag{A.7}$$

For values of S less than or greater than unity, simple multiplication may be used.

Figure A.4 assists in a quick visual appreciation of these problems by providing stoichiometric quantities under the assumption of ideal mixing conditions of vapor and air. Here again, an air-mixing factor (K) may be necessary to increase capacity. Industrial Ventilation, A Manual of Recommended Practice (1970) and Sax, N. I. (1968) provides guideposts for the selection of K values.

EXAMPLE: A worker is operating a process vessel in which carbon bisulfide is being handled. What is the toxicity ventilation rate if 2 lb per 8 hr are being discharged and if the worker is exposed over the full 8-hr workshift? The molecular weight of CS_2 is 76.13 and its MAC (TLV) value is 20 ppm.

SOLUTION: Referring to Fig. A.4, enter at the bottom at MAC = 20 and move vertically to meet line M = 76 (interpolation required). Now cross over to the left scale and read 5.6×10^2, or 560 cfm/lb. For 2 lb the answer becomes 1,120 cfm. This is the ideal rate, which must be corrected upward, depending on ventilation efficiency, operation, and the particular system application.

General System Design Precautions

In all calculations regarding safety and health hazards, good judgment and the intelligent use of safety factors must be exercised.

For occupied spaces, the volume of dilution air becomes so large and unweildly to handle that local exhaust (as opposed to dilution or general ventilation) systems are necessary to keep down air quantities and to reduce heat losses by exhausting smaller quantities of air.

In dilution-ventilation instances, exhaust openings should be located near the sources of contamination. Also, for dilution methods to be effective, the air supply and exhaust outlet must be located so that the entire air flow is replaced by makeup air (heated in the winter). The air-flow pattern within the room should be from across the back of the operator to the exhaust opening. To avoid recirculating vitiated exhaust air, its discharge should take place above adjacent roof lines.

Because of the effect of toxic vapors and gases handled in industry, not only do workers need to be examined periodically but the atmosphere around processing equipment should be routinely sampled. Good instruments are available* that permit gas sampling and the determination of vapor concentrations in a practical way.

Air-flow switches in the exhaust stacks of vented equipment should be included in the total-system design. Adjustable to certain air flows, the equipment can be connected to an alarm or a safety switch that will stop the processing equipment if any change occurs in the amount of exhaust air (after the dampers for air flow are set)) These alarms or switches will indicate any change in the exhaust system because of exhaust fan motor failure belt slippage on fan drives, plugging up of exhaust ducts, incorrect setting of dampers, or an accidental change in damper setting.

In plant areas or for expensive and critical processing equipment, it may be advisable to install permanently recording or indicating explosimeters. It is also good practice to apply fans and motors that meet the rigid requirements for hazardous areas. See the National Safety Council's Accident Prevention Manual for Industrial Operations (1964).

---

*Such as those made by Mine Safety Appliance Co., Pittsburgh, Pennsylvania, and Davis Emergency Equipment Co., Newark, New Jersey.

A.3. CALCULATING SOUND LEVELS FROM OCTAVE-BAND ANALYSES

To avoid the obvious difficulty of enforcing a maximum-noise standard with complex requirements, OSHA has chosen a simple, single-number standard that takes the entire frequency spectrum into account: the A-scale on a standard sound-level meter using a weighted* electrical network that makes the meter respond to sound as the human ear. Thus, 90 dBA—set by the Occupational Safety and Health Act (OSHA) as the maximum level to which workers may be exposed in an 8-hr day—actually describes a contour line as in the dBA curves of Fig. A.5.

However, the various sources that contribute to the overall noise of plants will rarely exhibit a smooth sound contour; and an octave-band analysis of the noise is frequently useful for identifying the contribution that each source makes to the total. This can be done by measurements taken with the "linear" scale of a standard sound-level meter. These readings will lie above and below the nearest A-scale curve and must be translated into dBA for study. One method is to plot the uncorrected band readings on a sound-pressure chart, as shown in Fig. A.5. Also, a numerical analysis can be obtained by dividing the corrected band readings by 10, treating these quotients as logarithms, and adding their antilogs. See Cheremisenoff, P. N. and Cheremisenoff, N. D. (1977).

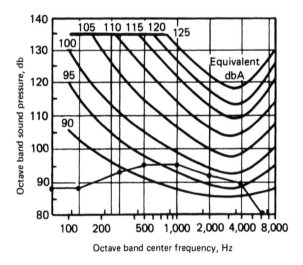

FIG. A.5. Tangent contour method of sound evaluation. (From Chemical Engineering, February 18, 1974.)

---

*Weighted and weighting used interchangeably.

TABLE A.2. Calculating Sound Levels from Octave-Band Analyses

Band	Center frequency (Hz)	Corrected sound pressure level (SPL) (dB)	SPL/10	Antilog of SPL/10
1	63	62	6.2	0.02×10^8
2	125	72	7.2	0.02×10^8
3	250	85	8.5	3.16×10^8
4	500	93	9.3	19.99×10^8
5	1000	96	9.6	39.81×10^8
6	2000	93	9.3	19.95×10^8
7	4000	90	9.0	10.00×10^8
8	8000	75	7.5	0.32×10^8
				93.41×10^8

Note: $\log 93.41 \times 10^8 = 9.97$; $10 \times 9.97 = 99.7$, equal approximately to 100 dBA.

EXAMPLE: The octave-band analysis of a noise gave the following results in terms of corrected sound pressure levels, dB. Corrections to sound-pressure readings are obtained from the instrument. These pressure levels are converted to antilogs, the antilogs are added, and the dBA is equated to the log of the sum in accordance with Table A.2.

A.4. HOW TO ESTIMATE EVAPORATION OF WATER FROM OPEN TANKS

Where moisture is released to the work space from open tanks, the problem often is to be able to estimate the rate of evaporation and thus provide for a reduction in moisture content of the room air. When considering steam, the escape rate is not too difficult a problem, but for hot water there has not been too much information disclosed for easy and rapid use by the design engineer. High room humidity affects worker comfort and, in some cases, worker health. It also presents quite a condensation problem with dripping from walls and roofs. See Carrier (1965) and Buffalo Forge (1970).

Typical industries in which this "wet heat" is found are

Textile: elimination of fog and condensation in dye houses, bleacheries, and finishing departments

TABLE A.3. The Rate of Evaporation from Open
Tanks Under Normal Room Conditions

Water temperature (°F)	Pound, water evaporated per hour per square foot
110	0.21-0.25
120	0.31-0.37
130	0.43-0.51
140	0.60-0.72
150	0.80-0.90
160	1.20-1.30
170	1.40-1.60
180	1.70-2.10
190	2.20-2.60
200	2.70-3.20

Paper and pulp mills: elimination of high vapor in machine, beater,
    and grinder rooms
Steel and metal goods: elimination of high vapor in pickling rooms
Food industries: control of high vapor in kettle, canning, blanch-
    ing, bottle washing, etc.

Under normal room conditions Table A.3 provides the engineer with
the rate of evaporation from open tanks.

A.5. AIR CONDITIONING SHOP AND MANUFACTURING
     AREAS

There is no shortage of published data regarding the advantages of air conditioning the shop and manufacturing areas. There are numerous publications that will provide the know-how of determining the air conditioning
load, but the matter of determining the sensible heat load from machinery
within these areas needs closer study because of the variations in the mode
of equipment usage. As an aid in calculating the internal sensible cooling
load from machine tools for a machine shop, Table A.4 will prove helpful.
It lists equipment usually available for machine ship operations, together
with a practical estimate of the use percentage for each piece, based on a
40-hr week (8 hr a day, 5 days a week). The table gives usages for normal

TABLE A.4. A Practical Estimate of the Use Percentage for Equipment
Usually Available for Machine Shop Operation

Equipment	Percent usage	
	Turnaround	Normal
1. Lathe, 16 × 24 in. swing, Southbend	40	20
2. Lathe, 20 × 78 in., Monarch	75	50
3. Lathe, 25 × 96 in., Monarch	70	40
4. Lathe, 28 in. × 50 ft long, sliding bed, Nebel	50	10
5. Grinder, pedestal	9	5
6. Saw, 26 in., Do-All	40	20
7. Threading machine, 1/4-2 in. bolts and pipe, Oster	70	10
8. Bandsaw, metal cutting, Kalamazoo #8	20	10
9. Hydraulic press, 25 ton	5	5
10. Milling machine, 3MI, Cincinnati	30	5
11. Grinder and buffer combination	10	5
12. Balancing machine, Trebel 6000	8	5
13. Safety valve test stand, Farris	90	25
14. Lapping machine, Lap Master	90	25
15. Drill press, 16 in., stand type	20	5
16. Oven, portable	5	2
17. Furnace, heat treating	5	2
18. Radial drill press, Carlton	50	20
19. Hydraulic press, 150 ton	25	5
20. Grinder, 6 ft × 3/4 in.	20	10
21. Abrasive cutter, Beaver Speed No. 4	25	3
22. Pantograph cutting machine	85	10
23. Grinder, pedestal, 12 × 12 in.	75	10
24. Welding machine, rectifier type, 600 A	20	3
25. Air compressor	100	100

TABLE A.4. (Continued)

Equipment	Percent usage	
	Turnaround	Normal
26. Welding positioner, 1000 lb	20	10
27. Heliarc welding machine	50	3
28. Submerged arc welding machine with control panel	50	3
29. Weld positioner, 3000 lb	20	10
30. Iron worker	75	25
31. Crimping and edging rolls	20	5
32. Sheet metal shear	20	5
33. Sheet metal roll	20	5
34. Sheet metal brake	20	5
35. Saw, 16 in., Do-All	50	20
36. Woodworking saw, Dewalt	70	20
37. Drill press	20	10
38. Wood planer	40	10
39. Masonry saw	10	2
40. Grinder	10	5
41. Grinder and tool cutter combination	25	10
42. Agitating chemical cleaner, Magnus	80	20

working conditions. For a major plant turn-around or complete plant servicing (shutdown conditions), higher usage factors are indicated. Anyone using the list can substitute similar equipment from other manufacturers without changing the effect. Calculation of the cooling load should be based on normal shop operating conditions. See Carrier (1965).

EXAMPLE: A machine shop is to be air conditioned. Equipment in use will include one each of items 3, 5, 7, 13, 15, 22, 24, 25, and 35, referring to list. How is the cooling load from equipment determined?

SOLUTION: For each piece of equipment, obtain the motor horse-power. Multiply each by 2545 Btuh/hp and then by the usage factor obtained from the list. Now add up the products of these calculations.

A.6. A DESIGN STANDARD FOR HEATING AND VENTILATING OF CHEMICAL PLANTS AND OIL REFINERY BUILDINGS

General

1. Scope
   a. This specification covers requirements for heating and ventilating fully enclosed buildings and rooms within process areas.
   b. This specification does not cover the requirements for air conditioning.
2. Modifications
   a. Any exceptions or additions to this specification shall be contained on the design data sheets.

Design

1. General
   a. Heating and ventilating requirements for buildings and rooms not specified on design data sheets shall be as shown on the building sketch and data sheets.
   b. Heating and ventilating systems, except as modified herein, shall be designed in accordance with the Guide and Data Book of the American Society of Heating, Refrigerating and Air Conditioning Engineers (ASHRAE).
      (1) The location of hazardous and nonhazardous areas and the requirements for positive pressure ventilation systems to reduce the degree of electrical hazard will be listed on the design data sheets for electrical systems.
2. Heating Systems
   a. Heating systems shall be designed to maintain the following average space temperatures during shut-down conditions, using the winter design dry bulb temperature indicated on the design data sheets:
      (1) Control, lavatory, office, and locker and maintenance rooms: 70°F.
      (2) Rooms housing equipment such as pumps, compressors, blowers, and switch gear: 50°F.
   b. Generally, the heating medium shall be steam at a nominal pressure of up to 50 psig for unit heaters and convectors and a

pressure of 15 psig for heating coils upstream of a steam control valve. Buildings and rooms remotely located may be heated electrically.

c. Steam and electrical unit heaters and central heating systems shall be thermostatically controlled; steam heating convectors and convection-type electrical heaters shall be manually controlled. General heating system controls shall consist of room and duct thermostats.

   (1) Room thermostats shall control heating medium to maintain space temperature.

   (2) Duct low limit thermostats shall control heating medium to prevent supply air temperature from dropping below a predetermined minimum.

3. Ventilating Systems

   a. Generally, ventilating systems shall be sized to supply the following minimum outside air quantities for summer ventilation. Quantities so determined may be reduced 50% or to the amount of exhaust, whichever is greater, for winter ventilation. These quantities are based on normal operation with no processing or piping system breakdowns.

      (1) Pump rooms, compressor rooms, and blower rooms: quantities for machinery in place and future shall be in accordance with Chapter 5, with the amounts for standby units reduced 25% below the operating quantities; quantities for unoccupied areas (exclusive of space required for future machinery) shall be 5 cfm/ft^2 of floor area in hot oil pump rooms, 3 cfm in cold oil pump rooms, and 2 cfm in compressor and blower rooms; quantities for other equipment shall be based on heat dissipation and dilution of toxic and flammable gases.

      (2) Other spaces: Table A.5.

   b. Outside air for mechanical ventilating systems shall be supplied through weatherproof louvers in outside walls. When buildings are located wholly in hazardous areas, air-tight stacks shall be used, with the intakes located in a nonhazardous area and provided with rainproof hoods.

   c. When buildings are located partly in a hazardous area and partly in a nonhazardous area, the air intakes shall be located high in outside building walls taking outside air from the nonhazardous area side of the building.

   d. When buildings are specified with positive pressure ventilation for the purpose of reducing the degree of electrical hazard, the positive pressure air system shall be designed in accordance with Chapter 9.

   e. Positive pressure ventilating systems shall contain the following features:

TABLE A.5. Ventilation Demand Rates

Space	Ventilation demand rate (cfm/ft^2 gross floor area)
Access spaces	2
Battery-charging rooms	2
Conference rooms	3
Control rooms	2
Cooking spaces	3
Corridors	1
Electrical shops	2
Instrument lead rooms	2
Instrument shops	2
Janitor closets	1
Laboratories	—[a]
Laboratory test areas	3
Locker rooms	3
Lunch rooms	3
Machine shops	3
Maintenance rooms (work shops)	3
Mechanical equipment rooms	2
General	3
Private	2
Shower rooms	3
Storage rooms	1
Switch rooms	2
Telephone rooms	2
Toilets	2
Turbo generator rooms	3
Utility rooms	2
Vaults	1
Vestibules	2

[a] 3 ft^3/ft^2 gross floor area plus all equipment requirements.

(1) A minimum number of doors to the outdoors shall be provided so that positive pressure can be maintained, while at the same time the number of doors shall be adequate for safe exit.

(2) Fixed window sash is not a requirement but may be used.

(3) Two complete ventilation units electrically interlocked to start-up one unit on failure of the other unit shall be furnished when type X purging is required. A spare unit is not furnished for types Y and Z purging.

(4) Either a space pressure switch or individual pressure switches on doors opening to the outside set at 0.1 in. w.g. (inches of water) with a 15 sec time delay (factory set) shall be furnished to activate the purging damper settings for the open condition.

(5) Recirculating dampers shall close and outside dampers open wide during the open condition so that an outward purge of 60 fpm is provided through openings.

4. Control Rooms

a. Control rooms provided with positive pressure ventilation systems to reduce the degree of electrical hazard shall be heated and ventilated by means of central systems consisting of a fan and steam-heating coils. Heating air shall be distributed through uninsulated ducts arranged to deliver air into the space below the hung ceiling and behind the instrument panelboard in the access space. Relief shall be through the adjustable counterbalance wall louvers above the hung ceiling level and by leakage through door cracks, windows, and walls.

b. All other control rooms shall be heated by steam convectors and ventilated by exhaust fans high in outside walls working in conjunction with windows, louvers, and grilles.

5. Office, Maintenance, Lavatory, and Locker Rooms

a. Office and maintenance rooms located in the same building with the control room provided with a central duct system shall be heated and ventilated by the system provided for the control room. Duct openings shall be provided with diffusers or grilles.

b. Office and maintenance rooms located in other buildings shall be heated by steam or electric convectors or unit heaters and ventilated by natural infiltration through doors and windows.

c. Lavatory and locker rooms shall be heated by steam convectors or unit heaters and ventilated as follows:

(1) Interior lavatory and locker rooms shall be ventilated by mechanical exhaust means. Makeup air shall be provided through louvered or undercut doors.

(2) Exterior lavatory and locker rooms shall be ventilated by natural infiltration through doors and windows.

6. Switch Rooms
   a. Switch rooms shall be heated by steam unit heaters at the ceiling. Under some conditions an alternate means of heating shall be by means of electric unit heaters.
   b. Switch rooms located in the same building with a control room provided with a central duct system shall be ventilated by exhaust fans and louvers high in the opposite outside walls.
   c. Switch rooms provided with positive pressure ventilation systems to reduce the degree of electrical hazard shall be ventilated as described in paragraphs 3d and 3e. Relief to the atmosphere shall be through an adjustable relief damper of the counterbalanced design and by leakage through door cracks and walls.
   d. All other switch rooms shall be ventilated by weatherproof downswept louvers and mechanical exhaust fans all located high in the opposite walls outside the building.
7. Equipment Rooms
   a. Pump, compressor, and blower rooms shall be heated by steam unit heaters thermostatically controlled and located high in exterior walls. Ventilation shall be by propeller-type wall exhaust fans located high in exterior walls. Outside air supply shall be through downswept louvers low in exterior walls.
8. Enclosures and Shelters
   a. Enclosures, such as elevator machinery or precipitator substation equipment, shall have no provision for heating. Ventilating shall be through weatherproof louvers and gravity roof ventilators.

Materials

1. General
   a. All equipment shall be of manufacturer's standard design for the required service.
   b. Fans, unit heaters, convectors, etc., shall conform to the ASHRAE and the Air Moving and Conditioning Association, Inc. (AMCA) standard codes for testing and rating.
   c. Insulation materials shall be in accordance with the specifications and data listed on the design data sheets for thermal insulation.
2. Fans, Unit Heaters, Convectors, and Heating Coils
   a. Positive pressure ventilation fans shall be of the nonoverloading type.
   b. Fans located in Division 1 areas shall have nonferrous or nonsparking wheels directly connected to explosionproof motors suitable for the class and group of the area. Fans located in Division 2 areas shall have nonferrous or nonsparking wheels

directly connected to nonsparking motors. Static conducting V-belt drives may be substituted for direct drive units in Division 1 and 2 areas.

c. Unit heaters shall be of the steam type, with propeller fans having nonferrous or nonsparking wheels directly connected to explosionproof motors in hazardous areas and to standard open-frame motors with standard wheels in nonhazardous areas. Steam coils shall be of the extended surface type (copper tubing with aluminum fins). All copper tubes and fins may be substituted here. The unit casing shall be provided with adjustable louvers and deflectors on vertical units.

d. Electric unit heaters, when used, shall be of the standard general purpose type for location in nonhazardous areas and as required by the classification for hazardous areas. See Chapter 3.

e. Electric convectors, when used, shall be of the standard general purpose type for location in nonhazardous areas and as required by the classification of hazardous areas. See Chapter 3.

f. Steam convectors shall be of the wall-mounted type having extended surface heating elements on steel tubing. The elements shall be enclosed in expanded metal covers.

g. Heating coils shall be of nonfreeze-type construction. Coils shall be of the extended surface type (copper tubing with aluminum fins) and arranged for even steam distribution. Coils shall be enclosed in heavy gauge galvanized steel channel-type castings.

3. Louvers, Registers, Grilles, and Roof Ventilators

a. Louvers shall be adjustable, stormproof, of No. 20 USS gauge galvanized steel sheet and furnished with 160°F fusible links for automatic closing. Wire mesh screens shall be provided at the louver interface. These shall be bird-screen-size mesh.

b. Grilles and registers shall be of steel.

c. Roof ventilators shall be of the gravity type, of galvanized No. 20 USS gauge (minimum) sheet steel and provided with flat, chain-operated dampers furnished with 160°F fusible links for automatic closing.

4. Ducts, Vanes, and Dampers

a. Ducts, vanes, and dampers for interior use shall be galvanized sheet steel No. 24 USS gauge for duct sizes less than 18 in., in width or depth and No. 22 USS gauge for sizes from 18 to 48 in.

5. Piping

a. Unless otherwise required by the equipment, piping in sizes 3 in. and smaller shall be threaded and 4 in. and larger shall be flanged. Pipe in sizes 1 1/4, 3 1/2, and 5 in. shall not be used.

  b. Pipe and fittings shall be of the following construction and
      materials:
      (1) Pipe: steel, black (ASTM A120) except that buried conden-
           sate lines shall be standard weight wrought iron (ASTM
           A72).
      (2) Flanges: ANSI 150 lb flat face slip-on steel (ASTM A181).
      (3) Threaded fittings: 150 lb banded malleable iron (ASTM
           A197). Plugs shall have square heads; unions shall have
           brass-to-iron seats.
      (4) Flanged fittings: ANSI 125 lb flat face cast iron (ASTM
           A126, Class B).
  c. Valve construction, and body and trim materials shall conform
      to manufacturer's standards for steam and water service and
      to the following:
      (1) Threaded valves shall be brass or bronze with a minimum
           saturated steam working pressure rating of 125 lb.
      (2) Flanged valves shall be cast iron with an ANSI rating of
           125 lb.
  d. Flange gaskets shall be 1/16-in. thick compressed asbestos
      full face flat rings.
  e. Flange bolting shall be machine bolts with nuts (ASTM A307,
      grade B).

Note: In today's chemical plants, oil refineries, and industrial plants in
general, air conditioning is provided for control rooms, administration
buildings, and offices as well as laboratories. Cooling and ventilation requirements are determined using ASHRAE sources and the Carrier Handbook of Air Conditioning System Design (1965). The reader is also referred
to the bibliography and reference sections of this book. Building pressurization techniques discussed in Chapter 9 may be applied.

A.7. COST ESTIMATING BY USE OF SIX-TENTHS FACTOR

Experience with a variety of equipment and plant costs provides a shortcut
as a quick estimating tool. When the cost of proposed equipment of certain
capacity is known, the cost of other sizes can be estimated, as long as the
equipment remains the same generically. The exponent-based technique
is simple and fast, yet it is reliable enough for making preliminary
evaluations.

    The "six-tenths" factor is useful in estimating the costs of mechanical
equipment and building construction and it lends itself to a quick graphic
solution. Stated briefly, the basis of the six-tenths rule is as follows: if
the cost of a given unit is known at one capacity and it is desired at some
capacity $\underline{X}$ times as great, the known cost multiplied by $X^{0.6}$ will provide
the cost of the second capacity.

Of course, this method should not be substituted for the detailed estimate needed for completely acceptable accuracy, and considerable care should be taken in its use by confining the scaling up or down to similar configurations and capacities. However, it does have its place in approximating costs quickly. See Chase, J. D. (1970) and Meckler, M. (1968).

Graphical Presentations

Correlation of equipment cost data has been done for many years by scientists and engineers who are responsible for costs and estimating. They have used one method of correlation in which they have plotted the cost of equipment against capacity on logarithmic scales. Since this approach produces straight-line plots, the general conclusion is that equipment costs may be correlated by equations of the form $Y = AX^b$, where Y is the cost, A is a constant for the type of equipment involved, X is the capacity of the unit, and b is also a constant. If we assume an equation of this type, then constant b will be the six-tenths factor.

Values of constants for various types of equipment are presented in Table A.6. If factor A is known, we can work from an existing unit to a proposed unit by letting X_1 = capacity of the first unit, X_2 = capacity of the second unit, Y_1 = cost of first unit, and Y_2 = cost of second unit. Then, statistical analysis of available cost data shows that

$$Y_2 = Y_1 \frac{X_2}{X_1}^b$$

In most cases, b again will be the six-tenths factor. Incidentally, when the exponent b is approximately 0.6, doubling size of equipment or capacity of a unit increases its cost by only 50%.

Typical Examples

To illustrate the method, assume that a 10-ton package air conditioner costs $2935. Now estimate the cost of a 15-ton machine of similar type, using 0.616 as the exponent. On the lower part of the accompanying Fig. A.6 read upward from the value of 1.5 for enlarged capacity ratio (15/10) to the oblique line representing a power of 0.616, then horizontally to find the value 1.29 on the scale at the right. Multiplying $2935 by 1.29 gives roughly $3790 as the scaled-up cost. Since the actual cost is $3900. this is close enough for a quick estimate.

In the reverse condition for a scaled-down cost using the same figures, enter the upper part of the graph at 0.667 (10/15), drop vertically to 0.616, and then proceed horizontally to find the value of 0.78 on the scale at left. Fractional capacity cost is $3900 × 0.78 = $3040, again a reasonable approximation compared to the actual cost of $2935.

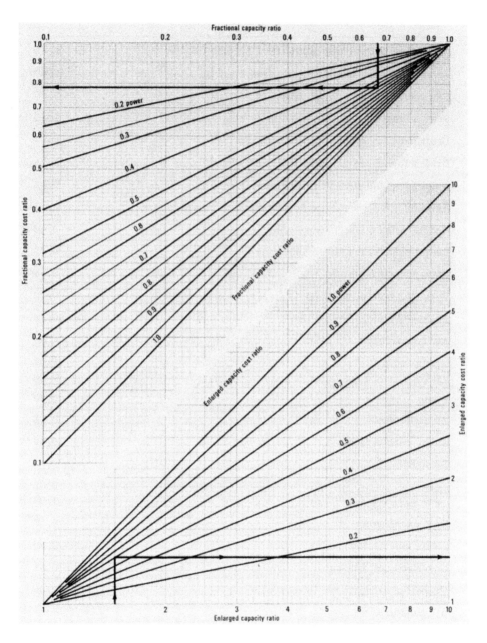

FIG. A.6. Cost estimating: cost-capacity ratio curves. (From Consulting Engineer, September 1973.)

TABLE A.6. Cost Factors for Various Types of Equipment for Use in Exponent-Base Preliminary Estimating

Centrifugal blower and motor, 3-7 1/2 hp	0.40
Centrifugal blower and motor, over 7 1/2 hp	0.90
Fan and motor, to 10,000 cfm	0.40
Fan and motor, over 10,000 cfm	0.66
Draft inducer, axial, 3000 to 6000 cfm	0.55
Draft inducer, axial, 6000 to 20,000 cfm	0.78
Axial duct fan, 4000 to 10,000 cfm	0.42
Axial duct fan, 10,000 to 50,000 cfm	0.76
Radial exhaust fan, to 5000 cfm	0.46
Radial exhaust fan, over 5000 cfm	0.77
High-pressure blower	0.64
Packaged boiler, to 30 hp	0.72
Packaged boiler, over 30 hp	0.52
Air compressor	
reciprocating	0.90
rotary	0.65
Pump	0.60
Electric motor	0.61
Tank, carbon steel	0.66
Burner	
oil	0.82
gas	1.06
Heat exchanger	0.55
Steam unit heater	0.60
Gas-fired unit heater	0.61
Propeller exhaust fan, panel type	0.66
Air handlers	
Draw through, 5 in. w.g. static pressure maximum fan section	
Draw through, 5 in. w.g. static pressure maximum, fan section section, 6-row direct expansion (DX) or chilled water coil, filter section, motor drive, vibration isolators	0.795

TABLE A.6. (Continued)

Air handlers (cont)	
Blow through, otherwise same equipment as item above, plus zone dampers	0.706
Air washers	
Capillary air washer with 6-row chilled water coil, 2-row hot water coil, recirculating spray pump	0.750
Lithium chloride chemical air washer	0.625
General distribution duct system complete with insulation, dampers, etc.	
Complicated system, high pressure, small zones, return air ducts, many fittings	0.961
Average system, low to medium pressure, medium size zones, moderate size cones	0.952
Simple systems, low pressure, large zones, no return ducts, few fittings	0.958
Air filtration	
99, 97% efficiency, DOP test	0.98
95%	0.70
35% mean efficiency, NBS test using atmospheric dust	0.716
Ultraviolet lamps in ductwork, 1500 fpm velocity	0.658
Bag houses, 4/1	0.80
Dust filtration, bag filter, mechanical shaker, 2:1 ratio	0.60
Shell and tube exchangers, carbon steel	
Less than 1500 ft^2	0.47
Greater than 1500 ft^2	0.78
All aluminum, 100–300 ft^2	0.49
All stainless, 25–500 ft^2	0.39
Air-cooled exchangers	
Carbon steel, 300–1500 ft^2	0.69
Stainless steel, 300–1500 ft^2	0.93
Vessels	
Storage tank, atmospheric, 200–1,000,000 gallons	0.46
Vacuum, 100–10,000 gallons	0.35
Pressure, 15–35 psig, 25–15,000 gallons	0.47
Agitators, 1–30 hp	0.54
Steam ejectors	0.54
Packed tower, stainless, 5–36 in. diam.	0.35
Packed tower, stainless, 36–100 in. diam.	0.85
Pilot plant equipment	
Autoclaves, 1200 psi	0.97
Tray dryers	0.53

TABLE A.6.   (Continued)

___

Air filtration   (cont)

Pilot plant equipment (cont)
Rotary dryers	0.53
Spray dryers	0.50
Dust collectors, cyclone bag, steel	0.80
	0.68
Evaporators	0.66
Filters	0.90
Hammer mills	0.56
Metering pumps	0.41
Jacketed reactors	0.50
Packed column scrubbers	0.73

Electronic precipitators
95%	0.584
97% NBS test using atmosphere dust	0.623
90%	0.455

Refrigeration equipment
Package liquid chillers	0.736
Water-cooled condensing units	0.712
Absorption water chillers	0.757
Open centrifugal water chillers, turbine driven	0.666
Hermetic centrifugal water chillers	0.616
Open centrifugal water chillers, motor driven	0.668
General mechanical equipment	0.60
Boilers	0.60
Buildings	0.60
Compressors, air and gas	0.90
Cooling towers	0.60
Electrical	0.60
Foundations	0.50
Furnaces	0.85
Heat exchangers	0.70
Paint and insulation	0.60
Piping	0.60
Pumps	0.60
Structural steel	0.50
Vessels	0.60

APPENDIX B

Problems

1. An analytical procedure requires a minimum of 5 mg of an offending material in a total sample in order to obtain satisfactory analytical accuracy. The TLV of this material is 75 ppm. It is suspected that the air concentration is 3 times greater than the TLV. Molecular weight of the material is 138. The sampling rate for the collecting device is 0.1 cfm. The temperature is 22°C and the barometric pressure is 750 mmHg. Determine the minimum time necessary to collect one air sample.

SOLUTION:

$$t = \frac{\text{(minimum amount of material)(22.4 L/gm-mol)}}{\text{(sampling rate)(TLV)(MW)}}$$

$$\times \frac{(10^6)(760/P(273 + C)/(273)}{(28.3 \text{ L/ft}^3)}$$

$$t = \frac{(5 \text{ mg})(0.001 \text{ g/mg})(22.4 \text{ L/g-mol})}{(0.1 \text{ ft}^3)(76)(138 \text{ g/g-mol})} \times \frac{(10^6)(760/750)(295/273)}{(28.3 \text{ l/ft}^3)}$$

$$t = 4.19 \text{ min}$$

2. A room of 100,000 ft^3 volume initially having a concentration of benzene equal to 1000 ppm is to have this concentration reduced to 25 ppm, using a 5 ppm benzene-air supply. The workroom has a ventilation system capable of delivering 50,000 cfm. Assume a 1/10 mixing factor. Determine the time necessary to dilute workroom air from 1000 ppm to 25 ppm. <u>Notation and Data</u>: Perfect mixing is rarely accomplished so that a mixing factor should normally be applied to the number of room air changes to approximate actual conditions. This mixing factor will depend on the gas or vapor toxicity, uniformity of contaminant distribution within the room, location of fans, construction of the room, and the room's population. This factor may vary from 1/3 to 1/10 and is used in conjunction with actual air changes to yield the number of effective air changes.

SOLUTION:

$$n = \frac{Qt}{R}$$

where

n = actual air changes

Q = air flow rate, cfm

t = time elapsed, min

R = space volume, ft^3

kn = number of effective air changes

Then,

$$C = C_s(1 - e^{-kn}) + C_i(e^{-kn}) \qquad (B.1)$$

$$C - C_s = (C_i - C_s)(e^{-kn}) = \text{diluted concentration} \qquad (B.2)$$

Where

C = concentration at time t

C_i = initial concentration at t = 0

e = naperian logarithmic base = 2.7182818

Substituting values from the problem in (B.2)

$$25 - 5 = (1000 - 5)(e^{-n/10})$$

$$= 995\,(e^{-n/10})$$

From which $n/10 = 3.9$ effective air changes. Finally,

$$t = \frac{nR}{Q} = \frac{(39)(100,000)}{50,000} = 78 \text{ min}$$

3. An air conditioning system is undergoing analysis. Fan cfm = 28,000, static pressure = 5.5 in. w.g., fan outlet velocity = 2,800 fpm. The system is a drawthrough configuration. (1) What is the temperature rise across the fan? (2) How many tons of refrigeration are needed to offset the temperature rise?

SOLUTION: a. Temperature rise across fan is given by

$$\frac{(5.19)(TP_2 - TP_1)}{(778)(C_p)(d_1)(FTE)} = °F$$

Where

TP_2 = downstream total pressure, in. w.g.

TP_1 = upstream total pressure, in. w.g.

FTE = Fan total efficiency

C_p = specific heat air = 0.24 Btu/lb

d_1 = upstream air density, lb/ft^3

Fan outlet velocity = 2800 fpm

Fan outlet velocity pressure = $(2800/4005)^2$ = 0.48 in. w.g.

Assume that the casing velocity pressure is negligible. It would normally be about 500 fpm, which is equivalent to 0.0156 in. w.g. Downstream total pressure = 0.49 + 5.5 = 5.99 in. w.g., say 6 in. Assume a reasonable fan total efficiency to be 84%. The total pressure on the upstream side of the fan is zero. Note that on any system where you have louvers, filters, and coils, TP_1 would be a negative number since the pressure when related to atmospheric pressure is negative. However, we have already calculated the required fan static pressure. Therefore, fan static pressure plus velocity pressure at the fan outlet gives us $TP_2 - TP_1$, neglecting the velocity pressure in the inlet plenum. Therefore, the temperature rise across the fan is

$$\frac{(5.19)(6)}{(778)(0.24)(0.075)(0.84)} = 2.65°F$$

b. Refrigeration required is

$$\frac{(28,000)(1.08)(2.65)}{12,000 \text{ Btuh/ton}} = 6.7 \text{ tons of refrigeration}$$

4. Ethyl ether is being evaporated from a product in a room temperature drying hood operated at atmospheric pressure. Solvent vapor must be removed at the rate of 46 lb/hr, and the solvent vapor concentration must be maintained below the 1.85% LEL. Calculate the air volume which must be supplied to the dryer. Room air is 75°F.

SOLUTION: This a gas dilution problem, and the solution is straightforward if you remember that gas analysis is based on percent by volume, i.e., for ideal gas mixtures, volume percent is proportional to the moles of each gas. The molecular weight of ethyl ether = 74.

Moles ether removed per hour = $(46)/(74)$ = 0.622

Since the LEL is given as 1.85% in air by volume, this is the same as saying 1.85 mol% ether in the exhaust air leaving the dryer. For each 1.85 moles of ether exhausted, 98.15 moles of air must dilute it. Then, the air leaving the dryer with 0.622 mol ether is $0.622/0.0185 = x/0.9815$, from which x is found to be 33 mol/hr. At standard conditions of 60°F and 14.7 psia, molal volume is 379 ft^3/lb-mol. Then, at a room temperature of 75°F, the volume per mole of air is

$$379 \, \frac{460 \, + \, 75}{460 \, + \, 60} \, = \, 390 \, ft^3/mol$$

Finally, the volume of air to be exhausted is

$$(33)(390) \, = \, 12,870 \, ft^3/hr$$

And this is the amount the air being supplied. This flow of air is the least permissible to prevent the LEL from being attained in the main bulk of the exhaust stream. However, local concentrations within the dryer itself may be explosive so that a sparkproof design is required.

5. An exposure chamber contains 50 ppm methyl chloride initially, and there is 100 ppm methyl chloride in the supplied air. The chamber is estimated to have a mixing factor of unity. What is the concentration in the chamber after 3 air changes?

SOLUTION: Using $kn = (3)(1) = 3$ effective air changes, Fig. 5.2 gives the fraction of supply concentration at 0.95. Thus, $(0.95)(100) = 95$ ppm in the chamber from the supply air. The contaminant remaining from the residual air is obtained from Fig. 5.2 by connecting $kn = 3$ on the left with $C_i = 50$ ppm on the right. The residual methyl chloride is then seen to equal 2.5 ppm. The answer is therefore the sum of these values, which equals $95 + 2.5 = 97.5$ ppm.

Note that if the initial concentration was zero (chamber initially filled with air alone), then the concentration is simply obtained by multiplying the fraction of supply concentration from Fig. 5.2 by the supply concentration. If there were no methyl chloride in the chamber initially, the concentration after 3 air changes would have been 95 ppm.

6. What are some other applications for Fig. 5.2?

SOLUTION: Figure 5.2 has applications in any system where the concept of logarithmic decay is valid, such as in natural radioactive decay or in a constant overflow system.

Natural radioactive decay is defined by a logarithmic decay equation of the form $N = N_i(e^{-\lambda t})$. Here problems may be solved with the chart by simply substituting the following values for the chart headings shown:

Let

$C = N$, the number of atoms at time t

$C_i = \lambda t$, the initial number of atoms at $t = 0$

kn = λt, the radioactive constant multiplied by the time elapsed, dimensionless

Another system meeting the logarithmic decay formula is a constant overflow system in which a pure liquid or liquid containing dissolved or suspended material is continuously added to a tank which itself contains either the same pure liquid or the same liquid containing some of the same material being fed. The concentration of material in the tank at any time could be determined with Fig. 5.2 by noting the similarity between the air and liquid systems. In the case just explained, the concentration terms C, C_s, and C_i would be the quantities of material in the liquid; the space or room volume R would be the tank volume; the air flow rate Q would be the liquid flow rate; the mixing factor k would be the liquid mixing factor; and the number of air changes n would be the number of liquid changes within the tank.

7. A glove box is being designed for a plutonium facility and is to be protected against fire by the injection of Halon 1301. The glove box volume is 25,000 ft^3 at 80°F. The volume of Halon 1301 injected into the room through suitable nozzles at constant temperature is 1800 ft^3 for adequate protection. Assume a homogeneous mixture after injection, and also assume constant temperature due to expansion cooling of Halon 1301, although there would be a tendency toward a drop in pressure. The molecular weight of Halon 1301 is 150. Assume no effect of the decomposition products: hydrogen fluoride, hydrogen bromide, bromine. Phosgene, generally feared as a byproduct of decomposed halogenated hydrocarbons, is not formed because no chlorine is present. Determine the pressure buildup inside the glove box due to Halogen 1301. Assume that the glove box is airtight.

SOLUTION: The basic equation is PV = WRT. Both temperature t and volume V are constant. Further, P = psia, V = volume (ft^3), W = weight (lb), R = gas constant for the mixture, and T = absolute temperature (°R).

The weight of atmospheric air in box is found

$$\frac{25,000}{13.8} = 1800 \text{ lb}$$

The weight of added Halon 1301 is

$$\frac{379}{150} \times \frac{460 + 80}{520} = 2.6 \text{ ft}^3/\text{lb}$$

$$\frac{1800}{2.6} = 690 \text{ lb Halon 1301}$$

The total weight of the gas mixture (air plus Halon 1301) in the glove box after Halon 1301 is injected is 1800 + 690 = 2490 lb.

Determine the gas mixture constant R = $1544/M_m$. But first determine the average molecular weight of the gas mixture M_m as follows:

$$\text{Moles of air} = \frac{1800}{29} = 63$$

$$\text{Moles Halon 1301} = \frac{690}{150} = 4.65$$

$$\text{Total moles} = 63 + 4.65 = 67.65$$

$$M_m = \frac{\text{total weight}}{\text{total moles}} = \frac{2490}{67.68} = 36.8$$

$$R_m = \frac{1544}{36.8} = 42$$

Now proceed to determine the resulting pressure due to injection, using $P = WR_m T/V$ thusly:

$$P = \frac{2490 \times 42 \times (460 + 80)}{25,000} = 2250 \text{ psfa}$$

Expressed in psia, 2250/144 = 15.6 psia, or 15.6 - 14.7 = 0.9 psi. This expressed in in. w.g. manometer = 2.31 X 12 X 0.9 = 25 in. Since normal glove pressure resistance is from 2 to 4 in. w.g., the pressure buildup within the glove box is excessive and could cause rupture and escape of radioactive materials. Develop new and sturdier glove material.

8. (1) Calculate a worker's daily 8-hr exposure to a solvent with a current threshold limit value (TLV) of 100 ppm if the worker spends 1 hr at an operation where the concentration is 250 ppm, 4 hr at 200 ppm, and 3 hr at 100 ppm. (2) If you returned to this same plant 2 weeks later and found similar exposures at the same operation, would you recommend that control measures be instituted? If so, why?

SOLUTION:

1. $\dfrac{(1 \times 250) + (4 \times 200) + (3 \times 100)}{8} = \dfrac{1350}{8} = 169 \text{ ppm}$

2. Control is necessary, since the 8-hr exposure exceeds the TLV of 100.

9. In a hammermill dust collector the air leaving the mill and entering the collector has the following conditions:

Total dry solids = 25 std (short tons per day)
Maximum moisture = 4%

Dry gas flow = 729 std, or 13,197 scfm
Water vapor = 31 std, or 904 scfm
Dry gas plus moisture = 760 std, or 14,101 scfm at 60°F dry bulb
  temperature
Dry bulb temperature of moisture is 130°F
Actual cfm (acfm) = 16,000 at 130°F
Operating conditions = sea level, or 14.7 psia
Collector sits in open air at 50°F dbt design conditions

1. Find the dew point of the mixture entering the collector.
2. Will condensation take place inside the steel plate collector
   walls and cause clogging?
3. Will jacketing the collector with insulation be necessary to prevent condensation?
4. What thickness of fiberglass insulation is necessary? The collector wall thickness is 1/8 in. steel.

SOLUTION:

1. Apply the humidity ratio (see Chap. 1) equation, letting
   pp = partial pressure of water vapor, psia. Set up the
   equation and solve for pp. Then refer to standard steam
   tables (saturated vapor); read the corresponding saturation temperature opposite pp. Molecular weight of water =
   18; molecular weight of air = 29.

$$\frac{11}{14.7 - pp} \times \frac{18}{29} = \frac{31}{729} = 0.042 \text{ lb water per lb dry air}$$

   from which pp = 0.93 psia. The corresponding saturation
   temperature is approximately 100°F. This is the dew
   point of the air-dust mixture.

2. Since 100°F is greater than 50°F, condensation will take
   place inside the collector and will cause clogging.

3. An insulation jacket is necessary to increase the wall
   temperature above 100°F. From tables in the ASHRAE
   handbook, 1/8-in.-thick steel plate with 1-in. rigid insulation has an overall coefficient U equal to 0.25 for a
   15-mph wind outside the shell. Assume inside shell coefficient = 1.65, and the overall resistance is (1/0.25) = 4.
   Then (1/1.65)/4 = 0.606/4 = 0.151. Now let T_i = 130°F
   inside temperature; T_{wi} = inside wall surface temperature,
   F. Also T_o = 50°F outside ambient temperature. Then

$$\frac{T_i - T_{wi}}{T_i - T_o} = 0.151$$

From which

$$T_i - T_{wi} = 0.151 (130 - 50) = 12$$

and it follows that $T_{wi} = 130 - 12 = 118°F$. This is the new inside wall surface temperature and is above 100°F dbt and vapor will not condense out inside the collector.

4. Use 1-in.-thick fiberglass rigid insulation. A common practice is to use 2-in. thick fiberglass rigid insulation as a minimum with an aluminum or stainless steel jacket overlapped at the joints and sealed against the weather.

10. You have collected three samples of a given fume using a portable electrostatic precipitator which you have assumed was operating at 3 cfm. Each sample was collected for 30 min, and on this basis the laboratory reported the following results:

No. 1: 0.085 mg/m^3
No. 2: 0.070 mg/m^3
No. 3: 0.040 mg/m^3

However, upon recalibrating the precipitator just after you returned from the field trip, you found it was operating at 2.75 cfm. What are the correct values of these three samples (1 ft^3 = 0.0283 m^3?

SOLUTION:

No. 1: $0.085 \times 3/2.75 = 0.093$ mg/m^3
No. 2: $0.070 \times 3/2.75 = 0.076$ mg/m^3
No. 3: $0.040 \times 3/2.75 = 0.044$ mg/m^3

11. Estimate the sound pressure level at 10 ft for the following vents:
Vent No. 1

Saturated steam
Valve size 4 in.
Temperature 400°F
Pressure 250 psig
Molecular weight 18

Vent No. 2

Air
Valve size 2 in.
Temperature 75°F
Pressure 250 psig
Molecular weight 29

Vent noise correction factor for saturated steam = -5.0, for air = 0. Vent sound pressure correction factor for 4-in.-diam. outlet = 12, for 2-in.-diam. outlet = 6.

SOLUTION: The sound pressure level is determined from L_p = $L_p(1) + L_p(2)$. Vent No. 1. $L_p(1) = 124$. This is the base sound pressure level at 10 ft. $L_p(2) = 12$ and $L_p(3) = -5$. And the total = $124 + 12 - 5 = 131$ dB sound pressure level at 10 ft.

The frequency of the maximum sound energy is F_0

$$F_0 = \frac{52.8}{d} \times \frac{T}{MW} = \frac{52.8}{4/12} \times \frac{860}{18} = 1000 \text{ Hz}$$

$$= 1000 \text{ Hz acoustic frequency}$$

Vent No. 2: $L_p(1) = 120$. This is the base sound pressure level at 10 ft at pressure.

$$L_p(2) = 6 \quad \text{and} \quad L_p(3) = 0$$

Total = 126 dB sound pressure level at 10 ft.

Thus

$$F_0 = \frac{52.8}{2/12} \times \frac{535}{29} = 1000 \text{ Hz acoustic frequency}$$

12. In a certain processing plant it is desired to determine the flow rate of a gas flowing through an irregularly shaped duct in which no measuring devices are installed and in which they cannot very well be used. Gas analysis shows that the gas contains 0.24% CO_2 by volume. It is decided to determine the flow rate by bleeding CO_2 into the gas stream from a small weighted cylinder or bottle. A constant rate is obtained by means of a flowmeter and after thorough mixing of the gases by passing through donut sections and bends, the average analysis of the mixture is found to contain 1.41% CO_2. The weight loss of the cylinder is 7.94 lb in 5 min, measured with a stop watch. The gas stream temperature mix is 120°F. What is the volume flow rate in cubic feet per minute?

SOLUTION: Ratio of CO_2 to CO_2-free gas in the original is $0.24/99.76 = 0.0024$, and the same ratio after mixing is $1.41/98.59 = 0.0143$. The increase in this ratio, $0.0143 - 0.0024 = 0.0119$, represents the moles CO_2 bled into the stream per mole of CO_2-free gas. Then the flow rate is

$$\frac{7.94}{5} \times \frac{1}{44} \times \frac{1}{0.0119} \times \frac{100}{99.76} \times 379 \times \frac{120 + 460}{60 + 460}$$

$$= 1275 \text{ cfm}$$

13. How many pounds of moisture must be added per hour to the air entering a building in which air is at 32°F and 60% relative humidity to produce an inside relative humidity of 30% and 70°F dBt? The building volume

is 500,000 ft^3 and there are 3 air changes per hour due to infiltration.
Take the specific volume of the mixture of air and water vapor as 13.8.

SOLUTION: Pressures are so low that the perfect gas law is
valid. Then, with the use of steam tables we see that at 32°F the
vapor pressure of water in the air at 60% relative humidity is
0.60 × 0.180 = 0.108 in. Hg. Now the humidity ratio becomes

$$\frac{0.108}{29.92 - 0.108} \times 0.622 = 0.00226 \text{ lb water per lb dry air}$$

This is equivalent to 0.00226/(1 + 0.0026) = 0.00224 lb water per
lb wet mix

At 70°F the vapor pressure of water is 0.739 in. Hg. The partial pressure of moisture in air at 30% relative humidity is 0.30 ×
0.739 = 0.221 in. Hg. The new humidity ratio becomes

$$\frac{0.221}{29.92 - 0.221} \times 0.622 = 0.00463 \text{ lb water per lb dry air}$$

This is now equivalent to 0.00463/(1 + 0.00463) = 0.00462 lb water
per lb mix. Water to be added is, therefore,

$$500,000 \times 3 \times \frac{0.00462 - 0.00224}{13.8} = 258 \text{ lb/hr}$$

or (258/500) = 0.515 gpm

14. A 1000 ft^3 tank containing 75 mol% hydrogen and 25 mol% carbon
dioxide is to have its hydrogen concentration reduced to 1 mol% by bleeding
in nitrogen at a constant rate. When the hydrogen content is down to 1% the
tank may be opened to the air and welding operations may proceed. How
long will it take to do this?

SOLUTION: Let

C_1 = 75 mol% hydrogen, initial

C_2 = 1 mol% hydrogen, final

V = tank volume = 1000 ft^3

R = purging rate, 30 cfm

Then

$$t = 2.303 \frac{V}{R} \log \frac{C_1}{C_2} = 2.303 \frac{1000}{30} \log \frac{75}{1}$$

t = 140 min required, or 2 hr and 20 min

This problem of dilution is common in pilot plant practice and operation and is recurrent also in large-scale work. In blending,

dilution of solutions, and purging of tank, a differential equation must be set up either

1. For calculating the necessary rate of diluting stream that will accomplish the desired concentration change in a definite time
2. For calculating the duration of the operation at a given rate of diluting stream that will accomplish the desired concentration change, or
3. For determining necessary initial and final concentrations for a given rate of diluting stream and a given duration time of operation.

In any case, it is necessary to assume instantaneous mixing, unless special data are at hand, and it is also necessary to set up and solve a separate differential equation for each step. The equation involved in the solution to such problems is

$$\int_{C_1}^{C_2} \frac{dC}{C} = \frac{R}{V} \int_0^t dt$$

Now

$$\ln \frac{C_1}{C_2} = \frac{Rt}{V}$$

Finally

$$t = 2.303 \frac{V}{R} \log \frac{C_1}{C_2}$$

From this development it is seen that C_1 and C_2 have the same units. R has the same volume unit as V and the same time unit as t.

15. Discuss the assumptions which are the basis for calculating theoretical exhaust volumes for dilution ventilation systems.

SOLUTION: The system will achieve equilibrium at a specific contaminant concentration regardless of the contaminant generation and air exhaust volume rates. Such equilibrium occurs when the contaminant generation rate equals the contaminant exhaust rate.

The contaminant exhaust rate equals the contaminant concentration multiplied by the exhaust air volume. Thus, equilibrium is attained when $R = C \times Q_e$, where R = contaminant generation rate at equilibrium (gr/min), C = fixed contaminant concentration (gr/ft^3), and Q_e = exhaust air volume (cfm).

A ventilation system is designed to maintain an inplant concentration at or below the TLV. Therefore, the TLV can be substituted for C, or $R = 0.000437(TLV)Q_e$, where $0.000437 =$ conversion factor from mg/ft^3 to gr/ft^3, and TLV = threshold limit value, mg/m^3.

Thus, the theoretical exhaust volume is

$$Q_e = \frac{R}{0.000437(TLV)} = \frac{2288(R)}{TLV} \text{ cfm}$$

This is based on the assumption that the contaminant is evenly distributed through the workspace.

16. A fan has the following characteristics: direct drive at 4800 rpm, air delivery at 2400 cfm, and 1/4 in. w.g.; it has 30 backward curved blades. What predominant frequency may be expected from the fan?

SOLUTION: The predominant frequency is that frequency for which attenuation design should be calculated when duct transmission is a problem. Thus,

$$\frac{4800 \text{ rpm} \times 30 \text{ blades}}{60 \text{ sec/min}} = 2400 \text{ cps (Hz)}$$

17. The acoustical treatment of a room has reduced the overall noise level by 3 dB. By what factor has the acoustical power been reduced?

SOLUTION: Reducing the overall noise level by 3 dB reduces the acoustical power by one-half. The basic formula is

$$W = 10 \log_{10} \frac{P_1}{P_2}$$

Then

$$3 \text{ dB} = 10 \log_{10} \frac{P_1}{P_2}$$

$$\frac{3}{10} = \log_{10} \frac{P_1}{P_2}$$

$$\frac{P_1}{P_2} = 10^{0.3}$$

$$\frac{P_1}{P_2} = 2 \quad \text{or} \quad P_2 = \frac{P_1}{2}$$

18. The following information on the thermal environment has been reported: globe temperature = 105°F, dry bulb or air temperature = 84°F,

wet bulb temperature = 70°F, air velocity = 100 fpm. What is the effective temperature corrected for radiation?

SOLUTION:

    a. Determine absolute humidity using dry and wet bulb temperatures from the psychrometric chart. This is found to be 84 gr per lb dry air.

    b. Determine the pseudo-wet bulb temperature using absolute humidity and globe temperature obtained from psychrometric chart. This is found to be 75.8°F.

    c. Determine the effective temperature corrected for radiation by using the pseudo-wet bulb temperature on the effective temperature chart.* Thus the effective temperature corrected for radiation = 84°F.

19. A material balance study indicates that two pints of toluene (toluol) are evaporated per 8-hr shift in a processing room at a plasticizer plant. What volume of dilution air for ventilation is required per shift to maintain the general air concentration at the current TLV of 200 ppm. Assume a K factor of 4.

SOLUTION: The volume of dilution ventilation required may be found by using the following formula:

$$\text{Cubic feet of air} = \frac{(403)(\text{specific gravity})(\text{pints evaporated})(10^6)(K)}{(\text{molecular weight})(\text{TLV})}$$

$$= \frac{(403)(0.87)(2)(10^6)(4)}{(92)(200)} = 152,360 \text{ ft}^3 \text{ per shift}$$

$$\text{Cfm equivalency} = (152,360)(8 \times 60) = 317 \text{ cfm}$$

20. 1250 cfm are to be exhausted through a round, freely suspended duct 6 in. in diameter. Calculate the expected velocity at a distance of 6 in. from the duct opening along the center line of the duct. A 6 in. flange is attached to the above duct at the intake end. What is the centerline velocity at 6 in. distance from the suction end?

SOLUTION:

    a. $V = Q/(10x^2 + A)$, where Q = 1250 cfm, x = 6 in. distance from intake plane, and A = area of 6 in. duct, or 0.1964 ft^2.

$$V = \frac{1250}{(10)(1/2)^2 + 0.1964} = 464 \text{ fpm (no flange)}$$

---

*Carrier (1965).

b. Flanged

$$V = \frac{Q}{(0.75)(10x^2 + A)} = \frac{464}{0.75} = 619 \text{ fpm}$$

21. A freely suspended hood, 2 in. wide and 72 in. long, exhausts 600 cfm. What is the velocity at a point 12 in. from the opening? What is the velocity at the same point after flanging?

SOLUTION:

1. Unflanged: $V = Q/(3.7 \times L) = 600/[3.7 \times (72/12)] = 27.0$ fpm fpm
2. Flanged: $Q/(2.8 \times L) = 600/[2.8 \times (72/12)] = 35.7$ fpm

22. Room air at 70°F is exhausted at 100 cfm per enclosure through each of 10 enclosures where a material is being fused. Within the enclosure the air rises to a temperature of 500°F before leaving the enclosure to the fan suction. The duct is well insulated so that there is no measureable temperature drop at the fan suction housing. What volume of air must the fan be able to handle? Assume ideal gas conditions.

SOLUTION:

$$\frac{(10 \text{ enclosures})(100 \text{ cfm})(500 + 460)}{460 + 70} = 1811 \text{ cfm}$$

The fan must handle 1811 cfm at 500°F.

REFERENCES

Note: Some of the data appearing in government and professional society sources are updated periodically and engineers are encouraged to contact the updated sources and obtain the newer data. However, the newer data should be compared and contrasted with the older data. This approach is more educational and they will be made more knowledgeable in the pursuit of their profession.

Alden, J. L., Design of Industrial Exhaust Systems, The Industrial Press, New York (1948).

Baumeister, T., Avallone, E. A., and Baumeister, T., 3rd., Marks Standard Handbook for Mechanical Engineers, McGraw-Hill, New York (1978).

Brief, R. S., Church, F. W., and Hendricks, N. V., Design and Selection of Laboratory Hoods, Air Engineering (October 1963).

Bruce, R. D., Workplace Noise Exposure Control—What are the Costs and Benefits? Sound & Vibration (October 1976).

Brumbaugh, A. K., Jr., Smokeless Burning of Refinery Vent Gases, Petroleum Processing (1947).

Buffalo Forge, Fan Engineering, 7th ed. (1970).

Bureau of Mines, Department of Agriculture, Report of Investigation No. 3751, Pittsburgh, Pennsylvania.

Carrier, Handbook of Air Conditioning System Design, McGraw-Hill, New York (1965).

Carroll, B. T., Controlling Humidity in the Plant, Plant Engineering (November 25, 1976).

Chase, J. D., Plant Costs vs. Capacity: New Way to Use Exponents, Chemical Engineering (April 6, 1970).

Cheremisenoff, P. N., and Cheremisenoff, N. P., Pollution Noise Glossary, Pollution Engineering (May 1973).

Cheremisenoff, P. N., and Cheremisenoff, N. P., Calculating Air Volume Requirements for Fume Exhaust Systems, Plant Engineering (March 18, 1976).

Cheremisenoff, P. N., and Cheremisenoff, N. P., Industrial Noise Control Handbook, Ann Arbor Science, Ann Arbor, Michigan (1977).

Cheremisenoff, P. N., and Young, R. A., Fans and Blowers, Pollution Engineering (July 1974).

Clarke, J. H., Design Requirements for Industrial Air Systems, ASHRAE Journal (September 1959).

Clarke, J. H., Air Flow Around Buildings, Heating, Piping & Air Conditioning (May 1967).

Constance, J. D., Putting the Lid on Boiler Plant Noise, Consulting Engineer (July 1980).

Coward, H. F. and Jones, G. W., Limits of Inflammability of Gases and Vapors, U.S. Bureau of Mines, Bull. 279 (1938).

Cowie, D., Upgrading Mechanical Dust Collection Systems, Plant Engineering (August 19, 1976).

Cutter, T. J., Testing Process Exhaust Systems, Plant Engineering (September 30, 1976).

Dalla Valle, J. M., Principles of Hood Design, USPHS, Washington, D.C. (1963).

Friedlander, S. K. et al., Handbook of Air Cleaning, U.S. Atomic Energy Commission, Washington, D.C. (1952).

Glitwitzky, W., Prevention of Acetylene-Air Explosions by Addition of Carbon Dioxide or Nitrogen, Berlin Autogene Metallbearbeitung, No. 1, 2-5 (1940).

Halitsky, J., Gas Diffusion Near Buildings, ASHRAE Transaction 69 (1963).

Hama, G. N., How Safe Are Direct-Fired Make-Up Air Heaters? Air Engineering (September 1962).

Hartmann, Irving, Recent Research on the Explosibility of Dust Dispersions, Industrial Engineering Chemistry, 40(4) (1947).

Heckert, F., Controlling Air Flow between Hospital Areas, Air Conditioning, Heating and Ventilating (December 1968).

Hemeon, W. C. L., Plant and Process Ventilation, The Industrial Press, New York (1964).

Hettig, S. B., A Project List of Safety Hazards, Chemical Engineering (December 19, 1966).

Hickes, W. F., Intrinsic Safety, Chemical Engineering (May 1, 1972).

Industrial Ventilation—Manual of Recommended Practice, 11th ed., American Conference of Governmental Industrial Hygienists, Committee on Industrial Ventilation, Lansing, Michigan (1970).

Karplus, H. B., and Bonvallet, G. L., A Noise Survey of Manufacturing Industries, American Industrial Hygiene Association Quarterly, 14 (1953).

Kravath, F. F., The Venturi Ejector for Handling Air, Heating and Ventilating (June 1940).

LeVine, R. Y., Electrical Safety in Process Plants, Chemical Engineering (May 1, 1972).

Lemke, R. C., Industrial Heat and Its Control, Air Engineering (October 1961).

Licht, W., Air Pollution Control Engineering: Basic Calculations for Particulate Collection, Marcel Dekker, Inc., New York (1980).

Marchello, J. M., Control of Air Pollution Sources, Marcel Dekker, Inc., New York (1970).

Marchello, J. M., and Kelly, J. J., Gas Cleaning for Air Quality Control: Industrial and Environmental Health and Safety Requirements, Marcel Dekker, Inc., New York (1975).

Marg, J., Comfort Conditioning the Plant with Evaporative Cooling, Plant Engineering (July 8, 1978).

McPartland, J., National Electrical Code Handbook, 16th ed., McGraw-Hill, New York (1979).

Meckler, M., Cost Estimating: Air Handling Equipment for Contamination Control, Air Conditioning, Heating & Ventilating (July 1968).

Miller, E. E., Danger—Explosive Vapors, Mechanical Engineering (December 1963).

National Safety Council, Accident Prevention Manual for Industrial Operations, 5th ed., Chicago, Illinois (1964).

Perry, R. E., Maintaining Centrifugal Fans, Plant Engineering, (June 10, 1976).

Perry, R. and Chilton, C., Chemical Engineers' Handbook, McGraw-Hill, New York (1978).

Polhemus, J., Controlling Worker Heat Stress, Plant Engineering, (March 3, 1977).

Sax, N. I., Dangerous Properties of Industrial Materials, Reinhold Publishing Corp., New York (1968).

Tomkins, S. S., Theoretical and Practical Considerations in Purging Practices, American Gas Association Proceedings, pp. 799-828 (1934).

Tuve, G. L. et al., The Use of Air Velocity Meters, ASHVE Transactions, 45; p. 645 (1939).

BIBLIOGRAPHY

Ackley, C. (Ed.), Air Pollution Handbook, McGraw-Hill, New York (1956).

Adams, R. L., Application of Baghouses in Electric Furnace Fume Control, JAPCA, 14(8), 299-302 (1964).

American Air Filter Company, Inc., American Filter Handbook (1958).

American Foundrymen's Society, Foundry Noise Manual (1972).

American Industrial Hygiene Association, Industrial Noise Manual (1966).

American Petroleum Institute (API), Evaporation Loss from Fixed-Roof Tanks (1962).

API, Evaporation from Floating-Roof Tanks (1962).

API, Evaporation Loss from Low-Pressure Tanks (1962).

API, Use of Plastic Foam to Reduce Evaporation Loss (1962).

API, Division of Refining, Manual on Disposal of Refinery Wastes (1951).

American Society of Heating and Air Conditioning Engineers, Inc., Heating, Ventilating, and Air Conditioning Guide, 37:142, New York (1959).

American Society of Heating, Refrigerating and Air Conditioning Engineers, (ASHRAE), Guide and Data Book, Fundamentals and Equipment, Chapter 16 (1981).

Anderson, C. E., Chemical Control of Odors, Pollution Engineering (August 1972).

Austin, P. R., and Timmerman, S. W., Design and Operation of Clean Rooms, Business News Publishing Co., Detroit, Mich. (1965).

Bedford, T., and Warner, C. G., The Globe Thermometer in Studies of Heating and Ventilation, Journal of Hygiene, 34(4), pp. 458-473.

Beranek, L., Acoustics, McGraw-Hill, New York (1954).

Beranek, L., Industrial Noise Control, Chemical Engineering Deskbook Issue (April 27, 1970).

Beranek, L., Noise and Vibration Control, McGraw-Hill, New York (1971).

Betz, G. M., Legal side of OSHA: What is "Unsafe" Handling of Hazardous Materials?, Plant Engineering (January 20, 1977).

Bloomfield, B. D., Air Pollution Control in Industry, Air Engineering (August 1963).

Bodurtha, F. T., Industrial Explosion Prevention and Protection, McGraw-Hill, New York (1980).

Botsford, J. H., Control of Industrial Noise Through Engineering, ASHA Reports, 4, The American Speech and Hearing Association, Washington, D.C. (February 1969).

Brandt, A. D., Industrial Health Engineering, John Wiley & Sons, New York (1947).

Callaghan, J. P., Designing Vent Systems for I-C Engine Room, Power (September, 1964).

Cheremisenoff, P. N., and Young, R. A., Materials and Methods for Noise Control, Sound and Vibration (August 1976).

Clarke, L. and Davidson, R. L., Manual for Process Engineering Calculations, McGraw-Hill, New York (1962).

Clayton, G. D. and Clayton, F. E., Patty's Industrial Hygiene and Toxicology, vols. 1, 2, and 3, John Wiley & Sons (Interscience Division), New York (1981).

Constance, J. A., Why Some Dust Control Exhaust Systems Don't Work, Pharmaceutical Engineering, (January/February 1983).

Constance, J. D., Estimating Fluid Friction in Ducts of Nonstandard Shapes, Chemical Engineering (February 22, 1971).

Constance, J. D., Calculating Masking Effects of Noise, Chemical Engineering (April 17, 1972).

Constance, J. D., Calculate Effective Stack Height Quickly, Chemical Engineering (September 4, 1972).

Constance, J. D., Estimating Fan Noise from Tip Speeds, Chemical Engineering (October 2, 1972).

Constance, J. D., Put Noise Criteria to Work in Your Plant, Power (April 1973).

Constance, J. D., Rate the Noise of Unducted HVAC Equipment by this Simple Step-by-Step Procedure, Power (February 1974).

Constance, J. D., Mechanical Engineering for Professional Engineers' Examinations, McGraw-Hill, New York (1978).

Cutter, T. J., Testing Open Hoods and Booths, Plant Engineering (September 16, 1976).

Drew, J. W. and Ginder, A. F., How to Estimate the Cost of Pilot Plant Equipment Chemical Engineering (February 9, 1970).

Encyclopedia of Instrumentation for Industrial Hygiene, Publication Distribution Service, Univ. of Michigan, Ann Arbor, Michigan (1956).

General Radio Company, Handbook of Noise Measurement, 6th ed., General Radio Co., Concord, Mass. (1967).

Heider, S. A., How to Design Fume Hoods, Exhaust Systems for Research Labs, Heating, Piping and Air Conditioning (March 1972).

Hougen, O. A., and Watson, K. M., Industrial Chemical Calculations, 2nd ed., John Wiley & Sons, New York (1936).

Jennings, H. R., and Rohrer, K. L., A Computerized Industrial Hygiene Program, Plant Engineering (October 14, 1976).

Kane, J. M., Manual of Exhaust Hood Designs, American Air Filter Company.

The C. M. Kemp Mfg. Co., Engineered Gas Systems Division, Kemp Gas Generator Technical Manual, Glen Burnie, Maryland.

Kent, R. T., Mechanical Engineers' Handbook, 12th ed., John Wiley & Sons, New York (1950).

Koroff, W. G., Gravity Ventilation for Industrial Buildings, Actual Specifying Engineer (October 1966).

Magill, P., Holden, F., and Ackley, C., Pollution Control Handbook, McGraw-Hill, New York (1956).

Matthews, C. W., Determining Heat Emitted by Motors, Electrical Construction and Maintenance (January 1967).

Meinhold, T. F., Facts About Noise Enclosures, Plant Engineering (September 16, 1976).

Mine Safety Appliances Co., Gascope Combustible Gas Indicator, Models 60 and 62, 600 Penn Center Boulevard, Pittsburgh, Pennsylvania.

National Board of Fire Underwriters Building Corp., Standard for Class A Ovens and Furnaces, Pamphlet 86, New York, New York.

National Fire Protection Association (NFPA), The Guide to OSHA Fire Protection Regulations, Boston, Mass.

Nelson, W., Petroleum Refinery Engineering, McGraw-Hill, New York (1958).

Pierce, D. E., Chemical Engineering for Production Supervision, McGraw-Hill, New York (1950).

Peterson, D., The OSHA Compliance Manual, McGraw-Hill, New York (1978).

Polhemus, J., Techniques for Identifying Noise Levels, Pollution Engineering (August 1976).

Precaustions in High Pressure Acetylene Work, B.I.O.S. Final Report No. 1162, Item No. 22, H. M. Stationery Office, London, S. O. Code 51-1275-62.

Purcell, W. E., Systems for Noise and Vibration Control, Sound and Vibration (August 1976).

Ramsey, M. A., Tested Solutions to Design Problems in Air Conditioning and Refrigeration, The Industrial Press, New York (1966).

Schmidt, E. M., How Safe is Your Industrial Ventilation?, Mechanical Engineering (January 1961).

Sessler, S. M., Designing Quiet into Equipment Rooms, Consulting Engineer (July 1980).

Short, W. A., Electrical Equipment for Hazardous Locations, Chemical Engineering (May 1, 1972).

Shreve, R., and Brink, J., Chemical Process Industries, McGraw-Hill, New York (1977).

Teplitzky, A. M., Electric Power Plant Noise Emission Controls, Sound and Vibration (September 1976).

Tetkora, S. G., Calculate Machinery Noise Problems Before Installation, Pollution Engineering (July 1976).

Thumann, A., and Miller, R. K., Secrets of Noise Control, Fairmont Press, New York (1976).

Trane Company, Acoustics in Air Conditioning, LaCrosse, Wisconsin.

Turk, A., Industrial Odor Control, Chemical Engineering Deskbook (April 27, 1970).

U.S. Dept. of Health, Education and Welfare, National Center of Pollution
    Control, Air Pollution Engineering Manual, No. 999-AP-40, Supt. of
    Documents, U.S. Government Printing Office, Washington, D.C. (1967).
Vatavuk, W. M., and Neveril, R. B., Estimating Costs of Air Pollution
    Control Systems, Chemical Engineering (October 6, November 3,
    December 1, and December 29, 1980).
Von Schwartz, Fire and Explosion Risks, Charles Griffin Co., Ltd.,
    London (1946).
Walsh, T. J., Various Systems for Measuring and Controlling Air Pollu-
    tion, Clapp and Poliak, Inc., New York (1972).
Weissenburger, J. T., Design Charts for Noise Reduction, Pollution Engi-
    neering (July 1974).
White, P. D., Give Them Air, The Plant (December 1952).
Witheridge, W. N., in Industrial Hygiene and Toxicology, 2nd ed., vol. 1
    (F. A. Patty, ed.) Interscience Publisher, Inc., New York (1958).
Zegel, W. C., Direct Flame Fume Incinerators, Plant Engineering
    (September 2, 1976).

INDEX

A

A-scale weighting network, 233
Aeration of industrial buildings, 55
  by natural means, 56
  general provisions for, 67
  need for openings, 66
Air-blowing operations, 28
Air-tight enclosures
  rate of CO_2 buildup, 65
Air cleaning, 109
  methods, 144
Air conditioning units
  filters for, 170
  package type, 170
Air contaminants
  emitted from piping and
    processing equipment, 26
Air distribution in laboratories, 190
Air currents
  effect on dilution, 123
Air entrainment effects, 89
Average molecular weight of a
  gas mixture, 12
Avogadro's law, 8
Atom
  defined, 3
  rate of weights (atomic)
    determination, 3

B

B-scale weighting network, 233
Barometric condensers, 29

Behavior of vapors and gases, 10
Blowers
  for enclosures, 176
  performance requirements, 176
Body cooling by
  air conditioning, 273
  air motion, 267
  conduction/convection, 266
  evaporation, 267, 272
  heat exchange, 266
  humidity control, 266
  radiation, 266
  radiant shielding, 271
  spot cooling, 268—271
Body heat, 266
Boiling point of a liquid, 7
Boyle's law, 8
Building condensation
  effect of higher humidities on, 64
  effect of mechanical exhaust on, 65
Buildings
  air conditioned, 162
  maintenance for dust control, 140
  removing moisture from, 222
  sealing of, 169
  ventilation with winter heating, 161
Bulk-loading facilities
  preventing emissions from, 27

C

C-scale weighting network, 233
Capture velocity, 72, 184

335

For Product Safety Concerns and Information please contact our EU
representative GPSR@taylorandfrancis.com
Taylor & Francis Verlag GmbH, Kaufingerstraße 24, 80331 München, Germany